LIOR VASKOV

The Day Our Paths Almost Missed

First edition

This book was professionally typeset on Reedsy.
Find out more at reedsy.com

Contents

I

TWO LIVES, TWO DIRECTION

1

A Morning That Changed Nothing

The morning sunlight filtered through the thin curtains of Evelyn Maran's tiny apartment, painting soft gold strips across her bedroom wall. If anyone else walked into the room, they would claim it looked peaceful—serene even—but Evelyn knew better. Peace didn't live here. Not anymore. Certainly not this morning.

Her alarm had already gone off twice, buzzing angrily like a tiny machine determined to make her life difficult. She reached out and slapped the snooze button harder than intended. Silence filled the room again, wrapping itself around her like an uninvited blanket.

It was another ordinary morning. Another predictable day. Another cycle that looked exactly like the one before it.

Evelyn rolled onto her back and stared at the ceiling. "Lord," she whispered, "if today is going to be just like yesterday... please, at least give me strength to smile through it."

She waited. For what, she didn't know—an answer? A sign? A sudden burst of energy?

Nothing.

Just the quiet hum of her fan and the distant Lagos traffic outside—horns blaring, people shouting, buses crawling. Life was moving. Somehow, she wasn't.

She finally pushed herself out of bed and shuffled toward the kitchen, tying her robe loosely around her waist. The kettle hissed as she filled it with water and set it on the stove. Her fingers lingered on the counter, tapping absentmindedly.

Her father used to tell her she had "the tapping fingers of someone who's waiting for something big." But she was twenty-nine now, and nothing "big" had come. Not the dream job. Not the grand breakthrough. Not the love story she once believed heaven had carved out for her.

She had gotten used to waiting.

Her phone buzzed. A message. Probably her friend Lara reminding her about the outreach planning meeting later that evening.

Evelyn sighed before even checking the screen. She wasn't in the mood.

But when she picked up the phone, the message wasn't from Lara. It was from her mother.

Mum:
Good morning my dear. Call me when you wake. It's important.

Important.

Her stomach tightened. That word rarely carried good news.

She didn't call immediately. Instead, she poured herself a cup of hot cocoa—her small comfort ritual—then walked to the window and slid it open. The morning breeze brushed against her face, warm and soft. She inhaled deeply, hoping fresh air might calm whatever storm her mother was preparing to unleash.

Her phone buzzed again—another message.

Mum:
Please don't forget. Call me.

Evelyn swallowed hard. She lifted the phone to dial—but stopped.

She needed a moment.

Her thoughts drifted to her life—how small it felt sometimes. Work, church, coming home. Work, church, coming home. Repeating like a scratched record. No excitement. No thrill. No surprises.

Just this.

Just nothing.

She wondered—not for the first time—if heaven had forgotten her address.

Her kettle whistled sharply, snapping her out of her thoughts. She turned off the stove, took another sip of her cocoa, and finally sat down, phone in hand.

"Okay," she whispered. "Let's hear it."

She dialed.

Her mother picked on the first ring.

"Evelyn?"

"Mum, I'm here."

"My daughter, good morning."

"Good morning. What's wrong?"

Her mother hesitated. The sound of it stirred anxiety in Evelyn's chest.

"It's your uncle," she said finally. "Your Uncle Samuel."

Evelyn stiffened. Her mother's eldest brother. The one who practically raised her during holidays. The one who never forgot her birthdays. The one who always had a story ready—funny, wise, comforting.

"What happened?" she asked, her voice barely stable.

"His blood pressure went very high last night," her mother explained. "They rushed him to the hospital. He's stable now, but the doctors said it was close."

Close.

The word landed heavily.

"I'm going to see him later today," her mother continued. "I thought you should know."

Evelyn pressed a hand against her forehead. "Is he… okay? Like, truly okay?"

"They said he'll need monitoring and rest. But he's conscious. Thank God."

Evelyn exhaled shakily. Relief, mixed with fear, swirled inside her chest. "I'll visit him today."

"Good," her mother said softly. "And Evelyn?"

"Yes, Mum?"

"You need to pray. You've been very quiet in your spirit lately."

Evelyn said nothing.

Her mother sighed, as though she could hear the silence thickening. "Life is not just passing you by. God is still writing your story."

Evelyn swallowed. "I know."

But she didn't know. Not really.

"Take care of yourself," her mother added, then ended the call.

Evelyn placed her phone down slowly, almost carefully, like it contained fragile emotions that might spill out. She sat still for a long time, listening to her heartbeat.

The morning looked the same. Felt the same. The same sunlight. The same cocoa. The same routine.

But her uncle's close call shook something loose inside her. A small realization. A whisper.

Life could change in a second.

But hers hadn't.

Not yet.

She glanced at the clock. She was already running late for work—which wasn't surprising, because she never felt motivated to hurry there. It wasn't a job she hated, but it wasn't one she loved either. It was just... life.

She showered quickly, dressed in a simple teal blouse and black trousers, and tied her hair into a low bun. As she reached for her bag, her eyes fell on the journal she kept on her dresser.

It was mostly empty.

She had written only seven pages since January. And even those pages felt like they were written by someone unsure of everything.

She opened it.

On the last written page, she had scribbled:

"Lord, I feel stuck. Please show me what's next... or at least show me You're here."

She stared at the sentence. It stared back.

"I'm trying," she whispered. "I really am."

Evelyn closed the journal, slipped it into her bag, grabbed her keys, and stepped out of her apartment. The air outside smelled of fried akara from the street vendor downstairs, mixed with dust and car exhaust. People moved with purpose—rushing, shouting, bargaining, living.

She envied them.

The moment she stepped out the gate, a motorcycle zoomed past her, nearly clipping her arm.

"For heaven's sake!" she gasped, jerking back.

The rider didn't even slow down.

"Rude," she muttered.

She flagged down a taxi, got in, and leaned back, watching the city blur past as the driver maneuvered through morning chaos.

Her mind drifted.

Would today change anything?

Probably not.

Her driver hit a pothole, jolting her sharply. She sighed. Even the roads didn't want to make life easy.

Then something strange happened.

As they approached the intersection near the old newspaper stand, Evelyn felt an odd tug in her chest. She glanced outside instinctively.

A man stood there.

Just a man. In a navy-blue shirt, sleeves rolled up, speaking to a vendor, his movements calm and purposeful. She couldn't see his face clearly, but something about him—his posture, the stillness around him—pulled her attention.

As though a thread had stretched between them.

She blinked.

Why am I staring?

The taxi moved again, turning left, and the man disappeared from view.

Evelyn frowned slightly. The moment felt… strange. Familiar, even though she didn't know him. Almost as if she was supposed to see him—supposed to meet him—but the city had swallowed him too quickly.

She shook her head.

"Random," she whispered to herself.

Just another day.

Just another morning.

A morning that changed nothing.

She arrived at work ten minutes late, stepped out of the taxi, and inhaled deeply. She could already hear her supervisor's voice echoing inside the building.

"Here we go," she muttered, straightening her blouse and pushing open the glass door.

As she entered, she had no idea—absolutely none—that her life had shifted in the smallest, quietest way.

That she had passed a man who would one day change everything.

That destiny had placed them in the same morning, same city, same intersection—and let them miss each other by seconds.

She walked into her office, believing nothing had changed.

But heaven had already begun moving pieces on the board.

And it started with a morning that looked like nothing.

A morning she would never forget.

Later.

2

He Was There, but I Didn't See Him

Daniel Adewale had always believed mornings were unpredictable—some began with clarity, some with chaos, and some with the kind of unsettling silence that followed him today. As he stepped out of his apartment, adjusting the strap of his leather bag over his shoulder, he felt a heaviness he couldn't explain.

It wasn't sadness.

It wasn't fear.

It was something in-between—like a whisper on the edge of his thoughts, an unfinished sentence lingering in his spirit.

He locked his door, took a deep breath, and started down the stairs of his apartment building. The world outside greeted him with a noisy warmth. A group of kids ran past him, laughing as they chased a worn-out football. An elderly woman swept her storefront with rhythmic swishes. A street preacher shouted verses from Psalms at anyone who would listen—or pretend to.

Daniel didn't stop to take any of it in. His mind was occupied.

Today wasn't just any day.

He was supposed to travel across town to meet a client—one he had been trying to impress for months. The meeting could open doors to new contracts, new partnerships, maybe even the expansion he had prayed for. But something was… off.

He kept checking his watch even though he was early. He kept patting his pocket even though he already felt the keys inside. He kept glancing behind him as though someone had tapped his shoulder.

He shook his head, chastising himself silently. "Daniel, focus."

But focus felt impossible.

He crossed the street and walked toward the bus stop. His phone vibrated in his pocket. He frowned and pulled it out.

A message from Tunde—his closest friend since secondary school.

Tunde:
Guy abeg, avoid Third Mainland Bridge this morning. Standstill traffic. Take another route if you can.

Daniel exhaled in relief. One crisis avoided.

Daniel:
Thanks. Heading towards Ojota instead.

Tunde:
Good. And calm your mind. God's got you.

Daniel stared at the message longer than necessary.

Calm your mind.

He wished he could. But the restlessness clung to him like wet fabric.

He reached the bus stop and joined the thin morning crowd. People stood in small clusters—office workers adjusting their ID cards, students scrolling through their phones, street vendors counting change. Life was happening loudly.

Daniel stepped aside, giving himself breathing space.

A bus pulled up, its conductor shouting destinations at a pitch that could fracture glass. People pushed forward. Daniel followed slowly, his thoughts still tangled.

He felt a sudden nudge at his elbow. He turned.

A young woman, maybe in her early twenties, was trying to balance a food warmer, a handbag, and a phone tucked between her shoulder and ear. She spoke hurriedly.

"No, Mummy! I said I'm already on the road! I'll reach school before eight o'clock na!"

Her scarf slipped slightly.

Daniel instinctively reached out to steady the food warmer she almost dropped.

"Oh! Thank you sir!" she gasped, flashing him a grateful smile before rushing toward the bus.

He nodded, offering a faint smile back. But just as he turned away, something—a very subtle sensation—pulled his gaze to the opposite side of the road.

A taxi had just passed. For a brief moment, through its window, he caught the outline of a woman—her profile soft, her gaze distant, almost melancholic.

Something in him paused.

He blinked.

But the taxi was gone.

He didn't see her face clearly. He couldn't have recognized her. But the moment—just a fraction of a second—felt strange. Like déjà vu from a memory that didn't belong to him.

"What was that?" he murmured under his breath.

He shook his head and climbed onto the next bus, squeezing into a window seat. The bus jerked forward, engine rattling, conductor still yelling. Daniel leaned his head back, closed his eyes, and breathed.

He tried to pray, but even that was difficult today. His thoughts scattered like loose papers.

"Lord," he whispered. "Please… settle my heart."

The bus swerved slightly, causing his eyes to snap open. He looked out the window, watching buildings blur past—shops, billboards, pedestrians, vendors shouting prices.

Everything looked normal.

Everything looked familiar.

Yet nothing felt right.

The bus arrived at Ojota, and he stepped out. He checked his watch again—still early. He exhaled, relieved, then started walking down the sidewalk.

That was when it happened.

A sudden gust of wind lifted a small sheet of paper from the ground, sending it tumbling toward him. Daniel reached down automatically and picked it up.

It was a flier for a charity outreach event—one happening later in the evening.

"Hands of Hope: Volunteer Today."

He recognized the logo. He had volunteered once, months ago. It was the same event where he had gotten an unexpected invitation from Lara, the coordinator. She had messaged him again last week, but he hadn't responded. He wasn't sure why.

He folded the flier and slipped it into his bag.

Maybe he would go.
Maybe he wouldn't.

He kept walking.

The client's office was located in a tall building near a busy junction. Daniel entered the lobby, greeted the receptionist, and waited for the elevator.

His phone buzzed again.

A new message.

From an unknown number.

He frowned. Opened it.

Unknown Number:
We need to talk. Please don't ignore this.

His chest tightened.

He knew that tone. That urgency.

It could only be one person.

His ex—Theresa.

He inhaled sharply and locked his phone. Not today. He didn't have time for ghosts from his past.

The elevator door slid open. Daniel stepped inside and pressed the fifth floor. As the elevator ascended, he caught his reflection in the mirrored walls.

Calm face.
Steady posture.
Eyes that tried too hard to hide worry.

"That chapter is closed," he whispered to himself. "You are not going back."

The elevator dinged.

He stepped out and entered the client's office. The secretary directed him to a waiting area. He sat, clasping his hands together.

His mind wandered again.

To the morning.
The strange heaviness he woke up with.
The sensation of being watched.
The sudden glance at the woman in the passing taxi.
The unexpected message from his ex.

Threads.
Disconnected but present.

He couldn't shake the feeling that something was shifting around him.

Something unseen.

Something approaching.

A door opened, pulling him from his thoughts.

"Mr. Adewale?" the secretary called.

Daniel stood. "Yes?"

"They're ready for you."

He smoothed his shirt, inhaled deeply, and walked toward the conference room.

As he entered, he caught a faint movement outside the glass window—a taxi stopping briefly.

He didn't know that inside that very taxi, just seconds earlier, Evelyn had driven past, unaware that he was only a few feet away.

They were in the same building.
At the same hour.
In the same city.

Twice that morning, their paths crossed without crossing.

He was there, but she didn't see him.

And he didn't see her.

Yet.

Daniel took his seat at the conference table. He tried to focus, but an unsettling truth hovered in his spirit, something he couldn't name.

The day was not ordinary.
The morning was not normal.
Something was shifting.

He just didn't know what.

Not yet.

3

Almost a Collision

The sky shifted from pale morning gold to a washed-out silver by the time Evelyn stepped out of her office building that afternoon. She stood under the small concrete shade near the entrance, holding her phone to her ear while trying to block out the chaos of break-time traffic. Her supervisor had dragged the entire team into a needless staff meeting, and her head throbbed with the weight of too many tasks and too little appetite for life.

“Lara, listen,” she said into the phone, “I’ll try to make it for the outreach meeting this evening, but I’m drained. Completely.”

Her friend chuckled on the other end. “You’re always drained. Come anyway. You need a change of scenery. Or… a change of destiny.”

“Destiny? Please.” Evelyn rolled her eyes. “Just send me the details. We’ll see.”

“You will come,” Lara insisted. “I know you.”

Before Evelyn could respond, someone pushed past her roughly, nearly knocking her phone out of her hand.

"Ah—excuse me!" she snapped, startled.

The culprit didn't even glance back. He rushed into the building, muttering something unintelligible.

"Evelyn? You okay?" Lara asked.

"Yes, yes," Evelyn sighed. "Talk later."

She ended the call and rubbed her arm where the stranger had hit her shoulder. People were becoming more impatient by the day, she thought.

Her stomach grumbled, reminding her she hadn't eaten anything since morning cocoa. She needed food—quickly. She crossed the compound and stepped onto the sidewalk where a line of food vendors lined the street. The aroma of rice, pepper stew, fried plantain, and grilled chicken filled the air, wrapping her in nostalgic warmth.

She picked the closest stall and ordered jollof rice and chicken, then waited while the vendor packaged it in a takeaway container.

While waiting, something—some invisible nudge—made her look across the street.

There he was.

The man she saw earlier that morning at the intersection.

The one whose face she never fully caught.

He was walking down the opposite sidewalk, holding a folder, speaking with someone beside him. He looked calm, focused, deliberate in his steps.

Evelyn blinked, unsure.

Was it really him?

Or was her mind replaying the strange moment from the taxi?

She tried to look away, but her eyes drifted back to him naturally, almost unwillingly. He had a presence—not loud, not flamboyant, just... steady. A quiet kind of strength.

Her food vendor cleared her throat loudly, drawing her attention. "Sister, your change."

"Oh—sorry." Evelyn fumbled the money. "Thank you."

By the time she looked up again, the man was gone.

Coincidence, she told herself.

Nothing more.

She didn't know heaven had a habit of repeating itself until humans finally paid attention.

—-

Daniel stepped out of the office complex feeling lighter than he had when he entered. The meeting had gone better than expected—his proposals accepted, his ideas supported, and even a follow-up appointment scheduled. For a brief moment, joy overpowered the restless heaviness he'd carried all morning.

He walked toward the sidewalk with the client's manager still talking beside him. The manager was explaining future projections, but Daniel's attention was divided. That strange tug—like something pulling him from the inside—had returned.

His eyes drifted across the road.

Something familiar.

Someone familiar.

But he couldn't place it.

"Mr. Adewale?" the manager called, jolting him. "Are you with me?"

Daniel blinked rapidly. "Yes, sir. Apologies."

But his eyes moved again—toward the food stalls across the road. A young woman stood there, holding a takeaway pack, her expression calm yet distant. He couldn't see her clearly through the moving cars, but something about her posture… that soft tilt of her neck… something about her presence tugged at him.

The bus passing between them blocked his view.

Then she disappeared.

Daniel shook himself. "What is wrong with me today?"

He wasn't someone prone to distraction. Yet the entire day had been one long string of odd sensations—fleeting glimpses, unfinished thoughts, things that felt familiar for no reason.

He breathed out and dismissed it.

Or tried to.

—-

Evelyn walked quickly, weaving through the afternoon crowd with her food in hand. She was already late returning to her desk, and her supervisor didn't exactly tolerate lateness with grace.

She turned a corner too sharply.

At the same moment, someone else turned into the same narrow path, also in a hurry.

A split second.

A miscalculated step.

A near accident.

Their bodies moved toward each other with the force of two rushing currents.

If the air could have screamed, it would have.

Evelyn gasped and jerked backward.

The man—Daniel—stopped short, stumbling slightly but catching himself by gripping the nearby signpost. Papers slipped from his folder and scattered across the walkway.

"Ah! I'm so—" Evelyn began, her voice shaking.

But neither of them collided.

They were an inch apart.

One inch.

Barely the length of a breath.

Close enough for her perfume to brush against him like a warm whisper.

Close enough for his cologne to drift toward her, soft and unintrusive.

Close enough for destiny to scream at the both of them, Look! LOOK! That's the one—right there!

But they both stepped back too quickly, too startled to think.

His gaze remained lowered as he bent to pick up his scattered documents. Her heart raced, but she fought the instinct to look too closely at him.

"Sorry," Daniel muttered without lifting his head.

"No, it's my fault," Evelyn said at the same time, also avoiding eye contact.

People around them flowed like water, brushing past, not noticing the almost-collision that nearly changed everything.

Evelyn knelt to help him gather his papers.

"Please don't worry," he said softly, reaching for a document just before she did.

Their fingers almost touched.

Almost.

A breath away.

A spark waiting, begging, dying to ignite.

She pulled her hand back sharply. "Sorry. I didn't mean to—"

"It's fine," he said quickly.

Neither looked up.

Because something strange was happening.

A familiarity.
A pull.
A weightless recognition neither of them could explain.

Daniel collected the last page and stood. Evelyn stood too, still holding her takeaway pack in a trembling hand.

"Are you alright?" she asked, forcing her voice to steady.

"Yes. You?" he asked, still avoiding her eyes.

"Yes. I'm fine."

An awkward pause stretched between them.

A meeting without meeting.
A recognition without recognition.
A whisper from heaven neither of them could hear clearly.

Evelyn stepped aside. "I should—go."

Daniel nodded. "Yes. Me too."

They walked in opposite directions.

Not looking back.

Not realizing they had come within one heartbeat of seeing each other fully.

Not realizing that destiny was getting irritated, tapping its invisible foot impatiently, saying:

Okay. Enough near misses. The next one, you two must NOT escape.

Evelyn rounded the corner and pressed a hand to her chest, steadying her breathing.

Why did that moment feel… strange?

Daniel walked straight until he found an empty bench. He sat down and stared at his hands.

Why did her presence feel like something he had experienced before?

He didn't know.

She didn't know.

Yet the world around them had already shifted—quietly, invisibly.

Their stories had brushed fingertips.

Their paths had crossed without crossing.

They had been one inch from colliding.

Almost.

Almost.

But heaven was far from finished.

4

A HEART TIRED OF WAITING

The soft hum of the refrigerator was the only sound filling the small kitchen as Amara stood barefoot on the cool tiles, staring blankly at the kettle steaming on the counter. She had boiled the water nearly five minutes ago, yet she hadn't moved to make the tea she claimed she wanted. Her mind was far too loud, replaying the same thoughts with relentless insistence.

She pressed her palms against the edge of the counter and exhaled sharply.

Why does life feel like it's moving without me?

The question floated through her mind, not new, not unfamiliar—just heavier today.

The sun was barely up, its rays soft and gentle through the lace curtains, but inside her chest, everything felt tight. She walked to the small dining table and sat slowly, brushing away a few crumbs from last night's hurried dinner. Her eyes drifted to the little vision board leaning against the wall—pictures of completed degrees, happy couples, wedding gowns, a little girl smiling in a park with curly hair she imagined her future daughter would have.

She blinked rapidly and looked away.

"God, I'm trying," she whispered, her voice cracking in the quiet room. "But I'm getting tired."

Tired of waiting.

Tired of pretending the waiting didn't hurt.

Tired of being hopeful with no evidence that her life was moving anywhere meaningful.

Her phone buzzed lightly on the table.

A message from Chisom.

CHISOM: Morning, love. Meeting at 10. Please don't come late again o. I don't have strength to cover for you today.

Amara sighed. At least Chisom's dramatic warnings always made her smile. She typed a quick reply and pushed her chair back to stand.

Then she froze.

Her stomach twisted sharply—not physically, but emotionally, the kind of jolt that reminded her of everything she was trying not to think about.

She opened her journal, the one she hid inside the kitchen drawer, and flipped through pages of prayers, confessions, frustrations, and dreams. Pages where she poured everything she couldn't tell anyone—not even Chisom.

She stopped on a page she had written exactly a year ago.

"Lord, I'm ready. Bring my husband."

Amara shut the journal quickly and leaned back in her chair as if the words were fire.

A year ago.

And nothing had changed.

Not even one step closer.

She tried to shake off the heaviness, but it clung to her. She walked back to the kettle, finally poured the water into her mug, added honey, and stirred lazily. The tea tasted like cardboard.

Her phone buzzed again.

This time, a call.

From her mother.

She groaned quietly before answering.

"Mummy, good morning."

"Amara, good morning," her mother replied warmly, though with that unmistakable undertone—concern blended with pressure. "How are you?"

"I'm fine."

"You don't sound fine."

"I'm okay, mummy."

There was a pause—long enough to confirm her mother didn't believe her.

"You know," her mother began slowly, "your cousin Nneka is getting married next month. She just sent me her invitation card. So beautiful."

Amara closed her eyes.

Here we go again.

"That's nice," she replied softly.

"Yes, it is. Nneka is just twenty-six. Very young. God is really helping her."

Another sharp twist in her chest.
Young — so what does that make me? Expired?

"Mummy, please don't start," Amara whispered, trying to keep her voice from shaking.

"I'm not starting anything o," her mother said defensively. "I'm only saying you should pray more. This thing… waiting… ehn… it can be spiritual—"

"Mummy, I have prayed," she interrupted, her throat tightening. "I pray every day. I'm just… waiting."

Her mother sighed deeply, as though she was the one carrying the burden.

"You know I want the best for you," she said gently. "I just don't want you to be alone for too long."

Alone.
That was the word she hated the most.
The one that stuck to her skin and followed her everywhere like a shadow.

"Mummy, please. I need to prepare for work."

"Okay, my daughter. We will talk later. God will do it. Don't worry."

Amara hung up and stood still for a few seconds, blinking rapidly to keep her tears from falling.

She wasn't angry at her mother. Not really. Her mother cared—deeply.

But sometimes, caring came with pressure that suffocated more than it comforted.

She finished the tasteless tea, stood up, and prepared for work. As she applied light makeup, she stared at herself in the mirror.

She looked fine.
Pretty, even.
There was nothing wrong with her.

So why did love seem so far away?

She shook her head, forcing her thoughts into silence.
Enough of this. She would get through the day. She always did.

She left her apartment, locked the door, and stepped into the fresh morning breeze. It was the kind of weather that could lift any mood—soft sunlight, cool air, faint hints of jasmine—yet her heart felt numb.

The bus stop wasn't far, just a six-minute walk. She walked briskly, forcing herself to breathe deeper and loosen her shoulders.

Halfway to the bus stop, she stopped abruptly.

There, at the fruit stand she always bought oranges from, stood a man. Tall, slightly slouched, wearing a grey shirt that clung comfortably to his frame. His back was turned to her, but something about the way he stood made her stare a second longer than necessary.

She frowned slightly. She didn't recognize him. And yet…

She felt something.
A pull.

A strange, sudden awareness.

She shook her head quickly and started walking again.

When she reached the bus stop, she checked her phone. No messages. No missed calls. Nothing from anyone special—because there was no special person.

A sigh escaped her before she could stop it.

Minutes later, a bus approached, sputtering loudly as it slowed down. People pushed forward, eager to enter. Amara stepped aside politely as usual, letting others go first.

But this time, she felt impatient.
She wanted the day to move faster.
She wanted life to move faster.

She stepped into the bus and found a window seat.

Two minutes later, just as the bus engine rumbled to life, someone climbed in.

Her heart kicked.
It was him.
The man she had seen at the fruit stand.

He didn't notice her. He simply paid the conductor and sat three seats ahead.

Amara leaned slightly forward, studying him.
Something about him felt… familiar.
Not in the I know you way, but in the I've felt you before way.

His shoulders were relaxed but heavy, like someone carrying invisible weight. His head hung slightly low, as though deep in thought. And every few seconds, he rubbed his thumb against his palm—a habit she found oddly calming to watch.

"Fine man," the woman beside her whispered. "But see as he looks sad."

Amara almost smiled.

Sad.

Yes. That was it.

He looked like someone who had lived through too many disappointments.

A mirror of her own heart.

The bus jerked forward, and she gripped the seat. She forced herself to look away from him, but some strange, magnetic pull kept drawing her gaze back.

She didn't know him.

He didn't know her.

Their worlds had never met.

And yet...

She felt seen.

Not by him—he hadn't glanced her way—

but by fate.

As if something was shifting ever so slightly.

As if the universe had paused and whispered:

Pay attention.

The bus continued down the road, neither of them aware that this ordinary morning—this morning that felt like nothing—was the beginning of everything.

Somewhere deep in her spirit, a soft whisper rose:

Maybe… maybe the waiting is not wasted. Maybe something is coming.

But Amara didn't hear it.
Not yet.

For now, she only knew one thing—

Her heart was tired of waiting…
but it had not stopped beating.
Not completely.
Not today.

And somewhere in the same bus, three seats ahead, a man with quiet eyes and an aching soul sat silently, unaware that destiny had just placed him dangerously close to the woman whose life would one day change his forever.

5

DANIEL'S QUIET BATTLE

Daniel sat motionless in the bus, staring at the blurry reflection of his face in the window as the city rolled by in streaks of color. His hands were clasped tightly together on his lap, so tightly his knuckles were turning white. He hadn't meant to grip that hard—it was simply how his body responded when his mind wandered into places he didn't want it to go.

This morning, he had woken up with that same gnawing heaviness that had clung to him for months—an invisible weight that rested on his chest before he even opened his eyes. He hated it. He hated waking up feeling defeated before the day even began. But it was becoming normal. Too normal.

He blinked, forcing his gaze away from his reflection.

Not today, he told himself silently. Just get through today.

The bus jolted over a bump, and Daniel inhaled sharply, grounding himself. He forced his attention to the chatter around him—the conductor shouting destinations, a baby crying at the back, two women arguing about the price of fish. Ordinary sounds. Simple. Familiar.

They reminded him that the world was still moving, even though he sometimes felt stuck.

He shifted slightly in his seat, rubbing his thumb against his palm again, a small movement he had picked up during the most stressful days of his life.

Days he never wanted to remember.

Days that still haunted him every time he closed his eyes.

His phone vibrated in his pocket.

He hesitated before pulling it out.

A message from his sister, Kendra.

KENDRA: Good morning big bro. Just checking in. Please don't shut me out today.

Daniel closed his eyes briefly.

She meant well. She always did.

But the constant checking... the worry in her voice... the unspoken fear that he might slip again...

He didn't blame her. He had earned her worry, though it hurt him to know he had become someone to be monitored.

He typed back quickly before he changed his mind.

ME: I'm fine. Heading to work.

Within seconds, she replied.

KENDRA: You sure?

Daniel swallowed. He didn't want to lie. He wasn't fine—not even close. But he didn't know how to say that without opening doors he was too tired to walk through.

So he just typed:

ME: Yes.

This time, she didn't respond. Perhaps she knew he was lying.

He slid the phone back into his pocket and straightened slightly. He didn't want pity from anyone—not even his sister. He didn't want anyone looking at him and seeing brokenness. He didn't want anyone reminding him of how badly he had failed, how terribly things had fallen apart.

He especially didn't want anyone reminding him of her.

His jaw tightened at the thought.

No. He would not think about Grace today.

But the moment he tried to push the memory away, her face appeared in his mind—her bright smile, the warmth in her eyes, the laughter they used to share, the promises they whispered late at night…

And the silence she left behind.

Daniel clenched his fists.

He could still hear the echo of her last words to him.

"You're not the man I thought you were."

He remembered the way she had said it—not angrily, not in bitterness, but in painful resignation. As though she had given up fighting for him. As though he wasn't worth the effort anymore.

He hadn't replied. He hadn't fought.

He hadn't tried to stop her from walking away.

Because deep down, he believed she was right.

He was not the man she thought he was.

Not then.

Not now.

The bus slowed to a stop, and Daniel looked up briefly. More people got in, squeezing past him. He shifted to give space but kept his gaze low.

That was when he sensed it.

A presence.

Soft, quiet, but strangely noticeable.

He didn't look back—he never liked drawing attention to himself—but something made the back of his neck prickle. Someone in the bus was watching him. Not in a threatening way… just observing. Curiously. Subtly.

He resisted the urge to turn around.

He didn't want to meet anyone's eyes.

He didn't want to open himself to conversation, questions, or small talk.

He just wanted the day to end.

He pressed his thumb against his palm again and exhaled slowly, letting the movement soothe him. The therapist had called it a regulation gesture. He called it survival.

The bus continued moving, and Daniel's thoughts drifted to the office.

The place he dreaded.

The place where he felt like a ghost moving through corridors, doing work he had stopped caring about. He had once been driven—ambitious, inspired, respected. But now, the spark had dimmed. His boss still trusted him, his colleagues still liked him, but Daniel felt… disconnected.

Like he was performing a version of himself rather than living his real life.

And every day, the fear grew that someday, someone would look closely enough and realize how hollow he had become.

His phone buzzed again.

This time, it wasn't Kendra.

It was his mother.

Daniel closed his eyes and prayed silently that she wouldn't ask the question he hated the most.

He answered.

"Good morning, Mum."

"Daniel," she said warmly. Too warmly. "I dreamt about you last night."

He winced internally.

His mother's dreams were always dramatic.

And always an excuse to preach.

"What did you dream, Mum?"

"You were standing alone on a bridge," she said, her voice tightening with meaning. "Dark clouds were gathering. Heavy ones. I had to pray endlessly before the clouds scattered. My son, you must be careful. You must stay connected to God. This season you are in—"

"Mum, please," he whispered, his voice strained. "Not this morning."

She paused, taken aback.
"Are you alright?"

"I'm fine."

"You don't sound fine."

"Mum. Please."

Another pause. A softer one this time.

"Come home this weekend," she said gently. "Just come. I want to see you."

When he didn't respond immediately, she added softly, "I miss you."

"I'll try," he said, though they both knew it meant maybe.

He ended the call and leaned back, rubbing his face with both hands. He felt drained already—and the day hadn't even begun.

He took a deep breath and let it out slowly.

He needed something—anything—to change.
But he didn't know what.
He didn't know how to start again.
He didn't know how to heal from wounds he never spoke about.

He was tired.

Of pretending.
Of failing.
Of being disappointed.
Of waking up with no sense of direction.

And yet he kept moving, because stopping felt dangerous.

The bus made another turn, and Daniel finally glanced to the side, letting his gaze wander aimlessly.

That was when he noticed her.

A woman seated several rows behind him.
He hadn't seen her earlier.
He didn't know why she caught his attention now.

She wasn't looking at him anymore; she was gazing out the window, her hand loosely holding her bag strap. Her expression was calm but… distant. As if she was fighting her own battles quietly.

Daniel stared for a brief moment, feeling a strange, unexpected tug in his chest.
Not attraction.
Not interest.
Just… recognition.

Two quiet souls riding the same bus, each carrying invisible weights.

He looked away quickly, unsettled by the thought.

Strangers shouldn't feel familiar.

He shook the feeling off and straightened, fixing his gaze ahead.

He didn't know her.
He probably wouldn't see her again.
It didn't matter.

He had enough problems of his own.

But even as he told himself that, something deep inside him whispered a different truth—soft, subtle, but persistent:

Your paths didn't cross by accident.

He ignored it, just as he ignored every whisper of hope these days.

He leaned his head against the window, closed his eyes, and braced himself for another long day.

Completely unaware that his quiet battle…
his hidden wounds…
his painful waiting…

…were guiding him toward a moment he was not prepared for.
A moment that would shift the direction of his life.

And that moment was closer than he thought.

6

THE MISSED BUS

The city woke slowly that morning, sunlight glinting off glass facades and puddles left from last night's rain. Evelyn Maran tightened the strap of her tote bag over her shoulder, the weight of yesterday still lingering in her bones. She had promised herself she wouldn't let the little disappointments of life dictate her mood today, but even as she stepped onto the sidewalk, she could feel it creeping back—the invisible pull of fatigue, the unspoken question of when will things finally move?

Her shoes tapped against the concrete rhythmically as she hurried toward the bus stop, glancing at the sky. It was a promising shade of blue, cloudless for once, but the wind brought a hint of chill that made her pull her cardigan closer. She usually liked the quiet hum of the early morning street, but today it felt louder than usual—car horns, shouting vendors, engines revving. She quickened her pace, anxious to reach the bus before it departed.

The bus stop was already crowded when she arrived, commuters fanning themselves with newspapers, umbrellas, or hands pressed against foreheads. Evelyn pushed through the group, her eyes scanning for the familiar yellow bus she relied on every day. She had barely caught sight of it turning the corner when she stumbled on a loose piece of pavement, nearly falling.

"Whoa!" she exclaimed, grabbing the arm of a nearby woman.

"Careful!" the woman said, frowning.

Evelyn steadied herself and dashed forward, but the bus was moving faster than she anticipated. By the time she reached the edge of the sidewalk, the bus had stopped at the curb for a few precious seconds. She ran with all her remaining energy, her chest tightening, her lungs burning, her tote bag swinging wildly against her side. She could see the driver waving passengers inside. A few people climbed aboard, the door starting to close.

And then—she missed it.

The bus door shut with a loud thunk just as she reached the steps, her hand slamming against the metal but sliding uselessly off. Evelyn froze for a heartbeat, staring at the departing vehicle as it moved away, her heart sinking. She felt a flush of frustration, embarrassment, and exhaustion wash over her. The people around her moved on, indifferent, leaving her standing alone on the damp pavement.

She leaned against the lamppost, breathing heavily, trying to regain composure. "Great," she muttered under her breath. "Just great. Why can't anything ever go right?"

Her phone vibrated in her pocket. She pulled it out, expecting a message from Lara about the outreach meeting. Instead, it was a notification from her bank—an alert she had ignored for too long. Her brow furrowed. She quickly unlocked the phone and read the message.

Insufficient funds: Transaction failed.

Evelyn groaned, gripping the phone tighter. She had been living paycheck to paycheck, careful with every naira, yet somehow it never seemed to be enough. Now, missing the bus and discovering her balance dangerously low felt like a cruel joke.

She slumped onto the curb, her bag sliding off her shoulder. She could feel the anxiety building—a familiar pressure in her chest that made breathing feel like a chore. She stared at the road ahead, watching cars weave through traffic, wondering how she would ever reach her office on time. Her supervisor would not tolerate this tardiness.

And then she saw him.

A man standing across the street, leaning casually against the railing of a small pedestrian bridge. He was looking down at something in his hands, oblivious to the chaos around him. Evelyn's first instinct was to look away—he was a stranger, after all—but something in his stance made her pause. There was a weight to him, a kind of quiet stillness in the middle of the bustling city.

Her gaze lingered. There was familiarity she couldn't explain, an unplaceable sense that she had seen him before. Perhaps it was the way his shoulders sloped, relaxed but deliberate, or the slight frown creasing his forehead as he concentrated. For a split second, Evelyn imagined herself walking toward him, introducing herself, breaking the routine of her own lonely life.

And then he looked up.

Their eyes met.

Her heart skipped a beat, and she instinctively stepped back from the curb. It wasn't recognition. She didn't know him, and yet—there was a spark of something that made her chest tighten. She couldn't look away, but the traffic in front of them demanded her attention. The moment was fleeting, gone as quickly as it arrived, leaving her breathless and disoriented.

The man glanced around briefly, then lowered his gaze, and Evelyn felt a strange pang in her chest. She didn't understand why, but she felt a sense of loss, as though she had just missed something important.

She shook her head, trying to focus on the problem at hand. She needed another bus, another way to get to work, but nothing seemed available immediately. She glanced down the street and saw another vehicle approaching—a minibus, crowded but willing to take passengers. Evelyn sprinted toward it, dodging a cyclist who nearly ran her over.

As she climbed aboard, she felt the strain of the chase in her legs, her lungs burning, her pulse racing. She clutched the handrail, trying to steady herself. The minibus driver frowned at her, muttering under his breath, but she ignored him.

Inside, the vehicle was packed. People pressed against each other, murmuring complaints, shifting uncomfortably as it swayed. Evelyn found a spot near the back, holding her bag close to her chest. She closed her eyes briefly, willing herself to calm down.

But the moment of reprieve was short-lived. A man entered the minibus, scanning the interior with sharp, calculating eyes. Evelyn felt a sudden jolt of recognition—could it be? Her mind raced, comparing the contours of his face, the set of his shoulders, the intensity in his eyes.

It was him—the same man from across the street.

He moved gracefully through the crowded aisle, nodding politely to a few passengers, his gaze briefly meeting hers before moving forward. Evelyn's stomach twisted. The universe had placed them in the same vehicle, yet the distance between them remained significant.

He didn't sit next to her; he chose a seat several rows ahead. She watched as he settled in, pulling a folder from his bag and laying it carefully on his lap. His attention was focused elsewhere, but she couldn't stop herself from glancing at him, memorizing the way he held himself, the way his fingers moved over the papers.

Her mind buzzed with questions she didn't have answers to. Why did this stranger's presence make her feel so… unsettled? So aware? She felt as though the missed bus this morning, the struggle to get here, and every small inconvenience had led to this moment—yet it felt like it was all happening just out of reach.

The minibus jerked forward, the engine grumbling, and Evelyn shifted in her seat, her bag pressed tightly against her. She tried to focus on the road ahead, on the buildings flashing by, on the rhythm of the city—but her eyes kept drifting back.

The man glanced briefly at her again, and this time their eyes locked for a fraction of a second longer. Evelyn's pulse quickened. She wanted to look away, to convince herself it was nothing, but she couldn't. There was a tension in the air, a current that made her feel both exposed and connected, though they had not spoken a word.

As the bus weaved through traffic, Evelyn felt a strange mix of excitement and apprehension. She had missed her usual bus, endured frustration, and faced delays—but somehow, everything had conspired to place her in the same vehicle as this man. The irony was not lost on her.

For the first time that morning, she allowed herself to wonder: Is this why I missed the bus? Was it meant to be?

The thought frightened her as much as it intrigued her. She wasn't used to surrendering to fate or serendipity; she had spent years relying on plans, schedules, and discipline. Yet here she was, in a crowded minibus, heart racing, watching a stranger who felt strangely familiar.

The man bent over slightly to adjust something in his folder, his movement deliberate, controlled, and almost unconscious. Evelyn felt an involuntary shiver. She looked away, pressed her forehead against the window, and tried to steady her breathing.

The minibus continued its journey, every bump in the road a reminder of the unpredictability of life. Evelyn couldn't help but think of how close she had come to not being here at all. The missed bus, the stumble on the pavement, the delay—all of it had pushed her toward this moment.

She didn't know him. She didn't know what his name was, or why he stirred something so profound in her chest. But in that quiet, suspended space, she realized that perhaps the universe had been conspiring quietly, deliberately, all morning.

Her hands tightened around her bag strap. The city roared outside, people moved, life continued—but inside her chest, time seemed to slow.

The missed bus had been more than an inconvenience. It had been an opening, a fracture in the ordinary, a doorway into something unanticipated. Evelyn could feel it in every nerve, every heartbeat, every breath.

And she knew, deep down, that this moment—fleeting as it was—would not be the last time their paths would intersect.

Because sometimes, life arranged collisions in its own slow, deliberate way.

And sometimes, you had to miss a bus to finally be in the right place at the right time.

Evelyn pressed her hand to her chest, feeling the rapid thrum of her heartbeat. She didn't know the name of the man ahead, she didn't know his story, and she didn't know if they would ever speak—but one thing was clear: the missed bus had changed something.

And she could feel, with a mix of fear and anticipation, that nothing would ever be the same again.

7

WHISPERS OF DESTINY

The city was alive with its usual symphony of sound, but to Daniel, it felt muted—like he was moving through a half-lit dream. The morning had started ordinary enough, but by the time he left his apartment, an unfamiliar weight had settled on his shoulders. He couldn't explain it, but there was a strange insistence in his thoughts, a sense that today, unlike any other, something would shift.

He stepped into the cool morning air and adjusted the strap of his leather bag. The sun glinted off passing cars, pedestrians hurried along the pavement, and vendors shouted over the traffic. All of it felt ordinary, yet there was a subtle hum under it, a rhythm he couldn't place.

Daniel walked in silence, hands deep in his pockets, eyes scanning the street without really seeing it. He had missed the early bus—the one he usually took to work—and it had thrown him off. At first, he had cursed his luck quietly, muttering to himself as he waited for the next vehicle. But now, as the minutes stretched and the buses crawled by in endless rows, he began to notice small details: a bird fluttering low over a puddle, a child's laughter bouncing off brick walls, the faint aroma of roasted peanuts and coffee drifting from a nearby vendor.

He shook his head. Focus, he reminded himself. Work. Meetings. Deadlines. Bills. Nothing else mattered.

And yet... he couldn't shake the feeling that the universe was whispering.

As he stepped closer to the corner of the street where he usually caught a bus, something caught his eye—a flash of color amidst the gray of morning traffic. A woman stood under the shade of a small awning, her tote bag clutched tightly against her side. She was staring across the street, oblivious to the cars and honking horns around her.

Daniel stopped mid-step. There was something striking about the way she held herself—poised yet weary, observant yet detached. He had never seen her before, and yet, his chest tightened in an inexplicable way. A peculiar sense of recognition stirred deep inside him.

He tried to shake it off. Just another commuter, he told himself. Nothing more.

The next bus approached, its engine growling as it slowed to a stop. Daniel stepped forward, and the woman moved toward the edge of the curb at the same time. Their eyes met for a brief moment as she glanced at him—just a fleeting glance—but it was enough. His heart skipped, a quiet jolt that left him feeling both grounded and adrift at the same time.

She didn't smile. She didn't speak. She didn't even linger in that moment. And yet, something in him knew that glance was significant.

The bus stopped, and she stepped aside, allowing Daniel to board first. He moved through the aisle, catching glimpses of her as she climbed on behind him. She found a seat several rows back, placing her bag carefully on her lap, her fingers resting lightly on its strap. She looked out the window, her expression unreadable, but Daniel couldn't look away.

The city blurred past the bus windows as Daniel sank into his seat, feeling the pull of something he didn't yet understand. It was a quiet, insistent tug—like the threads of destiny weaving themselves invisibly between two people who had yet to realize they were bound together.

He tried to focus on the mundane—checking his emails, scrolling through messages, the familiar rhythm of life he relied on to keep himself grounded—but every few seconds, his gaze drifted back to her.

There was an aura around her, subtle yet undeniable, that seemed to brush against the edges of his consciousness. He wasn't sure what it was—an energy, a presence, a familiarity he couldn't name—but it made him restless.

She shifted slightly, pulling a strand of hair from her face, and Daniel felt a shiver run down his spine. She was unaware of him, yet he felt intimately aware of her. It was as though the world had narrowed, leaving only the two of them suspended in a quiet, vibrating space that existed apart from time.

The bus jerked to a halt at another stop. Commuters pushed and shoved, stepping on each other's heels in their rush to board. Daniel noticed her hands tighten on her bag, the subtle gesture revealing her tension, her fatigue, her patience stretched thin. He wanted to reach out, to speak, to ask if she was alright—but he didn't. He couldn't.

The quiet pull between them was fragile, easily broken by words, by movement, by the noise of the world. And yet, it persisted.

Daniel's thoughts drifted again, this time to the morning he had spent alone in his apartment. The letters he had left unread, the missed calls from his sister, the quiet solitude that had enveloped him like a heavy cloak. He realized, with startling clarity, that he had been waiting—not for something specific, but for a change, for a sign, for a moment that would shift the trajectory of his life.

And now, in the crowded bus, with the city rushing past, he felt it.

A whisper of destiny.

It wasn't loud. It wasn't dramatic. It didn't announce itself with fanfare. It was subtle, insistent, undeniable. It threaded through his chest, brushed against his heart, and spoke directly to the quiet corners of his soul that had been waiting for years without knowing it.

He didn't know her name. He didn't know her story. He didn't know what her presence meant. But he knew, as surely as he knew the sun would rise, that she was part of something larger—a moment orchestrated by forces he couldn't see, but could feel.

The bus turned a corner sharply, jolting him slightly, and the spell of the moment broke. He glanced down at his hands, still pressed together in his lap, and exhaled slowly. The rational part of his mind argued that he was overthinking, imagining connections that didn't exist. But the deeper part of him—the part that had endured years of quiet struggle, loneliness, and disappointment—knew better.

She was more than a stranger.

And he had a sense that their lives were about to intersect in ways neither of them could anticipate.

Evelyn shifted in her seat, looking down at her phone briefly, her fingers tapping absentmindedly against the screen. She didn't notice him watching. She didn't notice the way his eyes followed her, careful not to stare too obviously, careful not to breach the unspoken boundaries of strangers sharing a crowded vehicle.

But she felt it anyway—the subtle weight of someone noticing her. A quiet vibration in the air, like a presence lingering just beyond perception. It made her pulse quicken slightly, though she didn't know why. She glanced toward the front of the bus, catching a fleeting shadow in her peripheral vision. She turned her head, but he was looking away.

And yet… there was something about him that stayed with her.

The bus continued down the road, and Daniel leaned back slightly, letting the rhythm of movement settle around him. His mind was unusually quiet, focused entirely on the small, almost imperceptible pull that tied him to the woman several rows behind. He couldn't explain it. He didn't want to. It was enough to feel it, to recognize that the universe was whispering, guiding, weaving paths together in ways that would reveal themselves in time.

For years, Daniel had fought battles quietly—personal struggles, professional setbacks, moments of despair he had hidden from everyone. He had learned to carry weight alone, to rely on discipline, reason, and a stubborn insistence on moving forward. But now, as he sat on the bus, he felt a shift in the air, a subtle reminder that life had a way of intervening when he least expected it.

Evelyn adjusted her bag, sliding it slightly to one side to rest against her knee. She looked out the window again, the city sprawling endlessly before her, streets converging and diverging like threads in an unseen tapestry. She felt a strange tension, a pull she couldn't name, as if she were on the edge of something significant. Something that had been waiting for her, just out of reach, for longer than she realized.

Daniel's gaze softened, almost instinctively, as he watched her adjust her posture. He didn't move, didn't speak, didn't make a single gesture. And yet, the connection—the quiet resonance between them—was undeniable.

It was in that suspended moment, in the crowded bus moving through the waking city, that both Daniel and Evelyn sensed the first whisper of destiny. Not a promise, not a guarantee, not even clarity—but a subtle, insistent presence that hovered just beyond perception, drawing them closer, threading their paths together with invisible strands.

Neither of them spoke. Neither of them acted. And yet, both of them were aware—aware that their lives had shifted in a small, imperceptible way. A shift that would grow, intensify, and pull them into a collision with fate that neither could ignore.

As the bus turned another corner, and the city stretched endlessly in front of them, Daniel exhaled slowly, a sense of anticipation coiling quietly in his chest. Evelyn leaned slightly forward, staring out the window, feeling the same invisible tug that had guided her here.

And somewhere deep inside, both of them knew—without words, without acknowledgment, without proof—that their lives were no longer entirely their own.

The whispers of destiny had begun.

And nothing would ever be the same again.

8

AN INVITATION HE ALMOST IGNORED

Daniel sat at his desk, staring at the blinking cursor on his laptop screen, wondering if it was mocking him. He had spent the morning wading through emails, signing off reports, and attending meetings that felt like echoes of themselves. Every word spoken around him seemed hollow, every request devoid of meaning. And yet, the city outside continued its relentless pace, indifferent to the storm quietly brewing in his chest.

It was during a brief lull—those rare moments when the office hummed but no one spoke—that he noticed the email notification flashing insistently in the corner of his screen. A simple subject line: Invitation.

He frowned. He didn't recognize the sender. It wasn't work-related. He hovered over it, a strange reluctance pressing against his curiosity. He almost ignored it. Almost deleted it. But something in the way the notification had appeared—soft yet insistent—made him pause.

Daniel clicked.

The email opened, and the words on the screen pulled him into a sudden, unshakable focus:

"You are invited to the Grace Community Outreach Evening. Your presence is requested to celebrate unity, inspiration, and the joy of meaningful connections."

A small detail caught his eye: a date. Tonight. And a location—a hall in the heart of the city he knew well, yet had never visited.

He leaned back in his chair, fingers pressing against the edge of the desk. Why me? he wondered. He had never attended such events. He had never sought social gatherings outside of work, preferring the solace of solitude. And yet, the invitation seemed… deliberate. Personal. Intentional.

He could almost hear a whisper in the quiet of his office: Go.

He shook his head, dismissing it. Invitations came and went every day. The world brimmed with events that didn't need his attention, didn't need his presence. He could simply ignore it and continue with the monotony of his life. That would be easier. That would be safe. That would be normal.

But the cursor blinked relentlessly, almost impatiently. He read the email again, slower this time, absorbing the rhythm of the words, the subtle suggestion woven through the polite phrasing.

"A night of purpose, connection, and discovery. Your presence is valued."

The phrasing tugged at him, a thread pulling at something buried deep in his chest. A part of him—a part he rarely acknowledged—recognized it. Something beyond logic, beyond reason, beyond the careful walls he had built to guard his quiet life.

He leaned forward, reading and rereading the details. The hall, the time, the names of a few speakers—all familiar in a way that unsettled him. He had never met these people, yet the setting stirred a distant memory he couldn't place. A sense of anticipation threaded through him, subtle but undeniable, like a soft pulse beneath the skin.

His fingers hovered over the keyboard, debating. Go. Don't go. Go. Don't go.

A call from his sister Kendra interrupted the mental tug-of-war.

"Daniel! Have you seen this?" she said immediately, her tone urgent but cheerful.

"See what?" he asked, a little tense, holding the email open for her to picture in his mind.

"This event at Grace Community Hall. They sent you an invite, right? I just got a flyer. Are you going?"

He paused. Her enthusiasm was infectious, almost annoyingly so. "I… I don't know," he admitted.

"You don't know? Daniel! It's tonight. They're celebrating the work of volunteers, community leaders… it's going to be inspiring!"

He rubbed his forehead. He wanted to shrug it off, tell her he was too busy, too drained, too indifferent to bother with such gatherings. But something in the tone of her voice—the insistence, the warmth, the soft encouragement—made him hesitate.

"I'm not sure, Kendra. I have work," he said finally.

"You always say that," she replied lightly, but not without concern. "Don't you want to do something different for once? Something that isn't emails, deadlines, and stress?"

Her words struck deeper than he expected. Daniel leaned back in his chair again, looking out the window at the city streets far below. Cars moved in orderly chaos, pedestrians bustled, and yet everything felt distant. He had spent so many days in a loop of routine, of predictable failures and quiet solitude, that the idea of stepping outside it—of embracing something unknown—felt terrifying.

And yet, exhilarating.

He closed his eyes, letting the memory drift in. The faint recollection of the woman from the bus surfaced—Evelyn. The fleeting glance, the subtle connection, the inexplicable pull. And a strange notion took root in his mind: she might be there. He had no reason to think so. No certainty. But something whispered that she could be.

Daniel opened his eyes sharply. Ridiculous, he told himself. She was a stranger. They had exchanged no words, no names. And yet... the thought of not seeing her again felt like a void he wasn't ready to accept.

Kendra's voice broke through his reverie again. "You should go. Trust me. Even if you think it's pointless, just go. Something tells me you need this."

He frowned. How did she know? How did anyone know?

"I'll... think about it," he said, though the words were weak, unsure.

"Daniel!" she said, a little firmer this time. "You're not going to let the opportunity slip because you're scared, are you?"

Her question lingered, echoing louder than he expected. Fear. That was it. He was scared. Scared of the unknown. Scared of breaking the routines that had kept him safe. Scared of what might happen if he ventured outside the predictable rhythms of his life.

And yet, a voice within—quieter but insistent—urged him to act. To move. To trust. To follow.

He sat silently, torn between inertia and impulse. He looked at the clock. He had just enough time to make it if he left now. If he chose to go.

His fingers hesitated over the keyboard, then moved. He replied to the email with a simple:

"I will attend. Thank you for the invitation."

He stared at the sent message, his heartbeat loud in the quiet office. The decision had been made, and yet a strange tension gripped him. Excitement mingled with apprehension. Anticipation wrestled with doubt.

He leaned back, closed his eyes, and let out a slow breath. For the first time in weeks, he felt a spark—something fragile, something tentative, but undeniable. A thread had been pulled, an invisible door had been nudged open.

For Daniel, the evening ahead promised uncertainty, yet a part of him welcomed it. He knew he was stepping into something larger than himself, something beyond his understanding. And as he rose from his chair, gathered his bag, and prepared to leave the office, he felt it—the subtle pull of destiny, the quiet insistence that his life was about to change.

Outside, the city hummed and breathed, unaware of the small but monumental decision that had been made. People passed by, lives intersected in fleeting moments, and the air carried the faint scent of possibilities waiting to be claimed.

Daniel took one final glance at his reflection in the window. There was weariness in his eyes, but also a spark—a hint of expectation, of hope, of readiness.

He didn't know what awaited him at Grace Community Hall. He didn't know if Evelyn would be there, if their paths would finally converge, or if the night would pass uneventfully.

But he had chosen to go.

And sometimes, Daniel realized, choosing to go—even when everything inside you screams to stay—is the first step toward rewriting destiny.

As he walked briskly toward the streets that would carry him to the hall, his heart thrummed with quiet urgency, a steady rhythm that seemed to echo the pulse of the universe itself. Every step felt deliberate, significant, charged with the electric tension of the unknown.

And in that moment, Daniel understood something he had long avoided acknowledging: life waits for no one. Opportunities appear once, sometimes twice, rarely more. And the invitation he had almost ignored—tonight—was not just an event. It was a threshold, a convergence, a whisper from fate that demanded action.

He didn't know the full story yet. He didn't know the faces he would see, the conversations he would have, or the decisions he would be forced to make. But he did know this: by stepping forward, by accepting what had been offered, he had opened the door to everything he had been waiting for, without even realizing it.

And as he moved toward the cab waiting at the curb, Daniel felt something shift within him—a quiet, unstoppable movement that whispered: tonight, nothing would remain the same.

9

A SIGN SHE COULDN'T INTERPRET

Evelyn walked through the glass doors of the Grace Community Hall with a sense of cautious anticipation. The evening air had cooled after the day's relentless sun, and she pulled her light cardigan closer around her shoulders. The hall was larger than she had imagined, its high ceilings and polished floors giving it a grandeur she didn't expect. Chandeliers hung like frozen constellations, casting warm light over the faces of people who were chatting, laughing, and moving through the space with purpose.

She paused at the entrance, adjusting the strap of her tote bag, and let her eyes sweep across the room. Volunteers were checking people in, offering programs and name tags, while musicians tuned their instruments for the opening performances. A faint buzz of energy filled the air, charged but not chaotic, welcoming yet unfamiliar.

Evelyn took a deep breath. She wasn't sure why she had come. She hadn't attended events like this in years, preferring solitude, routine, and the safety of predictability. But something—a quiet insistence she couldn't name—had drawn her here. Her heartbeat quickened at the thought, a mixture of excitement and apprehension swirling within her.

She wandered deeper into the hall, moving past groups of people she didn't recognize, until she found a quiet corner near the windows. From here, she could watch without being watched, observe without engaging. She rested her bag on the ledge, letting her hands linger over it, and tried to calm the fluttering in her chest.

And then she saw it.

A small table near the center of the room, decorated with a modest bouquet of white lilies and soft candlelight, had a single envelope lying atop it. It wasn't addressed in the conventional sense—there was no name, no signature—but something about it made her pause. The envelope was simple, cream-colored, with edges slightly raised as if it contained more than a sheet of paper.

Evelyn's breath caught. She didn't know why she was drawn to it. Logic told her to ignore it—someone had probably left it there accidentally, or it belonged to the organizers. Yet, a strange, magnetic pull tugged at her. She walked slowly toward it, her fingers brushing the edges of the envelope as if the touch itself might answer the unspoken questions swirling in her mind.

She picked it up, her fingers trembling ever so slightly. The envelope was light, almost weightless, but it felt oddly significant in her hands. She turned it over, studying the smooth surface, the faint scent of lavender clinging to it.

There was no indication of who had placed it there, no hint of intention. And yet, Evelyn felt certain it had been left for her. She didn't understand why she felt that certainty, only that it resonated deep within her chest, brushing against the tender edges of a curiosity she had long kept dormant.

She opened the envelope with deliberate care, letting the paper slide out smoothly. On it was a short note, written in neat, flowing handwriting:

"Tonight is the beginning. Pay attention to what you almost miss."

Evelyn's brow furrowed. The words were cryptic, almost elusive, and she had no context to interpret them. Who had written this? Why was it here? How had they known she would come? She read it again, her pulse quickening.

"Tonight is the beginning. Pay attention to what you almost miss."

Her mind raced, trying to assign meaning. Was it a message meant for someone else? A motivational note from the organizers? Or... something more personal, more intentional? The uncertainty gnawed at her, a blend of intrigue and unease that left her chest tight.

She held the paper, her eyes scanning the words over and over, trying to decode the hidden message. And yet, the meaning eluded her, slipping just beyond her understanding. She felt a quiet thrill mixed with fear—a sensation she hadn't felt in years.

Evelyn placed the note back into the envelope and slipped it into her bag, determined not to let the uncertainty distract her from the evening's proceedings. But she couldn't shake the feeling that the note was significant. That it was meant to steer her toward something she had yet to recognize.

Her gaze wandered across the room, and she felt the pull again—like an invisible thread tugging her toward the center of the hall. People were beginning to take their seats for the opening ceremony. Volunteers were bustling about, arranging chairs and guiding attendees. Music swelled softly from the stage, the notes weaving through the air, settling gently in the quiet corners of the room.

Evelyn moved slowly, trying to understand the strange tension within her. The note, the envelope, the pull—it was all disorienting, unfamiliar, and yet undeniably compelling. She found an empty seat near the side, close enough to see the stage but not so close as to be conspicuous.

As she sat, she felt a strange sensation—a sense of anticipation, as if something important was hovering just out of reach. Her heart beat faster, not from exertion, but from a quiet, insistent awareness that tonight was different. That tonight was not ordinary. That something—or someone—was waiting, and she might almost miss it if she didn't pay attention.

She tried to focus on the performance beginning on stage, but her mind kept drifting back to the note. Pay attention to what you almost miss. The words echoed in her head, repeating like a refrain she couldn't fully interpret. What could she almost miss in a room filled with strangers?

Then she noticed a movement across the hall—subtle, almost imperceptible. A man had entered. Tall, composed, carrying himself with a quiet intensity. He scanned the room briefly, eyes moving over the crowd with calm purpose. And then, their eyes met.

Evelyn's breath caught. The man—Daniel—stood several feet away, yet she felt an instant recognition, a jolt that made her heart tighten. The pull she had felt on the bus, the fleeting glance that lingered too long in her memory, all of it surged forward, undeniable and insistent.

He walked slowly toward a seat near the front, moving with deliberate steps that somehow made the crowd around him blur into insignificance. Evelyn's gaze followed him, her chest tightening with a mixture of anticipation and confusion.

The note in her bag seemed to pulse in response to his presence, a quiet affirmation of something she didn't yet understand. Tonight is the beginning. She realized she was beginning to see the truth in the cryptic words. But what it meant, she still could not interpret.

Daniel lowered himself into the seat, careful not to draw attention. He glanced around briefly, his eyes scanning the crowd, and for a fleeting moment, they locked with Evelyn's again. The connection was brief, almost imperceptible to anyone else, but it was enough. Enough to ignite a spark of curiosity, a flicker of understanding that destiny was at work in ways neither of them could fully grasp.

Evelyn leaned back in her seat, clutching her tote bag tightly. Her mind raced, trying to process the significance of the moment. The note. The man. The pull she couldn't name. Everything pointed toward a convergence she didn't yet understand, a moment that demanded her attention even as its meaning remained elusive.

She glanced at the stage, at the lights, at the performers, but her awareness kept returning to Daniel. There was a quiet intensity in him, a presence that made her senses sharper, her thoughts clearer, and yet left her feeling completely unprepared.

She didn't understand the sign. She couldn't interpret it. But deep down, she knew—she could not ignore it.

The music swelled, the lights danced across the hall, and the audience clapped politely. Yet Evelyn's focus remained divided, tethered to the envelope in her bag, to the cryptic words she couldn't decode, and to the man who seemed to carry an invisible pull.

Tonight was not ordinary. She felt it. She sensed it. And the note, which had appeared so mysteriously, had prepared her for this awareness. But the meaning—the full weight of it—remained just out of reach, teasing her like a shadow she could not touch.

The hall seemed to shrink around her, the lights dimming as the opening speaker took the stage. Evelyn's pulse raced. Every instinct told her to stay calm, to watch, to observe. But every instinct also screamed that she was on the verge of encountering something pivotal, something that might shift her life in ways she could not yet anticipate.

She exhaled slowly, letting the note's words echo once more in her mind: Pay attention to what you almost miss.

And she realized, with a mix of fear and anticipation, that she was about to.

10

THE FIRST TIME HE SPOKE HER NAME

The hall was alive with low murmurs, the gentle rustle of programs, and the distant hum of music from the stage. Evelyn sat rigidly in her seat, hands clasped over her tote bag, her mind cycling relentlessly over the cryptic note she had received earlier. Pay attention to what you almost miss. She didn't understand it, and yet the sensation it left in her chest was undeniable, like an electric current that refused to fade.

Her eyes flicked toward the front of the room, where the opening speaker was about to begin. Daniel was there, seated several rows ahead, almost perfectly still except for the occasional tilt of his head as he scanned the crowd. The earlier spark of recognition—the fleeting moment on the bus, the unspoken connection—lingered in the air between them. It was subtle, intangible, and yet undeniable. Evelyn's pulse quickened at the thought of him, though she had no rational reason for it.

The speaker's voice cut through the quiet, calm yet commanding, introducing the evening's purpose: community, connection, and the celebration of human resilience. Applause followed, polite and encouraging, but Evelyn found herself barely hearing it. Her attention was anchored, pulled irresistibly toward Daniel.

Minutes passed. The speech continued, and the first performances began—soft music, a choir, and readings from volunteers' experiences. Evelyn clutched her bag tighter, the weight of the envelope in her lap a constant reminder of the cryptic message she had yet to interpret. And then, as the room dimmed for a spotlight performance, a sudden hush fell over the audience.

It was at that moment, amidst the quiet, that she heard it—soft, deliberate, and unnervingly close.

"Evelyn."

Her heart stopped.

The voice was unmistakable. Calm, low, deliberate. Carried just enough across the hall to reach her ears without being loud. It was a name she had not heard spoken aloud by anyone other than her family, a name that had always sounded ordinary, until now. Spoken by him, Daniel, it felt like something entirely new—charged with intention, weight, and an unspoken acknowledgment that shifted the very air around her.

Her head jerked toward him. Daniel stood near the edge of the stage, a slight frown creasing his forehead as if he had been searching for someone. His eyes met hers immediately, and in that instant, the room around her seemed to fade. The music, the chatter, the applause—all of it became background noise, a distant hum. There was only the two of them.

Evelyn's fingers tightened on her bag. She didn't move. She couldn't. Every rational thought in her mind screamed that this was impossible. He didn't know her. They had never spoken. And yet—he knew her name. And the very fact that he had said it aloud sent a ripple of something deep through her chest, something she couldn't name.

Daniel took a deliberate step forward, moving along the aisle toward her. Each movement was measured, purposeful, yet casual enough that no one else in the room seemed to notice. But Evelyn noticed. She noticed the quiet authority in the way he walked, the subtle tension in his shoulders, and the way his eyes held hers like a thread that refused to break.

"Evelyn," he said again, this time slightly louder, though still under his breath. The sound of her name on his lips resonated in her ears, sending shivers down her spine.

She swallowed, suddenly conscious of the tightness in her chest and the rapid pulse in her veins. Her mind scrambled for explanations—how did he know her name? Why did he speak it like it carried weight, like it mattered in a way she had never known?

Daniel stopped a few feet away, careful not to draw attention from the crowd, yet close enough that she could see the subtle lines of his face—the tension in his jaw, the intensity in his eyes, and the faint shadow of a smile tugging at the corners of his lips.

"You—uh—you received the note?" he asked, his voice low, almost intimate, meant only for her.

Evelyn's eyebrows shot up. He knew. He knew about the envelope, the cryptic message. Her fingers instinctively went to her bag, to the cream-colored paper she had been gripping since arriving. She felt exposed, vulnerable, yet a thrill coursed through her, mingling with confusion.

"Yes," she replied cautiously, her voice barely above a whisper. "I… I did."

Daniel nodded, a subtle acknowledgment, like he had expected this answer, like her hesitation was understood. “It’s not meant to be ignored,” he said softly, almost conspiratorially. “It’s meant to guide you. And you—Evelyn—are meant to notice.”

Her chest tightened again. His tone wasn’t commanding, not in a way that demanded obedience, but in a way that carried certainty. A certainty she found inexplicably disarming. How could a man she had never spoken to, barely known, speak to her with such awareness? And yet she felt it—this unspoken recognition that something important was happening, something she couldn’t ignore.

The music swelled, and the spotlight shifted. Evelyn felt torn. Part of her wanted to run, to retreat into the safety of anonymity, to ignore the pull that had drawn her here. But another part—a deeper, quieter part—urged her to remain, to pay attention, to respond.

Daniel’s gaze softened, just slightly, as he waited for her reaction. “You’ve been noticing things,” he said, almost conversationally. “Small things you might dismiss, moments that almost pass you by. The note—it’s a reminder. Tonight… it matters more than you realize.”

Evelyn’s fingers trembled slightly. She wasn’t sure what to say, what to ask, what to understand. She only knew that her heart had begun to race in a way that defied reason, a rhythm that matched the subtle urgency in his voice.

“And you…” Daniel paused, the words heavy with unspoken weight. “I’ve seen you notice. Even before the note. You have a way of observing, of catching the details that others miss. It’s… rare.”

Her breath caught again. It wasn’t flattery—it wasn’t meant to charm. It was acknowledgment. Recognition. Something she had never received from anyone outside herself, and it shook her more than she expected.

"I… I don't understand," she admitted, her voice barely audible, her words trembling slightly. "I don't know why I'm here. Or… or why the note… why you… why any of this."

Daniel smiled faintly, a softness that seemed to draw the room into shadows around them, leaving only the space between their quiet connection. "That's the point," he said, his tone almost a whisper meant solely for her. "Sometimes, the things that happen around us, the moments that brush past, the almosts… they carry meaning we can't immediately interpret. But that's why we pay attention."

Evelyn's eyes were wide, her fingers clutching her bag strap so tightly her knuckles turned white. Her mind spun, trying to make sense of the strange, intoxicating tension that filled the space between them. She didn't know what he meant, and yet she felt it—every word, every glance, every subtle movement carried significance she could feel but not name.

Daniel stepped closer, though still careful to maintain distance from the curious eyes of the crowd. He lowered his voice further, so low that it brushed against her consciousness like a secret. "Evelyn… I've been looking for this moment. Not knowing exactly why, not knowing exactly how. But when I saw you… I knew."

Her heart thundered, her breath catching in her throat. The vulnerability, the tension, the impossibility of it—it all crashed into her chest at once. She had not expected this, had not planned for this, and yet it felt inevitable, undeniable, and terrifyingly real.

"I… I don't know what to say," she whispered, barely able to meet his gaze.

"You don't have to say anything," he replied, his voice calm but infused with gravity. "Just… notice. That's all you need to do tonight."

Evelyn felt a tremor run through her. She wanted to speak, to ask questions, to unravel the mystery, but her instincts told her to stay silent, to simply absorb this improbable, breathtaking moment. Daniel spoke her name, not casually, not in passing, but with intention, weight, and meaning. For the first time in her life, hearing it aloud felt like it belonged to someone else as much as it belonged to her.

And in that moment, with the crowd, the music, and the lights blurring around them, Evelyn realized she was no longer just an observer. She was part of a story being written before her eyes, a story whose significance she could not yet interpret—but whose presence she could no longer ignore.

The first time he spoke her name, everything shifted. The world tilted imperceptibly. And neither of them could deny that something extraordinary had begun.

II

THE FIRST REAL MEETING

11

ONE CHANCE APPOINTMENT

The night had deepened outside Grace Community Hall, the city lights glimmering like distant stars in a low, golden haze. Evelyn stepped out onto the quiet street, clutching her bag close as the cool evening air wrapped around her. The notes of music from the hall lingered faintly behind her, a soft echo of the energy that had filled the room. She had left before the evening formally ended, claiming fatigue and an early morning ahead, but in truth, she was unsettled—her mind replaying the moments that had transpired, especially the rare, electrifying moment when Daniel had spoken her name.

The envelope, the cryptic note, the impossible recognition—all of it was tangled in her thoughts. She felt as though she had been nudged into a story that had been quietly waiting for her, a narrative where the rules were unknown, the paths uncertain, and yet impossible to ignore. Her pulse still throbbed at the memory of his voice—low, deliberate, and intimate, despite the distance and anonymity of the crowded hall.

Evelyn's steps slowed as she approached the corner where a small café stood, its soft light spilling onto the pavement. The sign read The Solace Café, unremarkable and familiar, but something compelled her to pause. Perhaps it was the quiet invitation of warmth, the sense of shelter, or perhaps it was her mind searching for a place to process the overwhelming events of the night.

Inside, the café smelled of freshly ground coffee and sugar, the air punctuated with the faint warmth of vanilla and cinnamon. She took a seat near the window, placing her tote bag on the chair beside her. The world outside seemed distant here, muted by glass and the soft buzz of conversation. She had only just settled when her phone vibrated—a single notification.

It was an email, its subject line simple, almost alarming in its brevity: Appointment: Tonight. 9:30 PM. Be on time.

Evelyn's heart caught in her chest. She opened it, her fingers trembling slightly. There were no names, no explanation, just a message that carried with it the same urgency and intentionality as the note in the hall.

She frowned, reading it over and over, trying to reconcile the logic of her life with the mounting strangeness of the evening. Who would know to send such a thing? Why tonight? Why now? The café seemed to shrink around her, her seat suddenly too small, the shadows too sharp.

Despite the confusion, she couldn't ignore the pull. Something told her this was important. Something told her that this appointment—whatever it was—was a crossroads. A pivotal moment that demanded attention.

The time ticked slowly. Each second felt laden with significance. Evelyn's mind raced, cataloging possibilities, rejecting most of them as implausible. But the tension refused to leave her chest. She felt drawn toward it, the quiet insistence of destiny whispering through her veins.

At 9:28 PM, she glanced toward the door. The bell jingled faintly as it opened, and she froze.

Daniel stepped inside.

It was as if the world had tilted slightly on its axis. The familiar pull she had felt earlier that night intensified tenfold. He moved with the same deliberate composure she had observed in the hall, yet there was something softer in his demeanor here, away from the formalities and noise of the event. His eyes found hers immediately, and for a heartbeat, the room vanished. There was only him, only her, only the quiet, almost tangible thread of connection that seemed to bind them together.

He approached her table slowly, as if testing the gravity of the moment. Evelyn's fingers instinctively tightened around her bag strap, her chest constricted with anticipation. She had never expected this—had never planned for a meeting that felt both fated and impossible. And yet here he was, moving toward her, confirming the impossible truth: she was part of a story that had begun before she realized it.

"Evelyn," he said, his voice low, carrying the same weight it had in the hall. The sound of her name made her pulse accelerate, her senses sharpen, and the world outside the café fade further. "You got the message?"

She nodded, unable to speak immediately. The envelope in her bag and the new email felt like two parts of the same puzzle, pieces that demanded attention she wasn't fully prepared to give.

"I did," she whispered finally. "I... I wasn't sure. I didn't know if it was real."

Daniel's gaze softened, a subtle acknowledgment of the confusion mirrored in her eyes. "I understand," he said. "It's... strange. Unusual. But it's important. That's why you're here."

Evelyn studied him, searching for hidden meanings, clues, or explanations. But Daniel's expression was honest, unguarded, carrying the kind of certainty that made it impossible to dismiss him. His presence alone conveyed significance, a subtle authority that demanded attention without force, a quiet gravity that drew her into the orbit of his certainty.

"What is this appointment?" she asked, her voice tentative. "Why now? Why… me?"

Daniel leaned slightly closer, though still careful to respect the distance between them. His eyes held hers with quiet intensity. "Because tonight matters," he said simply. "There are moments that come once in a lifetime—moments that you cannot anticipate, cannot plan for, and yet they shape everything. You almost missed the first. This is the next. One chance. That's all you get."

Evelyn's heart skipped again. The idea of a singular opportunity, a rare intersection of fate, made her chest tighten. One chance to act, to respond, to notice—it carried weight far beyond the simplicity of the words. She felt the gravity of it pressing into her, an invisible force compelling her attention.

"You're serious," she murmured, more to herself than to him.

Daniel's eyes softened further. "I wouldn't bring you here if it weren't. Everything depends on being present in this moment, on noticing the subtle currents you might otherwise ignore. Life… it gives us these moments, but only once. One chance appointment. Miss it, and it's gone."

Evelyn shivered slightly, a mixture of fear, anticipation, and exhilaration coursing through her. She had spent so long observing life from the edges, hesitant, cautious, unwilling to step into uncertainty. And now, here was the living embodiment of that uncertainty, of possibility, waiting in front of her, asking her to choose—to accept or to retreat.

The café was quiet around them. The soft hum of conversation, the clinking of coffee cups, the distant rumble of the city—all of it seemed to exist in a separate reality, removed from the weight of the moment between them. Evelyn felt as though she had stepped out of time itself, into a suspended bubble where destiny whispered its fragile insistence.

Daniel reached into his coat pocket and produced a small card, sliding it across the table to her. Evelyn picked it up, reading the details: an address, a time, and a single line in Daniel's unmistakable handwriting: "Be ready. Don't miss it."

Her pulse quickened. The message was direct, urgent, impossible to ignore. And yet, a part of her hesitated, questioning the reason, the legitimacy, the safety. But the deeper part—the part attuned to subtle currents, to whispers of destiny, to moments almost missed—urged her to act. To move forward. To step into the unknown.

She looked up, meeting his gaze. The air between them was thick with unspoken understanding. No explanations were necessary. No rationalizations. The tension, the anticipation, the rare acknowledgment of a shared understanding—was enough.

Daniel nodded once, a quiet, deliberate gesture. "One chance," he reminded her. "That's all there is. The rest… will unfold only if you choose to be present."

Evelyn nodded, the card trembling slightly in her hand. She felt a strange, thrilling fear, a magnetic pull that made her chest constrict and her mind sharpen simultaneously. One chance. Only one. And somehow, she knew the moment he spoke of was about far more than a mere appointment—it was about possibility, about fate, about the subtle intersections that could change everything.

She stood, smoothing the cardigan around her shoulders, the card still clutched tightly in her hand. The cool night air greeted her again as she stepped outside, her mind a whirlwind of anticipation. Daniel followed, matching her pace as they walked down the quiet street together, neither speaking, both acutely aware of the significance of the moment.

Every step felt deliberate, every breath loaded with unspoken promise. Evelyn realized she was standing at the threshold of something immense, fragile, and impossible to ignore. The one chance appointment had arrived. And she was present.

The night stretched before them, filled with the weight of anticipation, the pulse of possibility, and the quiet insistence of destiny. Evelyn couldn't yet interpret all the signs, couldn't yet understand the full gravity of the moment, but she knew one thing with clarity: she would not let this chance slip away.

And as Daniel walked beside her, the first faint sparks of what could only be described as fate beginning to ignite, Evelyn felt the delicate thrill of stepping into the unknown—a path she had long avoided, now illuminated by the quiet certainty that some moments only happen once.

Tonight. Tonight, everything could change.

12

A CONVERSATION THAT DIDN'T END

The café had emptied almost completely, leaving behind only the faint scent of coffee and the muted hum of the city beyond the windows. Evelyn and Daniel remained, seated across from each other at the small table near the back, the flickering light of a single lamp casting long shadows across their faces. Neither spoke at first. The tension was thick, palpable, an invisible cord winding tightly between them, vibrating with unspoken possibilities and questions that neither could yet articulate.

Evelyn fidgeted with the edge of her tote bag, her fingers tracing the stitching as though it could offer answers she didn't have. The card Daniel had given her burned faintly in her pocket, a reminder of the strange, impossible evening that had brought them here. A one-chance appointment, he had said. And yet, once seated together, it was clear that the moment would stretch far beyond any expectation—fluid, elastic, and uncontainable.

"Do you… do you always do this?" Evelyn asked finally, her voice barely above a whisper. She gestured vaguely toward him, to the certainty in his posture, the quiet authority in his presence. “Appear at the exact right moment? Speak a name like you’ve known it forever? Send messages that… that feel impossible to ignore?”

Daniel’s lips curved slightly, a half-smile that was almost amusement, almost sympathy. He leaned back in his chair, hands clasped loosely on the table. “I don’t think of it as doing anything,” he said calmly. “I think of it as noticing. Paying attention to what almost goes unseen. To what almost passes by without consequence.”

Evelyn’s brow furrowed. “Noticing?”

“Yes,” Daniel said, his voice soft but unwavering. “Life is made of these small, almost imperceptible moments. One glance, one word, one subtle movement—and everything can shift. Sometimes we catch them, sometimes we don’t. That’s all the note, the card, everything—you almost missed it, Evelyn. And that’s why you’re here now.”

Her hands trembled slightly as she processed his words. It was as though the very air around them had changed, charged with the energy of something she had always believed existed but had never truly encountered: deliberate purpose, undeniable connection, and the quiet weight of choice.

“I still don’t understand why you’re here,” she murmured, her voice wavering. “Why me? Out of everyone in the hall, out of everyone in the city… why now? Why this conversation?”

Daniel’s gaze softened, steady and unwavering. “Because sometimes,” he said slowly, “there are moments that demand presence, moments that cannot be postponed or repeated. They demand that we step into the unknown, that we acknowledge possibilities before they slip away. And you—Evelyn—you’ve been stepping into them without even realizing it.”

Her pulse quickened. The words sounded profound, almost prophetic, and yet they carried a simplicity that made her heart ache. She wanted to argue, to question, to retreat into reason, but every instinct—the part of her that had felt the pull all night—told her to remain. To listen. To pay attention.

Daniel leaned slightly forward, elbows resting lightly on the table, his hands loosely clasped. "I've been watching, in a way," he admitted quietly. "Not in a way that's intrusive, but in a way that notices—the small ways people move, the details others might overlook. And I noticed you. Even before the note, even before tonight."

Evelyn blinked, caught off guard. She felt a strange mixture of embarrassment, curiosity, and something deeper, almost reverential, stirring inside her. "Before the note?" she repeated. "You... you knew me?"

"Not in the conventional sense," Daniel said, shaking his head slowly. "I knew you in the way that matters for moments like this. The way that recognizes patterns, choices, and the small shifts in a person's attention that hint at destiny."

Evelyn's chest tightened. The words were abstract, almost incomprehensible, and yet they resonated in her soul, vibrating in the hollow spaces she had long ignored. She felt as though she had been staring at a puzzle for years and had just been handed a piece that didn't fit anywhere—yet demanded to be understood.

"You make it sound like fate," she whispered.

Daniel's gaze met hers, unwavering. "I don't believe in fate as something that forces our hands," he said carefully. "I believe in awareness, in noticing, in taking action when the moment presents itself. You almost missed the first moment. I couldn't let the next pass by unnoticed."

Her fingers pressed against the edge of the table, knuckles white. "And now?" she asked, her voice fragile. "What happens now?"

Daniel's smile was gentle, almost tender, yet carried the gravity of truth. "Now, we continue noticing. Now, we engage. Now, we choose to step fully into the moment rather than retreat from it. Conversations like this—they don't have to end. And sometimes, when they don't end, they change everything."

Evelyn's mind raced. The words were like fire in her chest—thrilling, terrifying, impossible to ignore. She had always been cautious, deliberate, careful not to step beyond the boundaries of what she knew. And yet, here was a man, speaking to her with certainty and clarity, about a world she had always sensed but never dared enter. A world where a single conversation could ripple through time and leave consequences she could neither anticipate nor dismiss.

The silence that followed was heavy, not awkward, but full of potential. Words seemed insufficient to describe the weight of the moment, the tension in the space between them, and the unspoken knowledge that this encounter was no ordinary meeting. The café lights flickered slightly, as if the universe itself were holding its breath.

Evelyn finally exhaled, her hands loosening slightly around her bag. "I feel like… like I'm on the edge of something," she admitted softly, almost to herself. "Something I can't define, can't predict. And yet, I can't step away from it."

Daniel nodded slowly, his eyes steady. "That's because you're noticing," he said. "You're aware, present, engaged. Most people never reach this level of awareness—they let moments slip by, opportunities vanish, connections dissolve. But you… you're here. Fully. Even when it's uncertain. Even when it's uncomfortable."

Her chest heaved slightly with the intensity of his words. She felt the pull of the moment—the kind of pull that demanded action, demanded attention, demanded acknowledgment. And in the depths of her awareness, she realized she had been waiting for this without knowing it, yearning for it without allowing herself to hope.

"Then... this conversation," she began cautiously, "it's not over?"

Daniel shook his head. "Not over," he confirmed. "And it doesn't have to be. It can continue, if we choose. But it will require honesty, attention, and courage. And you've already shown the first two, just by being here, by being present, by noticing."

Evelyn's fingers fidgeted in her lap. Courage. That was the word that struck her hardest. She had always measured herself against what was safe, expected, familiar. But here, with him, courage was something fragile and essential—a choice she had to make with every heartbeat.

"I... I want to continue," she whispered finally. Her voice carried a quiet determination, a tentative step toward the unknown. "Even if I don't fully understand it. Even if I'm afraid."

Daniel's expression softened further, relief and warmth mingling with the familiar intensity in his gaze. "Then we continue," he said simply. "No end. Just... noticing, speaking, engaging. One moment at a time. That's all it takes."

The world outside the café continued its slow rhythm, but inside, the small room seemed suspended in time. Words flowed between them, tentative at first, then more fluid, more natural. They spoke of inconsequential things—music, books, the city at night—yet every sentence carried weight, every glance conveyed understanding, every pause pulsed with unspoken acknowledgment.

Hours passed unnoticed. The hum of the refrigerator behind the counter, the soft footsteps of the barista cleaning up, the occasional honk of distant traffic—all faded into irrelevance. There was only the conversation, the thread that connected them, the unbroken line of presence and awareness.

Evelyn realized, with a quiet thrill, that this was more than mere dialogue. It was a communion of attention, an exchange of recognition, a silent agreement to inhabit the moment fully, without distraction, without fear, without reservation.

And for the first time that evening, she understood a fraction of the note's meaning, the weight of the card, the urgency in Daniel's actions. Moments like this—fleeting, fragile, charged with possibility—were rare. Almost impossible. And yet, they existed, waiting for those who were willing to notice, willing to step into the unknown, willing to speak and listen with their whole selves.

The conversation between them didn't end. And in that refusal to end, in that quiet persistence, Evelyn felt the unmistakable pulse of destiny beginning to weave itself around her life, pulling her forward, drawing her into the narrative she had almost missed.

Tonight was not a beginning in isolation. Tonight was the continuation of something vast, invisible, and unstoppable—something that would not allow itself to be ignored, and that would demand every ounce of attention and courage she could summon.

And as they spoke into the night, the café emptied completely, leaving only the two of them in the glow of the lamp, two people tethered by coincidence, by fate, by a conversation that refused to end, stretching into a future neither could yet imagine.

13

THE SMILE HE TRIED NOT TO NOTICE

The night air was crisp as Evelyn stepped out of the dimly lit café, the quiet streets stretching before her like a promise and a challenge all at once. Her heart was still racing from the conversation she and Daniel had shared—long, fluid, and intoxicatingly alive. Every word, every glance, every subtle gesture had felt deliberate, as though time itself had paused to accommodate the fragile gravity between them.

Daniel walked beside her, a few paces behind, his hands tucked into his coat pockets. The streetlights painted the pavement in patches of gold, illuminating their paths in intermittent bursts. He was quiet, and she noticed that his silence was different from ordinary quiet—it was watchful, deliberate, as if every step, every flicker of movement, was cataloged in a way that seemed almost instinctive.

Evelyn's mind replayed fragments of their conversation—the way he had spoken her name, the certainty in his gaze, the words about noticing, about moments almost missed. It had left her unsettled, exhilarated, and strangely vulnerable all at once. And yet, she couldn't ignore the faint thrill of anticipation that threaded through her chest, tightening with each step.

They reached a small park at the edge of the street, its path lined with ancient trees whose leaves rustled softly in the breeze. The park was nearly empty, save for a couple walking a dog in the distance and the occasional sound of a night bird calling from the shadows. It was private enough, she realized, private enough to feel the intensity of proximity without intrusion.

Daniel slowed, allowing her to move slightly ahead, though not too far. There was a subtle tension in his posture, an almost imperceptible shift in his shoulders, as if he were weighing something inside him, resisting it, and yet unable to completely suppress it. Evelyn noticed it, of course. She always noticed small things—tics, shifts in weight, subtle changes in expression—and that was part of the reason this connection felt so electric.

As she walked, she caught a glimpse of him from the corner of her eye. He was looking at her. Not casually, not with simple observation, but with that focused intensity that had first drawn her attention days before. And then she noticed it—a flicker, almost imperceptible at first, a slight twitch at the corner of his mouth that threatened to become a smile.

He was trying not to notice it.

Evelyn's chest tightened. There was something dangerously intimate in watching him struggle with something as simple, as human, as a smile. It suggested restraint, self-awareness, awareness of the gravity of the moment—an internal tug-of-war that only heightened the tension. She felt simultaneously curious, amused, and slightly disarmed by it.

The smile, when it emerged briefly, was subtle, almost shy, yet it carried a warmth and an energy that seemed to ripple through the space between them. It was not the kind of smile one gave casually or as a courtesy; it was a smile that belonged to someone who had just caught sight of something they hadn't expected but had secretly hoped to see.

Daniel's eyes met hers as the smile threatened to widen. He quickly suppressed it, masking it behind a slight cough, a turn of the head, a subtle shift in his stance. But Evelyn had seen it, and that was enough. She felt her own lips curve involuntarily, a reflexive response to the rare, fleeting glimpse of something so human and so revealing.

"You—" she started, her voice tentative, almost teasing, "you smiled. I saw it."

Daniel froze, the faintest trace of surprise crossing his face. He had clearly thought himself careful, cautious, unobserved, yet her words stripped the moment bare. He blinked once, twice, and finally allowed himself a controlled exhale, a slight concession.

"I... maybe," he said slowly, carefully, "I didn't mean to."

Evelyn laughed softly, the sound low and melodious, carrying with it an irrepressible lightness that belied the tension between them. "It's okay," she said, her voice gentle, coaxing. "I noticed. And I think it's... nice."

Daniel's gaze softened, though the faint line of tension in his jaw remained. He glanced away for a moment, then back at her, and finally, after a long pause, allowed the smile to surface fully, though restrained, subtle, controlled, but unmistakably present. It was as if he were testing boundaries, daring the moment to exist without judgment or restraint.

Evelyn felt a ripple of warmth spread through her chest. That smile—fleeting, imperfect, restrained—was laden with meaning. It spoke of attraction, curiosity, amusement, and a cautious acknowledgment of the connection they were threading together. More than words, more than gestures, it conveyed something elemental: an unspoken truth neither could yet articulate, but both understood.

“Why do you try not to smile?” she asked softly, her gaze holding his.

Daniel’s eyes darkened slightly, a shadow of thought flickering across his features. “Because… sometimes,” he began carefully, “when you smile, even just a little, it changes everything. It changes the way people notice you, the way moments unfold, the way… feelings form. And I can’t afford for everything to shift too quickly.”

Evelyn tilted her head, intrigued. “Shift too quickly?”

“Yes,” he said, his voice low, deliberate, almost confessional. “Some things… some connections… they need time. Observation. Patience. Not everything can—or should—be rushed. And yet, you make it difficult not to notice. To feel. To respond.”

She felt heat rise to her cheeks. His words were neither teasing nor casual—they carried an intimate weight, a deliberate awareness of the impact he had on her, and perhaps, the impact she had on him. The tension in the air thickened, as if the night itself had become a living presence, aware of their proximity, their unspoken desires, their mutual restraint.

They continued walking along the dimly lit path, side by side now, the unspoken thread of connection pulling taut between them with each step. Evelyn’s thoughts were a swirl of anticipation, curiosity, and something deeper—something that felt like the quiet recognition of inevitability. She realized that each glance, each gesture, each subtle smile held more weight than ordinary interactions.

Daniel glanced at her again, and for a moment, the smile surfaced once more, fleeting but undeniable. He quickly suppressed it, but the residue of warmth lingered in the space between them. Evelyn caught it, and she understood instinctively: he was as affected by her as she was by him.

"Do you always try to control yourself like this?" she asked, a teasing note in her voice.

He chuckled softly, a low sound that vibrated in his chest before escaping his lips. "Not always," he admitted. "But with certain things... certain people... it's necessary. To avoid mistakes. To avoid jumping too far ahead."

Evelyn's chest tightened. She had expected charm, casual conversation, or perhaps a spark of flirtation. But this—this careful, deliberate restraint—was intoxicating in a way she hadn't anticipated. It was as though every suppressed smile, every fleeting glance, carried more meaning than a hundred overt gestures ever could.

They reached the edge of the park, where the street opened into the quieter residential area. The night was still, the shadows longer, the occasional distant car the only reminder that the city continued its rhythm beyond their moment. Evelyn felt the pull of the evening's significance—the conversations, the notes, the impossible appointments, and now this restrained, deliberate smile that conveyed so much without speaking a word.

"You're difficult to read," she murmured, her voice low, thoughtful.

Daniel's eyes twinkled faintly, the hint of a smile tugging at the corners of his lips once more. "Maybe," he said quietly, "but maybe that's part of noticing, part of paying attention. You don't notice what's obvious. You notice what's subtle, fleeting, almost missed. And that... that's rare."

Evelyn's lips curved into a small, genuine smile. "Maybe," she said softly, "that's why I noticed your smile."

Daniel's jaw loosened slightly, and he allowed himself to chuckle—a controlled, deliberate sound that held warmth without surrender. The smile remained, faint but persistent, carrying with it the promise of attention, understanding, and the potential for moments yet to come.

For Evelyn, the evening had shifted again. The note, the card, the impossible appointment—all of it led here, to this subtle, restrained smile, to the fragile acknowledgment of something neither could fully articulate but both felt profoundly. And she realized, with a quiet thrill, that the smallest gestures—the almost smiles, the suppressed acknowledgments, the deliberate glances—often carried the heaviest weight.

And Daniel—he was learning, struggling, attempting to contain something that refused containment. And in that struggle, in that quiet tension, Evelyn felt the gravity of the moment deepen, pulling her closer into a story that was unfolding in the space between gestures, in the quietness of restraint, in the almost imperceptible smiles that spoke louder than words ever could.

Tonight, she realized, would be remembered not for what was said, but for what was almost revealed.

The night stretched before them, endless, filled with possibility, charged with anticipation, and alive with the subtle pulse of a connection neither could ignore. And Daniel—despite himself—was beginning to notice that some things were impossible to hide.

Even a smile.

14

WHY HER PRESENCE FELT FAMILIAR

The night had grown colder, the wind moving through the streets in restless currents, curling around the edges of the dimly lit lampposts. Evelyn pulled her cardigan tighter around her shoulders, the crisp air making her shiver slightly, though the tension in her chest, a different kind of heat, kept her alert. Daniel walked beside her, quiet but attentive, the earlier restraint giving way to something subtler—an almost imperceptible ease in his posture, as though he were finally allowing himself to notice everything without fear.

Evelyn's mind was a whirlwind of questions, impressions, and an unsettling awareness that tonight was not ordinary. Every step, every glance, every breath felt charged, saturated with a gravity she could not yet name. She had felt it before, fleetingly—the sudden recognition of a place, a face, a moment—and she realized now that it was happening again, this time with him.

As they turned onto a quieter street, the yellow glow of the lamps casting long shadows along the cracked sidewalks, Evelyn noticed something peculiar about Daniel. He wasn't just observing her—he was remembering.

Something about the way he looked at her, the pauses in his speech, the subtle shifts in his body language, suggested that her presence stirred a memory, a sensation, or an echo of a moment long past.

"Do you feel it too?" she asked suddenly, breaking the silence. Her voice was tentative, almost hesitant, as though daring to give form to the uneasy sensation in her chest.

Daniel glanced at her, eyebrows slightly furrowed, and then shook his head slowly. "I don't know," he admitted, his tone careful. "It's strange… I feel… familiarity. Not just in the way I notice you, but in the way… being near you feels like it should be remembered. Like something inside me recognizes you before my mind does."

Evelyn's heart skipped a beat. She had never heard anyone articulate that before—not like this, not so precisely, so consciously. She felt the weight of it pressing into her chest, a subtle tug of destiny she couldn't yet interpret.

"Familiarity?" she echoed, curiosity tinged with wonder. "Do you mean… like déjà vu?"

"No," Daniel said softly, his eyes fixed on a patch of cracked pavement ahead. "Déjà vu is fleeting. This… this feels deeper. It's not just memory—it's recognition. Something my soul remembers, even if my mind cannot place it. It's as if… as if our paths have crossed before, in ways I cannot fully comprehend, yet my instincts recall."

Evelyn's fingers tightened around the strap of her bag. The idea was impossible, improbable, yet it resonated with a hidden part of her that had always sensed that life contained invisible threads, connections that defied ordinary explanation. She had felt something similar when she had first noticed him in the hall, when he had spoken her name, and again at the café. Now, walking beside him in the night, the feeling had grown, rippling through her consciousness with quiet insistence.

"Do you think... we've met before?" she asked, her voice barely above a whisper. She feared the answer, yet part of her longed for it.

Daniel hesitated. He tilted his head slightly, the expression on his face serious, searching. "I don't know in the conventional sense," he said slowly. "I can't place a moment in time or space where I've seen you before. But I know the sensation—the awareness of your presence—it's ancient, somehow. As if a thread between us existed long before tonight."

Evelyn felt a shiver run down her spine. There was a quiet intensity in his voice, the kind that left no room for triviality, no room for doubt. It wasn't mere attraction or curiosity—it was an acknowledgment of something deeper, something that transcended casual connection. Something that felt like destiny but carried the weight of memory.

They continued walking in silence for a few moments, the faint crunch of gravel under their shoes filling the gaps in conversation. Evelyn's mind wandered, sifting through fragments of memory, fleeting impressions she could not place. Faces in crowds, fleeting glances, moments almost forgotten—yet now they seemed to shimmer with new significance. Her heart pounded with the possibility that Daniel's presence, too, had been imprinted in the hidden corners of her life, a lingering echo she had not consciously recognized.

"You feel it too, don't you?" she asked again, more insistently this time, her curiosity a quiet demand.

Daniel's eyes met hers, steady and unwavering. "Yes," he said finally. "It's subtle, almost imperceptible, but it's there. Your presence... it feels like a door I've been searching for, a door I didn't know existed until now. And the moment I noticed it, everything else fell into place. Almost like the universe was reminding me of something I had almost forgotten."

Evelyn's chest tightened. The weight of his words pressed into her heart, but not in a suffocating way—rather, it was a pull, a tether, a magnetic force drawing her closer to understanding, even as the details remained obscured. She felt the thrill of recognition, the quiet electricity of moments almost missed, and the strange vulnerability of standing at the edge of something immense and invisible.

They paused near a small fountain in the center of a quiet square, the water trickling softly, reflecting the muted light of the surrounding lamps. The world seemed to shrink around them, leaving only the two of them and the fragile, electric thread that connected their awareness. Evelyn noticed the way Daniel's eyes lingered on her, the subtle shift of his stance as if he were holding himself back from reaching closer.

"Do you ever wonder," she asked softly, "why some people feel familiar, even when you've never met them? Why some faces, some voices, some gestures... resonate like echoes of something you've lost or forgotten?"

Daniel's expression darkened slightly, contemplative. "I do," he admitted. "More than I used to. Because sometimes, when someone feels familiar, it's not just about memory. It's about recognition—of patterns, of presence, of energy. It's a quiet, undeniable certainty that this moment... this person... matters in ways you cannot yet explain."

Evelyn swallowed hard. The idea resonated with her, aligning with the strange, unshakable certainty she had felt since the first encounter: in the hall, on the street, at the café. Daniel's presence had never felt ordinary. It carried a gravity, a subtle insistence, a recognition that seemed to bypass reason and touch the very core of her being.

"I've felt it before," she whispered, almost to herself. "This... feeling. That someone's presence can change everything without even speaking. That moments have weight, even if you can't see it. That some connections… refuse to be ignored."

Daniel's gaze softened. "Exactly," he said quietly. "And that's why noticing matters. That's why presence matters. Because these fleeting recognitions, these almost forgotten connections, they guide us. They point us toward the moments we are meant to encounter—sometimes only once, sometimes only in small glimpses. And your presence… Evelyn… it's one of those moments I cannot ignore."

Her fingers tightened around the edge of her cardigan, her chest heaving with a mix of anticipation, fear, and something deeper—a raw awareness that her life, her understanding of connection, her perception of destiny, had shifted irreversibly. She realized, with sudden clarity, that the sensation of familiarity was not just about the past—it was about alignment, about resonance, about the quiet threads that wove together moments, people, and choices into patterns that defied ordinary understanding.

The wind picked up slightly, rustling the leaves in the trees overhead. Evelyn shivered, though the chill was more a reflection of the intensity of the moment than the temperature. She looked at Daniel, and for the first time, she allowed herself to fully acknowledge the truth of his presence, the undeniable weight of the recognition, and the fragile, exhilarating thrill of being seen in a way that transcended ordinary awareness.

"Then… this isn't just coincidence?" she asked softly, her voice barely audible above the trickle of the fountain.

"No," Daniel said, his tone deliberate and unwavering. "It never is. Not for moments like this. Not for connections like ours. There is a reason your presence feels familiar. And that reason… will unfold, if we notice it carefully enough, if we remain present enough, if we allow ourselves to recognize it without fear."

Evelyn's chest tightened again, a mixture of excitement, apprehension, and awe. The night had revealed truths she could not yet name, and yet she understood the essential core: Daniel's awareness of her, the quiet familiarity that pulsed between them, and the tension of recognition, were all part of something larger, something beyond chance, something that demanded attention, courage, and subtle surrender.

They stood there for a long moment, silent, eyes meeting, hearts aware of the invisible thread binding them. Neither moved closer, yet the proximity, the recognition, and the shared awareness made every second pulse with significance. Evelyn realized she was standing on the edge of understanding, facing something she could not yet fully grasp, yet could no longer ignore.

And in the quiet, in the soft rustle of leaves, in the trickle of the fountain, Evelyn understood a truth that both terrified and exhilarated her: some presences, some connections, some encounters are never ordinary. They are familiar before they are known, recognized before they are understood, and powerful enough to shift the very course of a life if one allows them to be noticed.

Her presence felt familiar to him. His presence felt impossible to ignore to her. And in that recognition, in that quiet awareness, the night seemed to pulse with possibility, ready to reveal the moments they had almost missed—and the ones they were only just beginning to understand.

15

THE UNEXPECTED RIDE HOME

The city had grown quiet as Evelyn and Daniel stepped out of the park, the wind carrying the faint scent of rain and distant asphalt. The night felt suspended, neither fully alive nor fully asleep, a space where time seemed pliable and ordinary rules didn't quite apply. Evelyn tugged her cardigan closer around her, though it was more a protective gesture than a practical one. She wasn't cold—at least, not in the usual sense—but her chest hummed with a tension that made each step feel deliberate, each breath purposeful.

Daniel walked beside her, hands in his coat pockets, his posture calm, composed, yet subtly alert. There was an energy about him that had shifted since their conversation in the park—a subtle relaxation, but also a deeper focus. He seemed attuned to everything: the sound of the night, the uneven pavement beneath their feet, the faint glimmer of the streetlights bouncing off puddles from an earlier rain. And, most importantly, to her.

They had been walking for nearly twenty minutes, the conversation flowing in fragments, interrupted by pauses that were weighted with unspoken understanding. Every now and then, Daniel's gaze would flicker, his eyes catching hers briefly before he quickly looked away, as if struggling to maintain composure. Evelyn noticed these small shifts, these almost imperceptible signs, and they made her pulse quicken. She understood that he was as aware of her as she was of him—and that awareness carried its own dangerous, intoxicating charge.

"I didn't expect to end up walking this far," Evelyn said softly, her voice careful, almost hesitant, as if speaking aloud might break the fragile tension enveloping them.

Daniel's lips curved into the faintest hint of a smile, restrained and controlled, as though he were aware of its power and unwilling to fully unleash it. "Neither did I," he admitted. "But sometimes the unexpected... carries the weight of intention. It's rarely random. You notice these things?"

Evelyn nodded, her fingers brushing against the strap of her bag. "I notice everything," she said. "Sometimes it's exhausting, but... I notice. And tonight... everything feels charged."

Daniel's gaze softened, his eyes holding a depth she couldn't quite name. "Charged... yes," he said. "That's one way to put it. Moments like these—they're fleeting. But they leave traces, impressions that linger long after the night ends. You can almost... feel them embedding themselves into your memory."

Evelyn's pulse quickened at the thought. She had felt that embedding all evening—the subtle, insistent pull of recognition, the almost imperceptible threads weaving her life toward something she couldn't yet define. She realized with a quiet thrill that it wasn't just the night, or the city, or even Daniel—it was the rare, almost imperceptible weight of moments that demanded presence.

As they reached the intersection near her apartment building, the streetlights flickered, casting shifting shadows along the pavement. Evelyn hesitated, glancing toward the crosswalk, then back at Daniel. She was about to step forward when a sound—sharp, sudden, unmistakable—made her freeze. A car horn blared from behind, the engine roaring to life with urgency.

Daniel reacted instantly, stepping slightly in front of her, a protective presence she hadn't consciously realized she craved. The horn sounded again, closer this time, and the driver's frustration was palpable. Evelyn's heart leapt into her throat. She felt the familiar, almost electric surge of danger—not from recklessness, but from the simple fragility of life, of the moment, of choice.

"Are you okay?" Daniel asked, his voice calm but threaded with concern.

She nodded quickly, trying to steady herself. "I—I'm fine," she stammered, though her fingers shook slightly.

He gave a subtle nod, eyes still scanning the street, before gesturing toward the corner. "Let's get you home," he said. "It's late, and… well, I don't think the night's finished with us yet."

Evelyn hesitated, uncertainty flickering in her chest. The suggestion, simple as it seemed, carried an unspoken weight. It was not an offer of protection, exactly, nor of intimacy—it was both and neither, hovering in the tension between safety and possibility.

"I don't want to trouble you," she murmured, her voice quiet, almost reverent.

"You're not," he said firmly, his eyes holding hers with an intensity that made it impossible to protest. "I insist. Consider it… part of noticing. Part of ensuring the moments that matter aren't missed."

Her chest tightened. The word insist carried weight. Authority. The unspoken acknowledgment that some opportunities could not, should not, be deferred. The subtle thread of destiny—or whatever it was—pulled her forward, and she allowed herself to nod.

They crossed the street together, the quiet hum of the city around them, and approached Daniel's car parked just a few paces away. He opened the passenger side door for her, a gesture that was courteous but also deliberate, controlled, layered with intent. Evelyn felt a thrill ripple through her. Each action, no matter how ordinary, seemed charged with subtle significance, a delicate tension that had built throughout the night.

As she settled into the seat, Daniel slid into the driver's side, the familiar click of the seatbelt closing around him echoing faintly in the stillness. He started the engine, the low rumble vibrating through the car, and for a moment, the two of them sat in silence, the hum of the city barely audible over the quiet that stretched like a living thing around them.

The drive began slowly, Daniel's hands steady on the wheel. Evelyn's eyes traced the contours of the city as it passed by: streetlights reflected in puddles, shutters closed on silent shops, the occasional flicker of neon from distant signs. And yet, she was acutely aware of Daniel, of his presence beside her, of the subtle tension that radiated from him in waves she could feel even without looking directly at him.

"You didn't mention your apartment earlier," he said, breaking the silence, his voice low, deliberate. "Is this… nearby?"

"Yes," Evelyn replied softly. "A few blocks away. I usually walk, but…" She trailed off, aware of how much had changed since the night had begun. How ordinary routines had shifted into something charged, something fragile, something dangerous in its intensity.

Daniel glanced at her briefly, his eyes catching the faint light from the dashboard, and she noticed a subtle shift in his expression. He was trying not to let the faintest trace of a smile or a reaction escape. The almost imperceptible tension in his jaw suggested he was aware, hyper-aware, of the proximity of her presence and the energy between them.

"Do you often accept unexpected rides home from strangers?" he asked lightly, though there was an undercurrent of something deeper—concern, curiosity, perhaps even caution.

Evelyn's lips curved into a faint smile, a reflexive acknowledgment of the irony. "Strangers? You're hardly a stranger now," she replied, her voice soft, layered with teasing and caution. "And no—I don't usually. But tonight… it feels… different."

Daniel's eyes flicked briefly to hers, and for the first time that night, she caught the faintest glimmer of emotion in his gaze. It wasn't overt, not a declaration, not a confession—but it was there. A spark, subtle and restrained, that threatened to ignite if either of them let it.

The car moved through the quiet streets, the hum of the tires against the asphalt a steady rhythm beneath the fragile tension in the cabin. Every glance, every movement, every subtle gesture was charged. Evelyn realized that this ride, unplanned, unexpected, carried with it the same weight as every other moment they had shared tonight—the weight of awareness, of possibility, of connection almost missed but now deliberately acknowledged.

As they approached her building, the streetlights reflected in the windows of the car, and Evelyn felt a sudden, startling realization: nothing about tonight had been ordinary. Every choice, every glance, every almost-missed moment had been orchestrated by something unseen, a quiet force she could not name. And now, this unexpected ride home, fraught with the tension of presence and proximity, felt like yet another thread in a tapestry she was only beginning to understand.

Daniel stopped the car in front of her building, the engine idling softly. The silence that followed was heavy, charged with unspoken acknowledgment. Evelyn turned to him, the weight of the night pressing into her chest.

"Thank you," she said softly, her voice almost a whisper, layered with gratitude, anticipation, and something deeper she could not yet name.

Daniel nodded, his eyes meeting hers with steady intensity. "Tonight isn't over," he said quietly, almost as if confessing. "This ride… it's just another part of noticing. Another step in moments that matter."

Evelyn felt her pulse quicken, the tension between them vibrating like a wire stretched taut. She realized with clarity that nothing tonight was ordinary—not the hall, not the café, not the conversation, not the subtle smiles, not even this unexpected ride home. Everything had been charged, deliberate, almost impossible to ignore.

And as she opened the car door, the cool night air rushing in, she understood a truth she could not yet articulate: the night was not finished with either of them, and neither would ever forget this ride—unexpected, suspenseful, and impossible to dismiss.

16

A NUMBER SAVED WITHOUT INTENTION

The night had thickened into a quiet darkness as Evelyn stepped into her apartment building, the faint hum of the city streets below fading into a distant murmur. Her footsteps echoed softly along the tiled corridor, a rhythm that seemed almost in sync with the rapid thrum of her pulse. She could still feel Daniel's presence lingering—the warmth of proximity, the subtle tension of shared awareness, and the faint echo of every word spoken during the night. Even though he had left, it was as if a piece of him remained, tucked invisibly into the folds of her mind.

Once inside her apartment, Evelyn closed the door with a gentle click and leaned against it for a moment, taking a slow, deliberate breath. Her mind was restless, replaying fragments of the evening: the park, the café, the near-collision on the street, the suppressed smiles, the unexpected ride home. Each memory pulsed with a resonance that made her chest tighten, a quiet insistence that tonight had been far more than chance.

She moved to her desk, flicking on a small lamp, and reached for her phone. It had been a casual gesture, almost unconscious, as though she were seeking a connection or a thread to hold onto after the whirlwind of the evening. Her thumb hovered over the screen, but she hadn't intended to save a number, hadn't even thought to ask for one. Yet there it was—his number, sent earlier in the day through a brief, almost perfunctory message: "In case noticing moments matters to you."

Evelyn stared at it, the digits glowing softly against the dark screen. She hadn't consciously made the decision to save it; her fingers moved almost on their own, tapping "Add Contact" and naming it simply: Daniel. The act felt insignificant, mundane even, but underneath it, she sensed a quiet shift—a subtle acknowledgment that she was opening herself to possibilities, whether she was ready for them or not.

Her heart raced as she realized the implications. Saving his number without intention was not a calculated move; it was instinctual, almost unconscious. And yet, it carried a weight she could not ignore, as if some part of her had always known she would do this, even before the moment arrived. The thought made her shiver.

She sank into her chair, phone in hand, and stared at the screen. A thousand questions swirled through her mind. Why did it feel so natural to save his number? Why did the simple act feel loaded with meaning, a marker of connection, a subtle declaration? And why, despite her best attempts to remain cautious, did her fingers tremble slightly as she set the phone down, fully aware that a single call or message could change everything?

Her thoughts were interrupted by a soft buzz from the phone. She looked down, startled, and saw a message notification from Daniel: "I hope the night wasn't too heavy for you."

Evelyn's breath caught. His words were brief, almost casual, yet they carried the weight of careful attention. He had noticed her, he had acknowledged the subtle tension of the evening, and he had extended a thread—delicate, almost invisible, yet impossible to ignore. Her fingers moved automatically, opening the message and crafting a response that balanced curiosity, caution, and the faint thrill of engagement:

"It wasn't heavy. It was… unforgettable."

She pressed send before she could second-guess herself, and immediately felt a rush of exhilaration. The exchange was small, almost insignificant in the eyes of the world, but for her, it carried the resonance of all the moments that had preceded it—the subtle gestures, the suppressed smiles, the near-misses, the careful observation. Each detail threaded into the next, forming a tapestry of awareness that was far too intricate to be dismissed as coincidence.

Her mind wandered, replaying his expression during the ride home, the quiet attention in his gaze, the almost imperceptible signs that he was measuring each moment, each movement. She remembered the brief hesitation before he spoke, the way he had glanced at her as though weighing whether or not to reveal the faintest hint of a smile. And she understood, in a deep, almost intuitive way, that the act of saving his number was a continuation of that delicate interplay—another subtle step in the dance neither of them fully controlled.

A knock at her apartment door startled her, and her pulse leapt. She hesitated, considering whether to answer, but quickly realized it was just the wind rattling the frame. Her laugh was soft, almost self-conscious, a release of tension she hadn't realized she had been holding. She sank back into her chair, phone still in hand, and felt the quiet gravity of the night pressing against her chest.

Daniel's message buzzed again: "There's more to tonight than we can unpack in one evening. I'm glad we didn't miss it."

Evelyn's fingers hovered over the screen, a thrill running through her as she considered the weight of his words. "We didn't miss it," she typed back, "but… what if we almost did?"

She hit send, and the phone rested in her lap, vibrating faintly with anticipation. The conversation, though brief and text-based, carried the same subtle tension as their encounters in person. It was a thread, fragile and tentative, that connected them across distance, across the quiet of the night, across the unspoken acknowledgment of something larger than either of them fully understood.

Her mind drifted to the idea of intention—or the lack thereof. Saving his number without consciously deciding to do so felt like surrendering to something outside her control, something invisible yet undeniable. It was as though a part of her was listening to a deeper rhythm, one that guided moments, nudged decisions, and connected people in ways that were impossible to orchestrate. She realized, with a mixture of awe and apprehension, that she had become part of that rhythm tonight, whether she intended to or not.

Evelyn leaned back in her chair, phone in hand, and reflected on the strange alchemy of the evening. The near-collisions, the café conversations, the suppressed smiles, the ride home—all had led to this moment, this simple act of saving a number without intention, and yet imbued with meaning. It was as if the night had been quietly orchestrated, each detail deliberate, each action layered with unseen significance. And the number—just a string of digits—was now a symbol, a key, a tether to moments yet to come.

Her thoughts were interrupted again by another message from Daniel: "Rest, if you can. Tomorrow may bring more moments we almost miss."

Evelyn felt a shiver run down her spine. The words were casual, almost playful, but beneath them lay the unmistakable tension of foresight. He wasn't speaking merely about tomorrow in the ordinary sense; he was speaking about anticipation, about presence, about the subtle weight of choices that could alter trajectories. Saving his number without intention suddenly felt like a pact, a quiet acknowledgment of participation in a story neither of them fully controlled.

Her fingers hovered over the phone again, but she didn't respond immediately. Instead, she set it down, her mind spinning with the possibilities. The act of saving the number had been unconscious, instinctual, yet it carried the gravity of intention. She realized that the smallest actions, the ones performed without thought, often carried the deepest consequences.

Evelyn moved to her window, looking out over the quiet city. Lights twinkled faintly in the distance, casting a soft glow over the buildings, streets, and shadows. The night felt alive with potential, charged with anticipation, and impossible to ignore. She understood that this evening, these encounters, these almost-moments, had shifted something fundamental within her. She had stepped across a threshold she hadn't known existed, and the number saved without intention was the first tangible sign that her life—and perhaps Daniel's—was no longer bound by ordinary routines.

The phone buzzed once more, briefly illuminating the room: "Good night, Evelyn. Until we notice again."

She stared at the message, a thrill of recognition pulsing through her. The night had not ended—it had only transformed. And in that transformation, she realized that the act of saving his number without intention was far more than a convenience or a casual gesture. It was an acknowledgment, a subtle surrender to awareness, to connection, to moments that demanded attention and courage.

Evelyn set the phone down beside her bed, her heart still racing, her mind alive with anticipation. She knew that the number was more than a series of digits—it was a tether to possibilities, a quiet key to doors she had only glimpsed, and a reminder that sometimes, even the smallest, most unconscious actions could alter the course of a life.

As she lay down, the night pressing gently against her windowpane, Evelyn felt a subtle, unshakable certainty. She had saved the number without intention, but the universe had noticed. And that, she realized, was enough to begin a story neither she nor Daniel could fully control, yet both would be compelled to follow.

Tonight, a number had been saved. And with it, a thread had been secured—a thread that would carry them into moments almost missed, near connections, and the subtle, suspenseful unfolding of something far larger than either of them had anticipated.

17

WHEN MESSAGES FEEL LIKE MORNING SUNSHINE

Evelyn woke to the soft glow of dawn filtering through the thin curtains of her bedroom. The city outside was slowly stirring, the distant hum of traffic and the faint chirping of birds blending into the quiet symphony of morning. She lay still for a few moments, wrapped in the cocoon of blankets, her mind already dancing with fragments of the previous night. The unexpected ride, the quiet intensity, the suppressed smiles, and the number she had saved without intention—they all hovered in her thoughts, lingering like a soft, persistent melody that refused to fade.

Then, her phone vibrated softly on the bedside table, pulling her from her reverie. She reached for it, half expecting a routine notification, half hoping it was something more. Her breath caught as she saw Daniel's name light up the screen. The message was simple, almost deceptively casual:

"Good morning, Evelyn. I hope the city greets you kindly today."

Evelyn's lips curved into a smile, soft and almost involuntary. There was a warmth in those words, a quiet attentiveness that felt almost tangible. It was like the first rays of sunshine sneaking through the blinds, gentle yet insistent, touching her consciousness with subtle but undeniable force. The way he phrased it—the city greets you kindly—wasn't just ordinary politeness; it carried the weight of observation, of consideration, of awareness that lingered long after the night had ended.

She responded carefully, fingers hovering over the keys before typing:

"Good morning, Daniel. The city seems brighter than usual... maybe it's because of your message."

She hit send, then leaned back against her pillow, savoring the quiet thrill that pulsed through her chest. Text messages could have been mundane, impersonal, and fleeting—but his words were different. They carried a resonance that made her heart quicken, a subtle energy that transformed the ordinary act of reading into an intimate connection. It was the way sunlight slants through the window at just the right angle, warming the room and illuminating every dust particle, making even the most mundane surfaces glow with quiet significance.

Her phone buzzed again, and she instinctively opened it, anticipating the reply even before seeing it.

"I'm glad to hear that. I had a feeling today would be better for you... though I must admit, my reasons for knowing are complicated."

Evelyn's pulse quickened. The cryptic nature of his message made her lean forward, curiosity wrapping around her like a delicate thread. What could he mean? Complicated reasons for knowing? Was it intuition, observation, or something deeper—something that neither of them had yet fully acknowledged? She felt a thrill of suspense, that same quiet tension that had colored the previous night, seeping into the new day like an invisible force guiding her attention.

She typed back, letting her fingers move almost instinctively:

"Complicated reasons? Now you have me intrigued… tell me more."

The reply came quickly, almost faster than she expected, and she felt a flutter of excitement at the immediacy.

"Some things are easier to notice than explain. Some connections… you can sense them before they exist fully in time. I think last night proved that."

Evelyn's heart raced. His words carried the same weight as his glances, the same subtle charge that had made every moment feel fragile, intense, and significant. It wasn't just flirtation; it wasn't casual charm. It was something deeper—an awareness that stretched beyond ordinary understanding, touching the edges of intuition, of recognition, of almost forgotten threads that had woven their lives together before either of them realized.

She couldn't help but respond with the same mixture of curiosity and vulnerability:

"I felt it too. Like something existed between us before last night… like a thread I hadn't noticed until it tugged at me."

Daniel's reply was nearly instantaneous, and she could almost hear the faint smile in his words:

"Exactly. That thread is persistent. It has a way of pulling, even when we don't fully understand why. I'm glad we didn't ignore it."

Evelyn leaned back, staring at the ceiling, the early morning light brushing her cheeks with soft warmth. Messages like these, brief and text-based, should have been inconsequential. Yet with Daniel, they were anything but.

Each word, each carefully chosen phrase, carried layers of meaning and subtle suspense. They were almost like tiny beacons, drawing her attention and curiosity, and creating a delicate anticipation for what might come next.

Her mind wandered to the way he had looked at her during the ride home—the restrained smiles, the glances held just long enough to notice but not linger. Every message now mirrored that same dynamic: delicate, precise, charged with intention without revealing all its secrets. It was as if their connection had moved into a new space, one where distance could no longer diminish the intensity, and where even the simplest exchange could carry the weight of unspoken truths.

Evelyn couldn't resist teasing him slightly, testing the boundaries of their evolving connection. She typed:

"Persistent threads can be dangerous, you know… they tug when we're least prepared."

A moment later, his reply came, measured but playful:

"Perhaps. But some dangers are worth noticing. Some threads… are worth following, even if they lead us to unexpected places."

The subtle flirtation, the almost imperceptible suspense woven into his words, made her pulse quicken. She realized, with a quiet thrill, that their exchanges were becoming a kind of ritual—a morning dance of awareness and restraint, curiosity and revelation, intention and unconscious action. Messages felt like sunlight because they illuminated unseen corners of her consciousness, revealing patterns and sensations she hadn't yet fully recognized.

As she scrolled through the conversation, Evelyn noticed something else: a rhythm, a cadence in his language that mirrored his presence in person. The pauses, the careful choice of words, the balance of playfulness and gravity—they all reflected the subtle tension she had felt throughout the night. It was almost uncanny, how a series of simple messages could recreate the same charged atmosphere as the park, the café, and the ride home.

Her thoughts drifted to the notion of intentionality—or the absence of it. Just as she had saved his number without thinking, she now realized that each response, each engagement with his words, was an unspoken participation in a delicate, unfolding story. Neither of them needed to consciously orchestrate it; the energy between them was sufficient to create the suspense, the connection, and the intimate awareness that made even simple messages feel like sunlight on her skin.

The phone buzzed again, drawing her back. This time, the message carried a different note—soft, personal, yet still tinged with subtle suspense:

"I hope your morning starts as bright as your awareness makes my night. And if today brings more threads, I hope we notice them together."

Evelyn's fingers froze above the keyboard. Notice them together. The phrase resonated, carrying the weight of shared attention and quiet intimacy. It was a simple suggestion, yet it implied partnership, presence, and anticipation—an acknowledgment that whatever lay ahead, they would face it with awareness, together. Her chest tightened with a mixture of anticipation and excitement.

She responded carefully, her own words carrying the same subtle balance of curiosity and restraint:

"I hope so too. And if the threads pull, I'll follow... but I'll need you to keep pace."

Almost immediately, his reply arrived:

"I'll keep pace. And maybe, if we're careful, we'll catch the threads before they slip away."

Evelyn smiled softly, leaning back against her pillow. She realized that the messages were more than conversation—they were a continuation of the night's unspoken tension, a bridge connecting moments, gestures, and almost-missed glances into a coherent, suspenseful whole. Each word carried significance, each phrase a subtle invitation to awareness, anticipation, and engagement.

She glanced out the window again, the morning light growing stronger, casting long, golden rays across the room. The city was waking, but Evelyn felt suspended in a space that was neither fully morning nor fully night—a place where the intensity of connection and the thrill of recognition persisted, where messages from Daniel felt like morning sunshine warming corners of her mind she hadn't yet explored.

As she set the phone down beside her, Evelyn understood something profound: the smallest gestures—the saved number, the carefully chosen words, the subtle timing of a message—had the power to transform ordinary life into something charged, suspenseful, and unforgettable. Each message was not just communication, but a thread, a pulse, a reminder that presence, attention, and intention—even unspoken or unconscious—could illuminate the world in unexpected ways.

And as the city fully awoke, Evelyn realized that this morning, unlike any before, had begun with light, warmth, and the subtle, thrilling awareness of connection—an awareness that would continue to unfold, one almost-moment, one subtle message, one delicate thread at a time.

18

THE COFFEE HE DIDN'T KNOW HE NEEDED

The morning had arrived with its usual clamor: car horns, the faint rustle of newspapers, and the low hum of a city waking slowly but insistently. Evelyn stepped out of her apartment building, the air crisp, carrying the faint scent of rain from the night before. The streets were already buzzing with pedestrians, hurried and focused, yet for her, the world had narrowed to a smaller radius—a radius that pulsed with anticipation. Every shadow, every movement seemed more vivid, more significant. She adjusted her scarf and stepped lightly toward the corner café she had been frequenting for weeks, drawn by the comforting routine and the ritual of solitude that she often sought in the early hours.

Daniel had not been mentioned, nor had she planned to think about him during her solitary morning ritual. Yet, as she approached the familiar wooden door of the café, the sensation of him—subtle, insistent, and lingering—made her stomach tighten. It was the same feeling she had experienced the night before, the same thread of awareness that refused to be ignored.

The bell above the door jingled softly as she stepped inside, the rich aroma of roasted coffee beans and the low murmur of conversation enveloping her. She moved past the counter and toward her usual corner table by the window, tucking herself into the small nook she had claimed as her own. She placed her bag carefully on the chair beside her, her mind wandering, half-conscious of the subtle tension that had become an undercurrent in her life.

Daniel, however, was nowhere to be seen. At least, she thought he wasn't. She ordered her usual—black coffee, no sugar, a hint of cream on the side—and settled in, pulling her notebook from her bag. She had intended to sketch, to write, to lose herself in the quiet world she had created for herself in this small corner of the city.

But the universe, it seemed, had other plans.

A low, familiar voice cut through the hum of conversation: "Evelyn?"

She looked up and froze. There he was—Daniel, standing near the counter, coffee in hand, scanning the room with that deliberate, measured attention she had come to recognize. The world seemed to narrow again, the chatter fading into a soft blur as her focus fixed entirely on him. His eyes, calm and searching, met hers, and for a fleeting second, the world outside the café ceased to exist.

He had a cup in his hand, the steam curling upward, and for a moment, the image struck her—Daniel, casually holding something as ordinary as a cup of coffee, and yet in that simplicity, he seemed impossibly magnetic. It wasn't just the sight of him; it was the quiet awareness that he, too, had come to this place, at this hour, and perhaps for reasons he didn't fully acknowledge—or understand.

Daniel approached, his movements controlled, yet there was a subtle ease in the way he carried himself, as if the space between them was both familiar and charged with suspense. "Mind if I join you?" he asked, his tone gentle but deliberate.

Evelyn shook her head, words caught in her throat. "Of course... please." Her voice was softer than intended, almost hesitant, betraying the subtle turbulence of anticipation running through her.

He slid into the seat across from her, setting his coffee down with a faint clink on the wooden table. For a moment, neither spoke, both of them caught in the weight of presence, the unspoken acknowledgment of awareness that had been growing steadily over the past nights. The quiet between them was dense, charged with possibility and curiosity.

Daniel took a slow sip from his cup, then set it down again. "I didn't plan to come here," he said finally, his eyes tracing the rim of his cup before meeting hers. "But something... drew me. Maybe it was the thought of noticing a moment I might have almost missed."

Evelyn's chest tightened. The words were simple, yet layered with subtle meaning. She understood immediately—he had come here without reason, without intention, yet with purpose. He had followed a thread he didn't fully understand, a thread that connected him to her in ways that were quiet, subtle, but impossible to ignore.

"I... I'm glad you did," she said softly, her fingers brushing the edge of her coffee cup. "It feels... unexpected, in a good way."

He nodded, a faint smile playing on his lips. "Unexpected is often where the most interesting moments hide. The things we don't plan... sometimes they matter the most."

Evelyn felt a thrill run through her at his words. The subtle undercurrent of suspense, the almost imperceptible tension in his gaze, made the ordinary act of sharing a table feel charged, intimate, and infinitely delicate. The coffee, steaming gently between them, became a silent witness to the quiet gravity of their connection.

"I didn't know I needed coffee," Daniel said suddenly, glancing at his cup, "until I realized… this one matters more than any I've had before."

Evelyn blinked, the weight of the words settling over her like sunlight through clouds. It wasn't just coffee he was referring to—it was the morning, the moment, the presence, the delicate and fragile tension that had been building silently between them. And she realized, with sudden clarity, that she had felt the same way—that ordinary rituals, mundane acts, could become charged with significance simply because of who shared them.

Their conversation flowed gently, punctuated by the subtle play of glances, half-smiles, and the small, almost imperceptible gestures that spoke louder than words. Daniel's hand occasionally brushed his cup, his fingers twitching slightly as if to resist reaching for hers. Evelyn noticed these moments, the restrained awareness that ran beneath his calm exterior, and felt a thrill of suspense that made her pulse quicken.

They spoke of ordinary things—plans for the week, fleeting observations about the weather, books and music—but every sentence carried layers of significance, every pause a calculated or unconscious acknowledgment of the delicate tension in the air. It was as if every word had been carefully chosen, not consciously, but by some subtle awareness of the shared gravity between them.

At one point, Daniel looked out the window, his gaze distant, almost as if he were measuring the world beyond the glass. "I never realized," he said quietly, "how much a moment like this—simple, ordinary, almost mundane—could carry… weight. Until now."

Evelyn's fingers curled around her cup. "It's strange," she said softly. "How ordinary things can feel... so extraordinary when someone is there to notice them with you."

He turned his gaze back to her, eyes steady and intentional. "Exactly. It's not the coffee itself—it's the noticing, the awareness, the presence. That's what makes it unforgettable."

The café around them continued to hum softly, patrons immersed in their own worlds, oblivious to the quiet tension unfolding at the small table near the window. And yet, for Evelyn and Daniel, the ordinary act of drinking coffee had become a nexus of suspense, curiosity, and unspoken connection. Each sip, each glance, each subtle movement carried the weight of awareness, of anticipation, of threads that had been woven long before they realized.

Evelyn felt herself leaning slightly forward, drawn by a gravity she could not name, a force as subtle as it was insistent. Daniel mirrored her movement unconsciously, their proximity shifting, but still measured, restrained. It was the tension of almost-touch, almost-reach, almost-confession—a suspense that made the air between them vibrate.

Minutes passed, though time seemed irrelevant. Every small detail—the steam rising from the coffee, the soft clink of a spoon against the cup, the faint murmur of conversation around them—was amplified by the awareness that they were sharing this moment deliberately and unconsciously, simultaneously aware and suspended in anticipation.

Finally, Daniel set his cup down and leaned back slightly. "I didn't know I needed this," he said again, softer this time, "until it happened. I didn't know I needed... noticing. Until I noticed you."

Evelyn's breath caught. The words were quiet, simple, yet they carried the full weight of every almost-moment, every unspoken glance, every subtle thread that had been tugging at them since their first encounter. Her fingers tightened around her own cup, and she felt a quiet, unstoppable pull of awareness, intimacy, and suspense.

She realized then, fully and unmistakably, that the coffee had been incidental. What mattered was the presence, the noticing, the shared awareness, the subtle gravity that had made a simple morning ritual feel extraordinary. She felt a thrill of anticipation, a shiver of understanding, and the faintest sense that this—this quiet, suspended, deliciously charged moment—was only the beginning.

And as they sat across from each other, steam curling lazily between them, Evelyn understood a truth she hadn't fully grasped until now: sometimes the things you don't know you need—the coffee, the conversation, the awareness—arrive precisely when they are meant to, and they change everything, quietly, irrevocably, and profoundly.

19

THE DAY HE REALIZED SHE WAS DIFFERENT

The city seemed to hold its breath that morning, caught between the restless energy of the day and the lingering hush of dawn. Daniel walked along the cobblestone streets with a careful pace, each step measured yet unconsciously quickened by a restless anticipation that had been growing inside him for days. Something about Evelyn had begun to shift the way he noticed the world. The usual rhythms of his life—the routine meetings, the precise timing of schedules, the familiar faces in predictable places—suddenly felt muted, almost flat, in comparison to the resonance she brought into his awareness.

It had started subtly, with small impressions he hadn't allowed himself to recognize until the threads were too tangled to ignore. Her laugh in the café, delicate yet honest, had lingered in his mind like a faint melody. Her way of noticing details, the slight tilts of her head, the way she leaned forward when listening—everything about her radiated awareness, a quiet intelligence paired with warmth that defied the usual masks people wore in his presence. And on that morning, walking toward the office with his thoughts heavy on her, Daniel realized the truth: Evelyn was different. Not in the obvious, striking sense of beauty or charm that often dominated fleeting impressions, but in a subtle, seismic way that unsettled him, intrigued him, and demanded his attention.

He paused at the corner of the street, briefly surveying the city as the morning sun broke through scattered clouds. Pedestrians moved in hurried lines, taxi horns pierced the hum of activity, and vendors called out greetings, their voices overlapping in the chaotic symphony of urban life. And yet, Daniel felt an unusual stillness in himself, a quiet focus that isolated him from the noise. He thought about her smile, the way she had leaned against the window of the café, tracing the rim of her coffee cup with delicate fingers, eyes alight with subtle amusement and awareness. He remembered the way she had spoken to him, words carefully chosen, infused with a weight that suggested thoughtfulness, depth, and—most disarming of all—an authenticity he rarely encountered.

As he walked, Daniel replayed moments in his mind, each memory pulling him deeper into the realization. The way she had saved his number without conscious thought, almost instinctively, and the way that act had carried more significance than many deliberate decisions he had witnessed in his own life. The quiet confidence in her presence that demanded recognition but never forced it. Her ability to notice without judgment, to observe without intrusion—qualities he had come to value without fully articulating until now.

By the time he reached the office, his mind was a whirlpool of impressions, subtle realizations, and the persistent hum of something unspoken yet undeniable. He lingered outside the building for a moment, his hand brushing the doorframe, eyes tracing the streets he had walked so often. Normally, mornings here were predictable, orderly, almost suffocating in their monotony. But this morning, as his thoughts remained tethered to Evelyn, the familiar streets seemed different, each detail sharper, each shadow more pronounced. The world had subtly shifted, and the shift was entirely her doing.

Inside the office, Daniel moved through the day with unusual distraction. Meetings, reports, emails—all proceeded as usual, yet he found his attention fracturing, constantly returning to the faint memory of her laugh, her precise observations, and the way her presence lingered in his awareness. It wasn't just attraction; it was recognition. She was someone whose existence resonated with the threads of his own life in a way he had not anticipated, nor allowed himself to anticipate.

During lunch, he found himself wandering to the café she frequented, almost without conscious thought. Each step was guided by the memory of her presence, the faint pull of awareness she had imprinted in his mind. And there she was—Evelyn, seated near the window, notebook open, her pen moving in deliberate, elegant strokes across the page. The sunlight caught in her hair, creating a halo of soft, golden light, and for a moment, Daniel stopped in his tracks, struck by a sudden, undeniable clarity.

It wasn't her physical presence that startled him—though she was undeniably captivating—it was the combination of awareness, grace, intelligence, and authenticity. She carried herself with a quiet authority that commanded attention without demanding it. She noticed details others overlooked and engaged with the world in a way that invited both participation and observation. The realization hit him like a surge of electricity: she wasn't just different in small, interesting ways—she was fundamentally unlike anyone he had ever encountered.

Daniel watched her, noting the subtle movements that he had subconsciously cataloged in his mind over the past few days. The way she tilted her head when thinking, the almost imperceptible hesitation before committing to a decision, the careful choice of words, the quiet laughter that seemed to ripple through her very presence. Each detail, each gesture, reinforced the stark truth: Evelyn was not ordinary. She was an anomaly in the best possible sense—an entity that defied his patterns, disrupted his expectations, and drew him into a realm of observation and awareness he had never permitted himself to inhabit so fully.

The thought made his chest tighten, a mixture of anticipation and something more fragile—something that hovered at the edges of possibility, too subtle to name. He realized that he had been unconsciously testing for this all along, measuring interactions, gauging reactions, and assessing authenticity in ways that now seemed almost preordained. And in Evelyn, he had discovered someone whose presence did not merely pass through his consciousness but embedded itself, insistently, in the quietest corners of his awareness.

Unable to resist, he approached the café slowly, careful not to startle her, yet conscious that every step carried weight. She looked up as he neared, her eyes meeting his with a faint, inquisitive smile. The recognition, the quiet awareness mirrored in her gaze, struck him with the force of revelation. She knew him as much as he knew her—perhaps not fully, not consciously—but enough to pull him into the shared, unspoken space that had been building since their first encounter.

"Daniel," she said softly, her voice warm but measured, as if she were aware of the quiet gravity that now hung between them.

"Evelyn," he replied, his voice steady but underscored with an almost imperceptible tension. For a moment, the world around them seemed to fade, leaving only the two of them, suspended in the delicate awareness of presence, anticipation, and recognition.

He took the seat across from her, eyes scanning her face, memorizing the subtleties that marked her as extraordinary. The tilt of her head, the slight curve of her lips, the intensity in her gaze—it all resonated with a clarity he had not expected. And in that moment, Daniel realized with undeniable certainty that he was encountering something rare, something profound: a connection that defied casual observation, a presence that demanded awareness, a person who was different in ways that would shape the trajectory of his life whether he chose to acknowledge it or not.

They spoke briefly, words carefully chosen, layered with subtle intention. Yet the conversation, mundane as it might have appeared to an outsider, carried a quiet suspense—the unspoken acknowledgment of mutual awareness, the delicate balance between recognition and restraint, the silent understanding that this encounter was far more significant than either would openly admit.

Daniel sipped his coffee, and in that simple act, he found clarity. It wasn't the caffeine, not the aroma, not even the warmth of the cup that mattered. It was the presence of Evelyn, the awareness she brought into every moment, the subtle ways she challenged perception, disrupted patterns, and demanded observation. The coffee had become incidental; she had become essential—a revelation he did not anticipate, could not ignore, and would not forget.

By the time he left the café, the city had shifted subtly in his perception. Streets seemed sharper, shadows deeper, colors richer. The morning had been ordinary, yet in the context of this realization, it felt extraordinary. He understood, with a quiet, almost terrifying clarity, that encountering Evelyn had altered the lens through which he perceived the world. She was different. Unique. Extraordinary in the most subtle, insidious, and undeniable ways.

And Daniel, for the first time in a long time, felt the thrilling, almost disorienting awareness that his life, his routine, and even his perception of himself would never be the same. Because she existed, and because he had noticed—and, perhaps more importantly, because he could not unnotice her—everything had shifted. The day he realized Evelyn was different was not marked by dramatic declarations or visible transformations. It was marked by the quiet, insistent recognition of subtle truths, by the suspension of ordinary perception, and by the profound understanding that some connections are destined to alter the trajectory of life itself, whether intended or not.

He walked back to his office, mind alive with possibilities, aware that the threads between them had tightened, that the subtle tension of anticipation had deepened, and that the realization of her difference was not a conclusion, but a beginning—a catalyst for moments that would be charged, suspenseful, and impossible to ignore.

For Daniel, the day he realized she was different was the day everything became sharper, quieter, more suspenseful—and infinitely more alive.

20

A SMALL GIFT WITH BIG MEANING

The late afternoon sun slanted through the windows of Evelyn's apartment, casting long, golden shafts of light across her living room. Dust particles floated lazily in the beams, illuminated like tiny sparks of magic dancing in the quiet air. She sat at her desk, pen in hand, but her thoughts refused to focus. The day had been a blur of ordinary tasks—emails, errands, calls—but there was an undercurrent of anticipation in her chest she could not ignore. It had started that morning, when a small, unexpected envelope had appeared on her doorstep. Its presence was subtle, almost unassuming, yet it radiated significance.

Evelyn had been skeptical at first. The envelope was plain, cream-colored, and sealed neatly. No stamp or sender name marked its surface, only her name written in neat, almost familiar handwriting. She had picked it up with cautious curiosity, her fingers brushing the smooth paper as if its texture could betray the secret it held. Something about it felt deliberate, intentional, and yet utterly understated—a paradox she could not easily reconcile.

She carried it to the desk, placing it gently on the polished wood, and sat down with a slow, measured breath. The envelope was light, almost weightless, but the tension in her chest made it feel heavy with expectation. She traced the edges with her fingertips, contemplating the act of opening it. There was a thrill in the hesitation, a suspense that teased her patience. Whoever had sent it had succeeded in catching her attention, drawing her into a moment that balanced on the edge of curiosity, anticipation, and unspoken significance.

Finally, with deliberate care, Evelyn broke the seal. The paper inside was folded meticulously, a single card resting atop a small object wrapped in soft tissue. She unfolded the card first, her eyes scanning the handwritten message:

"For noticing the small threads that others often miss. May this remind you that attention carries meaning, and presence has power."

The handwriting was unmistakable—Daniel's. Her breath caught, a thrill running through her chest, both exhilarating and nerve-wracking. It was brief, concise, yet packed with layers of intention, meaning, and subtle acknowledgment. The card alone would have been enough to unsettle her equilibrium, but the object beneath promised something more.

Carefully, she unwrapped the tissue, revealing a small pendant, delicate and understated, yet exquisite in its craftsmanship. It was a simple silver charm, shaped like a thread subtly entwined with a tiny, faceted gemstone. The design was elegant in its subtlety, symbolic in ways that spoke to her deeply. The charm seemed to encapsulate the essence of her connection with Daniel—a delicate thread, woven with attention and care, infused with significance beyond the visible.

Evelyn lifted it carefully, turning it over in her fingers. The craftsmanship was meticulous, almost reverential in the way the metal twisted around the gemstone. It was not flashy or ostentatious, but in its simplicity lay profound meaning. The small gift carried the weight of awareness, attention, and intent—the very qualities she had come to associate with him.

Her mind raced, replaying moments from the past weeks—the café encounters, the near-collisions, the almost-glances, the whispered conversations, and the messages that had felt like morning sunshine. Each moment had been a thread, subtle but persistent, weaving an intricate pattern she had not yet fully understood. And now, in her hands, the pendant symbolized that pattern, crystallized into a tangible form she could hold, examine, and, in a way, possess.

Evelyn placed the pendant around her neck, the cool metal resting lightly against her skin. The weight was small, almost negligible, yet it felt substantial in its impact. She caught her reflection in the window, the afternoon light casting soft shadows across her face, and realized that the pendant was more than a gift—it was a reminder, a marker, a silent acknowledgment of awareness and presence that could not be articulated in ordinary conversation.

Her thoughts turned to Daniel, and she felt a thrill of curiosity mixed with suspense. Why had he chosen this particular gift? Why had he sent it in such a quiet, understated manner rather than delivering it personally? The anonymity of its arrival only heightened the sense of mystery and significance. The gift was a puzzle, and each layer—handwriting, message, pendant—was a clue that required careful attention to decode.

She imagined him choosing the gift, considering every detail, weighing every nuance. The pendant was delicate, reflective of his own measured approach to life. The card was precise yet intimate, balancing attention and restraint, observation and participation. Everything about the small package screamed intentionality, a deliberate acknowledgment of connection and awareness, and it made her pulse quicken with the thrill of suspended possibility.

Evelyn traced the chain with her fingers, feeling the subtle twists and curves of the pendant, and realized that she was holding more than a physical object. She was holding the essence of Daniel's awareness, crystallized into a tangible form. It was a small gift, yes, but its meaning stretched far beyond its physical dimensions. It was a tangible manifestation of the subtle threads that had begun to bind them together—threads of attention, recognition, curiosity, and unspoken understanding.

Her thoughts wandered to the idea of intention versus unconscious action. The act of sending the gift could have been deliberate, calculated, or perhaps spontaneous—but either way, it carried weight. The pendant and the card were more than gifts; they were symbols, markers of presence and awareness, small catalysts with the power to shift perception, elevate attention, and deepen connection.

The suspense in Evelyn's chest did not dissipate; rather, it intensified. She understood, in a way that was almost frightening, that this small gesture could alter the trajectory of their relationship in ways neither of them could fully anticipate. The simplicity of the gift belied the magnitude of its implications. It was not about the pendant itself, or even the gemstone, but about the acknowledgment of being seen, noticed, and understood in ways that transcended ordinary interaction.

She lifted the card again, reading the message aloud softly, as if speaking it would anchor the meaning more deeply:

"For noticing the small threads that others often miss. May this remind you that attention carries meaning, and presence has power."

Her fingers tightened around the card, the weight of the words settling over her. Attention carries meaning. Presence has power. These were not just casual observations—they were declarations, subtle yet profound, charged with the kind of awareness that had characterized every encounter with Daniel. The small gift, she realized, was a tangible manifestation of those principles, a reminder that their connection was built not on grand gestures or overt declarations, but on the quiet, persistent awareness that defined their interactions.

Evelyn felt an almost reverent excitement as she fastened the chain around her neck fully, letting the pendant rest against her chest. It was a symbol she could carry everywhere, a private acknowledgment of a growing bond, and a reminder that subtle actions could carry consequences and meaning far beyond what was immediately visible. The suspense, the anticipation, and the thrill of recognition were all encapsulated in this small, delicate object.

Her mind returned to the day's ordinary routines, which now seemed suddenly charged with possibility. She imagined Daniel walking through the city, selecting the gift, imagining her reaction, and realizing the quiet impact it would have. The thought made her chest tighten with a combination of excitement and suspense. Everything about their connection—the small threads, the almost-moments, the quiet anticipation—was intensified by this gift, a reminder that even seemingly insignificant actions could carry profound meaning.

Evelyn placed the card and tissue paper carefully back in the envelope, treating it with the same reverence she had shown the pendant. She understood that this gift, though small, was monumental in significance. It was a bridge, a connector, a tangible manifestation of the subtle forces that had been guiding their interactions. And she knew, with quiet certainty, that it was the beginning of something larger—an unfolding story of awareness, recognition, and suspenseful intimacy.

She lingered at her desk, tracing the edges of the pendant with her fingers, feeling the weight and the texture, and allowing herself to imagine the possibilities that lay ahead. Every detail—from the choice of the gift to the timing of its arrival—felt deliberate, intentional, and yet wrapped in mystery. The suspense in her chest was almost unbearable, a quiet tension that hinted at more revelations to come, more moments of recognition, and the slow, thrilling unraveling of a connection neither of them could fully control.

The small gift had arrived unexpectedly, yet it carried weight far beyond its size. It was more than a pendant, more than a card. It was a declaration of attention, a subtle acknowledgment of shared awareness, a quiet promise of the threads that would continue to pull them closer together. And as Evelyn held it in her hands, she realized that some gifts, though physically small, could carry the power to change perception, alter awareness, and deepen connection in ways that words alone could never achieve.

Tonight, she would leave it around her neck, a constant reminder of the delicate, suspenseful, and profoundly significant bond that was quietly growing between her and Daniel. The small gift had arrived without fanfare, yet its impact was undeniable, transforming an ordinary afternoon into a charged, meaningful moment that would linger in her awareness long after the sun had set.

III

CHEMISTRY & CONFLICT

21

FEELINGS THEY PRETENDED NOT TO FEEL

The evening had settled over the city like a velvet curtain, the lights of buildings and streetlamps flickering to life in a rhythm that mirrored the heartbeat of the streets below. Evelyn sat at her desk, the pendant Daniel had given her still resting lightly against her chest, a quiet weight that seemed to pulse in time with her emotions. She had not yet taken it off, not because it was physically necessary, but because the presence it represented lingered in her awareness, a subtle but insistent reminder of the threads binding them.

Her phone vibrated softly, breaking the stillness. Daniel's name lit up the screen. Her fingers hovered for a moment, a mixture of anticipation and hesitation tightening her chest. She opened the message slowly, as if prolonging the moment would make it sweeter, more significant.

"Are you free tonight? There's something I think we need to say... even if it's just between the spaces words usually avoid."

Evelyn's pulse quickened. The phrasing was deliberate, layered, and suspenseful, a subtle acknowledgment of unspoken tensions that had been building for weeks. The message carried weight, the weight of expectation and the potential for revelation. She replied almost immediately, though her fingers trembled slightly:

"I'm free. But are we really ready for the spaces words avoid?"

His response was instantaneous, a line that made her chest ache with anticipation:

"Sometimes the spaces speak louder than words. Let's find out."

By the time Daniel arrived, Evelyn had moved to the living room, her hands twisting lightly in her lap as she tried to steady the fluttering of her heart. The doorbell rang, crisp and deliberate, and she took a slow breath before answering. There he was—Daniel—standing in the doorway with a subtle smile, eyes glinting with awareness and restraint. He carried nothing with him, not a gesture, not a gift, not a sign of overt intention, yet his presence alone was charged, suspended with tension.

"Evelyn," he said softly, stepping inside. His voice was low, measured, almost reverent in the way it caressed her name.

"Daniel," she replied, her own tone quieter than she intended. The sound of his name left her lips like a whispered confession, a subtle surrender to the awareness that had been building between them.

They sat down across from each other, a small coffee table between them, both aware that the evening was not about mundane conversation. The air carried an unspoken understanding, a suspenseful gravity that made the simplest gestures—hands resting on the table, the tilt of a head, the shift of a chair—loaded with meaning.

Daniel's eyes held her gaze, steady, searching, as if measuring not her words but the spaces between them, the unspoken truths lurking beneath polite conversation. "Evelyn," he began, his tone soft but deliberate, "I think... we've been pretending."

Evelyn's breath caught. "Pretending?" she repeated, her voice fragile, almost betraying the quickening in her chest.

"Yes," he said slowly, leaning forward slightly. "Pretending that the tension, the awareness, the moments that stretch between us... don't mean anything. Pretending that we can ignore it, that it's convenient or coincidental, that it can be managed by polite distance."

Her fingers brushed the edge of the pendant, a grounding ritual, a tactile connection to the presence of meaning it represented. She had felt it—every subtle look, every whispered message, every near-touch—but to hear it articulated, to have the unspoken named aloud, sent a thrill of suspense through her chest.

"I... I think I've been pretending too," she admitted, her voice barely above a whisper. "Pretending that I can remain composed, unaffected, as if the moments between us were nothing more than coincidence or fleeting circumstance."

Daniel nodded, his expression softening, though the tension in his eyes did not entirely fade. "And yet," he said, "we can't pretend anymore. Every glance, every smile, every word carefully chosen... it all carries meaning. And pretending we don't notice doesn't make the tension vanish. It only intensifies it."

The words hung between them, electric, dense with suspended energy. Evelyn felt a shiver of recognition. He was right. The tension, the anticipation, the subtle awareness—they had been cultivating a silent, mutual acknowledgment of each other's presence for weeks. And now, named aloud, it became a tangible reality, almost impossible to ignore.

"I've tried," she admitted, her voice trembling slightly, "to pretend that it's just... coincidence. That the way we notice each other, the way moments stretch, the way... everything feels different when you're around... it doesn't matter."

Daniel's hand twitched slightly, as if resisting the urge to reach across the table. "I've tried the same," he said softly. "Pretending that the quiet moments, the almost-glances, the messages that linger like sunlight... pretending that they're insignificant. But they aren't. And neither are you."

Evelyn's heart raced, each word a pulse, a silent drumbeat echoing through the space between them. She realized how much weight they had carried in pretending—pretending that proximity didn't awaken something fragile and undeniable, pretending that their mutual awareness could be dismissed as coincidence, pretending that the threads tugging at them could be ignored without consequence.

Daniel leaned back slightly, his gaze fixed on her with a soft intensity. "And now that we've acknowledged it..." he said, voice low, deliberate, "...we can't go back. Pretending is no longer an option. Every small interaction, every shared moment, every unspoken glance—it will carry weight from now on. Because we've both felt it. Even when we acted otherwise."

The suspense in the room was palpable, a quiet charge that made the mundane air of the living room feel almost sacred. Evelyn's fingers trembled slightly as she traced the edge of her pendant. Each word from Daniel felt like a thread tugging at the heart of the tension they had maintained in careful balance.

"I've felt it," she whispered, "every day. The subtle awareness, the anticipation, the... the moments that feel suspended just for us. I've pretended not to notice, but I can't anymore."

A slow, almost imperceptible smile curved Daniel's lips, a mixture of relief and acknowledgment. "Neither can I," he admitted. "And the truth... the truth is that these feelings—quiet, deliberate, undeniable—have been growing. And pretending not to feel them... it only made them stronger."

Evelyn's eyes softened, her chest tightening with the weight of mutual recognition. The suspense was no longer about uncertainty, but about acknowledgment—acknowledgment of a connection that had grown quietly, insistently, beyond the reach of ordinary explanation.

"Then we stop pretending," she said, her voice steadier now, though still delicate. "We stop pretending that we don't notice, that it's inconsequential, that it doesn't matter. Because it does. It always has."

Daniel reached forward slowly, his hand hovering over the table for a fleeting moment before resting lightly on hers. The touch was gentle, deliberate, a physical manifestation of the acknowledgment they had just spoken aloud. The tension between them, the anticipation, the suspense of unspoken feelings—all converged in that single contact, a bridge from denial to awareness, from pretension to recognition.

"Then we allow ourselves," he said softly, "to feel what we've been pretending not to feel. And we see where it leads, without reservation, without hesitation, without fear."

Evelyn's breath caught. The room seemed suspended in that moment, the city outside a muted blur of light and shadow. For the first time, the tension between them was no longer just a whisper of anticipation or subtle awareness. It was articulated, acknowledged, and reciprocated. The feelings they had been guarding, managing, and hiding—deliberately or unconsciously—were now free to exist, charged with the energy of mutual recognition and suspenseful possibility.

She nodded slowly, a soft smile curving her lips. "Then we feel it," she whispered back, her voice carrying a fragile certainty. "We let ourselves notice, acknowledge, and embrace it. No pretending. No hiding. Just... presence. Awareness. Us."

Daniel's fingers tightened slightly over hers, the warmth of contact grounding the intensity of the moment. "Us," he repeated, the single word heavy with meaning, charged with anticipation, and layered with the suspense of what would come next.

For a long moment, they simply sat there, hands touching, eyes locked, the silence between them filled with unspoken acknowledgments, the weight of suspended emotions, and the quiet thrill of recognition. Every glance, every subtle movement, every pulse of breath carried the weight of feelings they had long pretended not to feel. And in that shared space, fragile yet charged, they allowed themselves to exist fully in the awareness of one another, letting the suspense of unspoken emotions transform into something tangible, deliberate, and profoundly intimate.

The city outside continued its rhythm, indifferent to the quiet intensity unfolding within the apartment. But inside, Evelyn and Daniel had crossed a threshold. The pretending was over. The suspense was no longer uncertainty, but possibility. The feelings they had long hidden, ignored, or denied were now alive, deliberate, and impossible to contain.

And in that charged awareness, in the acknowledgment of emotions that had once been whispered only in the spaces between words, they found a new kind of intimacy—a suspenseful, thrilling, and delicate connection that neither time, distance, nor pretense could undo.

22

WHEN MISSING SOMEONE FEELS TOO SOON

The afternoon was unusually quiet, the city humming in a soft, subdued rhythm that made Evelyn acutely aware of each passing moment. She sat by the window of her apartment, legs tucked beneath her, the light casting a warm glow across the pages of the book she pretended to read. Her eyes, however, were not on the words. They were on the street below, where pedestrians passed in hurried, indifferent waves, oblivious to the subtle unrest stirring in her chest.

It had been only hours since Daniel had left, a brief farewell at the café, his presence lingering like the faint scent of rain on the city streets. She had watched him walk away, each step deliberate, carrying him out of sight, yet leaving a quiet echo in the air that refused to dissipate. Evelyn had thought she would feel relief, or at least composure, after the intensity of their shared morning, the acknowledgement of feelings they had long pretended not to feel. But instead, an unfamiliar ache had settled in her chest—a prelude to longing that felt disproportionate to the time they had spent together.

She traced the rim of her coffee mug absentmindedly, the warmth seeping into her palms, but it did little to anchor her. The ache was in her mind, a pulse of absence that had begun to dominate her awareness, making every shadow in the room seem heavier, every noise from the street sharper. She realized, with a jolt of both excitement and apprehension, that missing someone could arrive with unsettling speed. Hours could be enough for absence to become a presence, for longing to develop roots in the quiet spaces of the day.

Her thoughts drifted to Daniel's smile, the subtle tilt of his head when he listened, the way his eyes lingered on hers as if memorizing the nuances of her expression. She recalled the slow, deliberate gestures of his hands, the quiet weight of his words, and the understated intensity that seemed to ripple through his every movement. Each memory was a thread, delicate yet insistent, weaving through her mind with a quiet insistence she could neither ignore nor suppress.

Evelyn pressed her hand to her chest, as if trying to contain the sudden surge of emotion that threatened to overwhelm her. How could she miss someone so acutely, so persistently, after only a few fleeting encounters? The thought was both thrilling and terrifying. She had known desire before, attraction before, even fleeting infatuations, but this—this immediacy, this depth of awareness—was something new, something she had not anticipated, something that carried its own suspenseful weight.

She picked up her phone almost unconsciously, scrolling through the brief flurry of messages exchanged that morning. Each text, each subtle phrase, each carefully chosen word had been a small thread, connecting them in a tapestry of awareness and unspoken acknowledgment. Yet the absence of his presence now made those messages feel insufficient, hollow even, compared to the warmth of shared space, the tactile sense of proximity, the unspoken intimacy of eyes meeting across a table, hands brushing almost by accident, the silent acknowledgment of attention and presence.

Evelyn leaned back in her chair, the pendant Daniel had given her resting lightly against her collarbone. Its weight, though physically minimal, carried with it an almost unbearable significance. Every small movement, every glance, every symbol embedded in that gift now felt magnified by absence. The pendant had become a tether, a fragile anchor to someone who was already occupying her mind in ways she could not fully articulate.

Time seemed elastic, stretching endlessly as the afternoon wore on. She found herself pacing the apartment, stopping at the window again and again to look for a familiar figure, for the silhouette of someone whose presence had already imprinted itself on her awareness. The city moved on, indifferent, but she remained suspended in a private bubble of expectation, longing, and the subtle tension of desire that had begun to flourish almost immediately.

Evelyn's mind wandered to moments from earlier in the day, the delicate weight of their conversation, the almost imperceptible touches, the intensity hidden in casual glances. Every detail replayed itself vividly, almost unbearably. She could remember the warmth of his hand near hers, the way he had paused mid-sentence as if sensing the gravity of what remained unspoken, the careful choice of words that allowed the tension to build without ever spilling over into overt confession. She realized with a thrill of suspense that every small moment had been a rehearsal, a precursor, a foundation for the ache she now felt so keenly.

A message appeared on her phone, a notification that made her heart leap in both anticipation and fear. She opened it with trembling fingers:

"I can't stop thinking about this morning. Every moment felt… important. Even the ones we almost pretended didn't exist."

The simplicity of the message struck her with unexpected force. Daniel had articulated what she herself had not dared to name, and in doing so, he magnified the suspense, the longing, and the awareness that had begun to dominate her day. She felt a shiver run down her spine, a mix of exhilaration and nervousness, the kind of thrill that comes from realizing that absence itself can speak, that missing someone can be a tangible, palpable force.

Her reply was almost instinctive, typed with fingers that trembled slightly:

"I've already started missing you. I didn't think it would feel this immediate, this… intense."

Seconds later, his response appeared, brief but charged:

"Then I guess we both feel it. And maybe… maybe that's not a bad thing."

Evelyn set the phone down, staring out the window once more. The streets below were busy, filled with people who were unaware of the private tension that had gripped her, the ache that made each moment feel heavier, each second more suspended. She realized, with quiet astonishment, that longing could arrive too soon, could take root before there was a right moment, before a connection had been fully defined. It was both cruel and exhilarating—a suspenseful reminder of how profoundly presence, absence, and awareness could intertwine.

She thought about the subtle ways Daniel had already changed her perception of ordinary moments. A morning cup of coffee, a brief conversation, a small gift—each had carried significance beyond the ordinary, and now absence itself carried weight. Missing someone too soon was a revelation, a force that demanded attention, reflection, and acknowledgment. She felt the thrill of suspense coursing through her, a heady mixture of excitement and apprehension.

Hours passed, and the city lights began to glow against the darkening sky. Evelyn remained by the window, watching the flow of traffic, the movement of pedestrians, the faint flicker of neon signs in the distance. Each shadow, each movement, each distant sound seemed heightened, amplified by the private ache in her chest, by the way absence had become a tangible presence. She realized she was suspended between desire and patience, between anticipation and uncertainty, and that every thought of him, every memory, every subtle sensation was a thread pulling her closer to a truth she could neither ignore nor fully articulate.

Her mind wandered back to Daniel, imagining him moving through his own evening, carrying the weight of awareness she knew he could not ignore. The thought made her pulse quicken. They were two threads in a complex weave, each tugging at the other with subtle insistence, each aware of the growing tension, each conscious of the impossibility of pretending that feelings could be contained. The suspense, the anticipation, the quiet ache of missing someone too soon—it was all evidence that the connection they shared had already begun to shape reality in ways neither could control.

Evelyn pressed the pendant to her chest again, feeling the cool metal, the smooth edges, the subtle weight. It was a symbol, a reminder, a tether to presence, awareness, and the subtle thrill of anticipation. And in that small, delicate object, she found both comfort and suspense—the knowledge that the ache of missing someone could be the prelude to something extraordinary, something profound, and something entirely unavoidable.

As night settled fully over the city, Evelyn sat quietly by the window, eyes tracing the pattern of lights below, thoughts occupied by the presence now defined by absence. She understood, with growing clarity, that missing someone too soon was not merely a symptom of desire—it was an acknowledgment of significance, a recognition of awareness, and a testament to the threads that had already begun to weave their lives together. The suspense, the longing, the thrill of anticipation—all of it was evidence that the story between them was unfolding, quietly, deliberately, and impossibly.

And as the first stars appeared in the night sky, Evelyn allowed herself to sit with the feeling, to honor the tension, to recognize the thrill of anticipation that only grew with every passing moment. Missing someone too soon was no longer a discomfort—it was proof that the connection, fragile and suspenseful, had already taken root.

23

THE PAST THAT WON'T STAY SILENT

The city streets were wet from an early evening drizzle, the air thick with the scent of rain and asphalt. Streetlights flickered in reflection on the slick pavement, casting long, wavering shadows that seemed to stretch toward the sky, as if reaching for something just beyond their grasp. Evelyn walked slowly along the sidewalk, her coat pulled tightly around her shoulders, the soft click of her shoes against the pavement the only sound she permitted herself to hear. Her mind was elsewhere, weighed down by thoughts she had tried to ignore all day: thoughts of the past, of memories she had tucked away in neat compartments, convinced they would stay buried if she didn't revisit them.

But the past, she realized with sudden clarity, had a persistence that demanded attention. It had a voice that refused silence, a presence that lingered in moments she had hoped would be untainted by its weight. And tonight, after the intensity of the hours she had spent with Daniel, after the quiet acknowledgment of feelings they had both tried to hide, her past seemed louder than ever—insistent, piercing, and impossible to ignore.

Evelyn's footsteps slowed as she approached a small park, one of the few places in the city where she allowed herself space to think, to breathe, and to confront the shadows she usually avoided. She stepped onto the damp path, the leaves scattered by the rain sticking to the soles of her shoes, each step releasing a faint, satisfying squelch. She sat on a bench, the wood cold and slick from the drizzle, and drew her knees close to her chest, her coat wrapped tightly around her. The pendant Daniel had given her, resting just above her heart, felt heavier tonight, not from its weight but from the significance it now carried—both a tether to the present and a subtle reminder that the past was still shaping her.

Her phone vibrated in her pocket, a brief message from Daniel lighting up the screen. "Thinking of you. Are you okay?"

She stared at it, fingers hovering over the screen, a quiet tension settling in her chest. She wanted to reply with the simple truth: that the past was loud tonight, that it refused to stay hidden, that memories she thought she had buried deep were clawing their way to the surface. But she didn't. Instead, she typed a measured response: "I'm… managing. Just needed a moment."

She sent it and slipped the phone back into her pocket, the act of restraint mirroring the control she tried to maintain over the emotions bubbling beneath the surface. But the past would not be managed. It had a way of seeping into the present, of coloring perceptions, of bending reality until the lines between then and now blurred. Evelyn closed her eyes, and in that darkness behind her eyelids, she allowed herself to remember.

Memories came unbidden, vivid and jagged. Childhood rooms, smells, sounds—faces she had loved and lost, mistakes she had made, moments of vulnerability that had taught her both caution and resilience. Each memory was a thread, fragile yet unrelenting, weaving a tapestry she could not fully escape. She realized that the past had a rhythm, a heartbeat of its own, and tonight it pulsed in synchrony with the suspense that had become a part of her life since Daniel's arrival.

Her mind returned to him, to his presence earlier that day, to the way his attention had felt like sunlight piercing through storm clouds. And yet, the juxtaposition of his quiet awareness with the roar of memories from her past created a tension she could not shake. The past demanded acknowledgment even as the present offered possibility. She felt herself caught between two currents, each pulling with equal force, each insisting on recognition.

A sudden memory of a conversation long ago surfaced—a conversation with someone who had meant the world at the time but who had left without explanation, leaving questions that had never been answered. Evelyn's chest tightened as she recalled the words, the tone, the weight of expectation and the subsequent silence. It had been a wound she thought she had stitched carefully, covering it with layers of distraction and discipline, but the quiet of this evening, the intensity of the connection with Daniel, had cracked the seam.

The pendant at her neck seemed to pulse in tandem with her thoughts, a tangible reminder that while the past had power, the present carried its own gravity. Daniel's influence in her life was quiet but insistent, a new thread interweaving with the old. And yet, the past refused to yield entirely. Memories pressed against her consciousness like fingers tracing her spine, cold and persistent, demanding acknowledgment, demanding reconciliation.

She remembered an old letter, folded neatly and stored in a drawer she hadn't opened in years. The letter had been from someone she had loved fiercely, someone whose absence had shaped her, whose silence had taught her caution. She had never read it again, yet its presence lingered in her subconscious, a ghost of unfinished stories and unresolved feelings. Evelyn realized that the past was not just memory—it was unfinished business, a collection of unresolved threads that had found their way into the quiet corners of her life, uninvited but undeniable.

Her fingers unconsciously brushed the pendant as she thought of Daniel. The small gift he had given her was a tether to the present, a reminder that even amid unresolved echoes, there was a possibility for new beginnings. Yet the tension was palpable. How could she reconcile the pull of the past with the weight of burgeoning feelings for someone who, in every subtle way, was reshaping her perception of the present?

A sudden gust of wind rattled the leaves, and Evelyn shivered, pulling her coat tighter. The sound seemed to echo the stirrings of memory, the whispers of the past that refused to stay silent. She realized that she was trembling not just from the cold but from the awareness that life was always a complex weave of past and present, of memory and possibility, of caution and courage.

Her phone buzzed again, Daniel's name appearing once more. "Are you still there? You've been quiet."

She stared at the screen, the suspense of the evening pressing against her ribs. She wanted to tell him everything—the ache of memories, the whisper of the past that wouldn't leave her alone, the fear that it could overshadow what they were building together. But she didn't. Instead, she typed, "Just thinking. The past has a loud way of speaking tonight."

She sent it, feeling the weight of honesty tempered by restraint. And then she leaned back, letting the cool air wash over her, the rain-slick streets reflecting the glow of city lights like shards of fragmented memories. She understood that the past, with all its weight, could not be erased. It had shaped her, informed her choices, taught her caution, and yet, it could coexist with possibility.

Evelyn realized that tonight, she was learning something profound: that acknowledging the past did not diminish the present. That memories, even the unresolved, could exist without consuming her entirely. That the suspense of unspoken stories, the weight of previous connections, and the ache of unfinished chapters could inform, rather than obstruct, the possibilities unfolding now with Daniel.

Her thoughts drifted to him once more. She imagined his face, the careful tilt of his head, the way his eyes lingered with unspoken curiosity, and she felt a thrill of anticipation. The past might whisper, it might claw at the edges of her awareness, it might insist on recognition—but the present had its own gravity, a force that was patient yet persistent, subtle yet undeniable.

Evelyn traced the pendant once more, feeling its cool surface, its subtle weight, the tiny gemstone reflecting the faint city lights. It was a symbol of the present, of connection, of quiet acknowledgment, of suspense that was not rooted in fear but in possibility. She realized that she could carry both: the past that wouldn't stay silent, and the present that demanded her attention. And in carrying both, she could navigate the tension, the suspense, the thrill of recognition, and the emerging awareness of feelings that were becoming impossible to ignore.

The rain slowed to a drizzle, and the city's hum softened. Evelyn remained on the bench, legs tucked beneath her, pendant resting against her heart, mind alive with memory and anticipation. She understood that the past would always have a voice, but it did not have to dictate her present or her future. And as the night deepened, she allowed herself to sit with the tension, the suspense, and the quiet thrill of possibility—the understanding that the past, though insistent, was not the only force shaping the moments to come.

In the distance, the city lights flickered, the streets shimmered with the aftermath of rain, and Evelyn closed her eyes, letting the past speak, letting the present pulse through her, and feeling, for the first time in a long while, that she could navigate both with awareness, courage, and the suspenseful thrill of what awaited.

24

EVADING THE TRUTH

The city had settled into the uneasy quiet of late evening, when the world seemed suspended between the remnants of daylight and the deep shadows of night. Streetlamps cast elongated, trembling streaks across the sidewalks, reflecting in puddles that had yet to evaporate from the afternoon's rain. Evelyn walked briskly along the familiar streets, her coat pulled tightly around her, not because of the cold, but because of the tension curling tight around her chest. She could feel it there—an invisible weight pressing on her shoulders, a rhythm of unease that refused to be ignored. Tonight, truth was an adversary she wasn't ready to face.

The day had been deceptively ordinary, filled with tasks she had executed with mechanical precision: work emails, errands, and the ritual of tidying her apartment. But beneath the surface, a storm churned. Daniel's presence lingered in her awareness like a persistent shadow, a subtle insistence she had tried to evade all afternoon. The past conversations, the almost-confessions, the lingering tension from their shared moments, were all threads pulling at her, threading through the careful armor she wore. And yet, despite every effort, the truth of her feelings was something she could not fully confront.

She paused at the corner of a narrow street, the dim glow of a nearby café spilling light onto the wet pavement. Through the window, she caught sight of a familiar silhouette—Daniel, seated at a corner table, alone, his phone resting lightly in his hand. His eyes were distant, focused somewhere beyond the glass, but there was a subtle tension in his posture, an energy that mirrored her own. Evelyn's heart stuttered, caught between desire and fear, anticipation and restraint. She considered entering, letting the moment demand confrontation, but a sudden impulse of caution held her back. Evading the truth, she realized, was easier from a distance, easier when she could control the narrative in her own mind.

She lingered in the shadows, unseen but fully aware, watching the play of light on his face, the slight movement of his hands, the way his brow creased with concentration. Daniel had always carried a quiet awareness, an energy that could command attention without needing to speak. And yet, in this moment, she sensed a vulnerability beneath the calm exterior—a subtle fracture in the carefully maintained composure he displayed so effortlessly. It made her chest ache. How could two people, so attuned to one another, remain caught in the delicate tension of evasion, each pretending to ignore what the other already knew?

Evelyn finally moved, her steps quiet, calculated, circling the café until she found herself inside, slipping into a booth across the room. Daniel did not notice her at first, absorbed in thought, but the subtle shift in the air when she entered—the almost imperceptible awareness of someone in the same space—was enough to make her pulse race. She pretended to look at her phone, adjusting her posture as if the moment were mundane, ordinary, easily managed. But her fingers trembled slightly as she scrolled, the act of avoidance itself a betrayal of the intensity simmering beneath her restraint.

Daniel finally looked up, eyes scanning the room, and for a brief moment, their gazes collided. The recognition was instantaneous, electric, charged with a tension that neither could deny. Yet neither moved, neither spoke. The truth between them hung like a suspended object, heavy, delicate, and impossible to navigate without acknowledgment. Evading it was no longer a choice—they were trapped by proximity, by awareness, by the subtle pull of feelings neither wanted to name aloud.

Evelyn's fingers tightened around her phone, the cool metal a grounding force as she forced herself to look away, to pretend that she had entered the café merely by coincidence. Daniel's gaze lingered a fraction too long, a subtle acknowledgment of the tension that threaded through the air. He took a slow sip of his coffee, the motion deliberate, almost ritualistic, as if buying time, as if giving himself the space to prepare for confrontation—or retreat.

She imagined the countless ways they could bridge the gap, the delicate steps of acknowledgment and confession that hovered at the edge of possibility. And yet, each path carried risk, each gesture demanded courage, and neither had yet summoned the resolve to traverse the space fully. Evading the truth, she realized, was not cowardice—it was preservation, a temporary shield against the intensity of recognition and the vulnerability that came with it.

Her mind drifted back to the past few weeks, to the subtle exchanges that had defined their interactions. The shared glances, the messages that felt like sunlight on a gray morning, the almost-touches that lingered in memory—each had been a thread weaving an invisible web, binding them closer with tension, anticipation, and unspoken awareness. And now, as they sat in proximity, the threads vibrated with possibility, pulling them toward acknowledgment even as their minds resisted.

Daniel's hand brushed against the rim of his coffee cup, a small, unconscious motion that betrayed the steadiness of his exterior. Evelyn's chest tightened. She had always noticed these subtle things—the minor habits, the almost-imperceptible gestures that revealed more than words could contain. It was part of why she felt this growing ache, this restless awareness of the truth she could no longer fully evade.

She looked around the café, noting the casual laughter of strangers, the clink of cups, the murmur of conversation, and felt a stark contrast between the ordinary life unfolding around them and the extraordinary tension suspended between herself and Daniel. It was as if they existed in a different temporal plane, a bubble of suspense where every glance, every shift, every subtle breath carried meaning.

Her fingers brushed against the pendant at her neck, the small silver charm now a talisman, a symbol of awareness, presence, and connection. Its weight reminded her that she could not fully detach from reality, that the threads pulling her toward Daniel were not abstract—they were tangible, persistent, and impossible to ignore. She realized, with a sharp thrill of apprehension, that evading the truth was only prolonging the inevitable, making the eventual confrontation more intense, more charged, more suspenseful.

Daniel finally spoke, his voice low, careful, almost hesitant. "Evelyn," he said, the single word carrying a weight that seemed to press into her chest. She looked up, heart stuttering, and met his gaze. "We can keep pretending, if you want. We can act as if this—whatever this is—doesn't exist. But you and I both know it does."

Evelyn's fingers tightened around the chain of her pendant. The words struck her with a force she had been resisting all day, a sudden confrontation with the very thing she had sought to avoid. Evading the truth, she realized, had only delayed the inevitable, and now, suspended in the fragile intimacy of acknowledgment, the reality of her feelings pressed in with undeniable clarity.

"I..." she began, voice trembling slightly, "I don't know if I'm ready. Not for... all of it. For the acknowledgment, for the risk, for the... vulnerability it demands."

Daniel nodded slowly, the subtle tension in his shoulders easing only slightly. "I understand," he said, voice measured. "I feel it too. That pull, the awareness, the tension between what we feel and what we can admit… it's intense. But pretending, evading… it doesn't make it go away."

Evelyn looked down at the table, her chest tightening with the mixture of anticipation and fear. The truth was a living thing between them, insistent and unyielding. Evading it had been a strategy, a temporary shield, a way to maintain control. But the longer she delayed, the more impossible it became to maintain composure. Every heartbeat, every subtle glance, every fraction of breath shared in proximity was a reminder that feelings, once acknowledged, could no longer be contained.

She lifted her gaze slowly, meeting Daniel's eyes with a fragile honesty. "Then… we can't keep evading it," she whispered. "Even if we're not ready for everything, even if we're scared, even if it's messy… we can't pretend it doesn't exist."

Daniel's lips curved slightly, a soft, deliberate acknowledgment. "I don't want to pretend anymore," he said. "I don't want to evade it. I want to face it with you, carefully, deliberately… whatever it takes."

The suspense that had charged the air between them shifted, no longer solely about avoidance but about the fragile threshold of acknowledgment. Evading the truth had been their shield, but in the quiet intensity of the moment, the possibility of confrontation carried its own thrilling weight, a suspense that was both frightening and intoxicating.

Evelyn's hand moved to the pendant at her neck, pressing it lightly, a grounding force in the whirlwind of emotions. She realized that truth, once confronted, was not an enemy but a guide—a delicate, suspenseful current that would steer them toward awareness, recognition, and connection. Evading it had served its purpose, but now the moment demanded courage, vulnerability, and the willingness to step into the intensity that had been building between them for weeks.

The café hummed with the ordinary rhythms of life around them, yet within the small space, Evelyn and Daniel existed suspended in their own reality—a fragile, charged, and suspenseful bubble where truth, once evaded, now demanded attention, recognition, and the quiet courage to face it together.

And as the night deepened, the rain softened to a whisper outside, Evelyn understood that evading the truth had been temporary, but the truth itself—suspended, palpable, undeniable—was a force they could no longer deny, a suspenseful current that would carry them into what neither of them could fully predict, yet both were beginning to desire.

25

THE MISUNDERSTOOD MESSAGE

The air was unusually still that evening, a heavy, almost tangible quiet that pressed against Evelyn's apartment walls. The city beyond her window was alive with the muted symphony of traffic lights, distant car horns, and the occasional hum of a bus rolling down the street, but inside, the world seemed suspended, as if time itself had slowed to a deliberate crawl. Evelyn sat cross-legged on her couch, her phone cradled in both hands, staring at the screen as if it could answer questions her heart had yet to articulate.

The message had arrived an hour ago, short, seemingly innocuous, yet it had set her mind racing in directions she was not prepared to explore. It was from Daniel, sent in the quiet hours of early evening:

"I think we need to talk. Soon."

On the surface, it was simple, almost ordinary, but the ambiguity of it carried a weight that pressed against her chest, making her pulse quicken. Was it a warning? An admission? A prelude to something she had both feared and anticipated? The vagueness was deliberate, a suspenseful pause that made her imagination spiral with possibilities, some thrilling, some terrifying.

Evelyn's fingers hovered over the screen, her thumb trembling slightly. She had learned to read Daniel's messages with nuance, to detect the subtle currents beneath the words he chose. And yet, this message eluded precise interpretation. Every angle she considered felt fragile, incomplete. Was it about the confession of feelings she both anticipated and feared? Or was it something else entirely, unrelated to the tension that had been building between them? The uncertainty gnawed at her, threading through every thought, every heartbeat.

She set the phone down briefly, trying to breathe, trying to anchor herself in the mundane—the hum of the refrigerator, the soft rustle of her coat as she shifted, the faint tick of the wall clock. But the message lingered like an uninvited specter, demanding attention, insisting on interpretation. Each second stretched, heavy with suspense, until the simplest action—replying, ignoring, or waiting—felt like a decision of profound consequence.

Finally, she typed a cautious response, deleting it twice before sending:

"I'm here. What do you want to talk about?"

The response was delayed, lingering for a moment before appearing like a faint pulse on the screen:

"It's complicated. I don't want to risk misunderstanding. Can we meet?"

Evelyn's heart stuttered. Complicated. Misunderstanding. The words were carefully chosen, precise, deliberate, yet vague. Her mind raced through every interaction they had shared in recent days—the subtle glances, the almost-touching hands, the conversations loaded with subtext. Could it be that Daniel feared she had misread him? Or perhaps he feared he had misread himself? The suspense was almost unbearable, a taut wire stretched across the quiet expanse of her apartment.

She left the couch, pacing slowly, fingers tracing the pendant at her neck, feeling its cool weight against her skin. Each small movement seemed to amplify the intensity of the anticipation, each step a drumbeat echoing in her chest. She tried to quiet her mind, tried to reason through the ambiguity, but the more she tried, the more elusive clarity became. She realized, with an almost painful awareness, that sometimes messages were more than words—they were vessels for unspoken tension, fragile threads connecting hearts yet teetering on the edge of misunderstanding.

Her phone buzzed again. Another message from Daniel, brief, almost cryptic:

“Meet me at the park near the old fountain. I’ll explain everything.”

Evelyn’s stomach twisted. The location was familiar, charged with history—the park where they had first walked together, where subtle acknowledgments had first been exchanged, where anticipation had first begun to bloom. To meet there now was to step into a space laden with shared memories, a setting perfectly designed to intensify suspense. She felt a shiver of both excitement and apprehension.

She grabbed her coat and stepped into the cool evening, the air damp with a lingering drizzle. The streets were alive with shadows and light, reflections from puddles dancing across the sidewalk, creating patterns that seemed almost deliberate, guiding her steps toward inevitability. Her mind spun with possibilities. What did he need to explain? What could possibly be complicated enough to demand a meeting in the shadows of memory-laden streets? The suspense was a living thing, crawling through her veins, making every step heavier, every heartbeat a percussion of anticipation.

The park was nearly empty, bathed in the soft glow of lampposts, the fountain at its center reflecting the fractured light like a mirror of memory and intention. Evelyn's pulse quickened as she spotted Daniel leaning against a tree, hands stuffed into his coat pockets, eyes scanning the quiet pathways with a vigilance that mirrored her own tension. His posture was calm, almost casual, but she could feel the electric charge emanating from him, a quiet acknowledgment of the importance of this encounter.

"Evelyn," he said as she approached, voice low, measured, deliberate. His gaze was fixed on hers, yet there was a weight beneath it, a tension she could almost reach out and touch.

"Daniel," she replied softly, keeping her distance, though instinctively moving closer. The night air was cool, but the space between them seemed charged with warmth, suspense, and anticipation.

He ran a hand through his hair, a subtle gesture of frustration or hesitation she couldn't yet determine. "I meant what I said," he began, "about misunderstanding. And about things being complicated." His voice trembled slightly, betraying the careful composure he tried to maintain. "There's something I need to clarify… because if I don't, everything could be misread. Everything between us could… shift in ways neither of us intends."

Evelyn felt a lump in her throat, a sudden constriction that made her chest ache. "Misunderstanding?" she asked, trying to sound calm, though the tremor in her voice betrayed her. "I… I don't understand. What could possibly be misunderstood?"

Daniel looked down at the fountain, the ripples reflecting in his eyes like fragments of memory. "It's not just what I say," he said, voice low. "It's what I do, how I act, the subtleties you've noticed, the attention, the glances… they're all real. But if I don't explain the context, the intentions… it could be misinterpreted. I could hurt you without meaning to."

Evelyn's breath caught. The suspense in the air thickened, almost tangible, as if each word he spoke carried the weight of inevitability. She realized that Daniel's careful choice of words, his deliberate pacing, and his almost apologetic tone were a manifestation of something far deeper: a fear that their mutual awareness, their unspoken connection, could be derailed by the fragile possibility of misunderstanding.

"Then tell me," she said softly, taking a tentative step closer. "Tell me everything. Don't leave anything unsaid."

Daniel's eyes met hers, vulnerability shining through the familiar steadiness that had always been his armor. "I... I was afraid," he admitted, voice barely above a whisper. "Afraid that I would say too much, that I would reveal more than you're ready for, that I'd... complicate what we've been building. And so I held back, evaded, even when my attention and my feelings were impossible to deny."

Evelyn felt a swell of emotion, a mixture of relief, anticipation, and the suspenseful thrill of clarity. "You were afraid," she repeated softly. "Of what, exactly?"

He shook his head slightly, a wry, almost sheepish smile tugging at his lips. "Of hurting you unintentionally. Of creating expectations. Of revealing the truth before either of us was ready. And... perhaps, of admitting that I've felt something stronger, more insistent, more impossible to ignore, than I ever expected."

Her heart raced, the suspense now mingling with an almost unbearable sweetness. The misunderstood message, the vague texts, the careful timing—they had been his way of navigating the delicate balance between evasion and revelation. And now, standing here, the tension between them stretched taut, she realized that the moment they had both been circling was finally unfolding.

"I... I think I understand," Evelyn said softly, voice trembling with emotion. "You didn't want to risk the wrong interpretation. You didn't want to... make things too intense too soon. But your message... it nearly drove me crazy trying to guess what it meant."

Daniel chuckled softly, a sound of both relief and embarrassment. "And I realize now," he said, stepping slightly closer, "that evading the truth, even to protect you, almost made it worse. Almost made us lose the thread connecting us."

Evelyn nodded, her fingers brushing against the pendant at her neck, the weight grounding her even as her chest fluttered with anticipation. The misunderstood message had been a spark, a delicate tension, a suspenseful precursor to revelation. And now, as the layers peeled away, the reality of connection—intentional, deliberate, and undeniably present—began to settle around them like a fragile but undeniable truth.

For the first time in hours, perhaps days, Evelyn felt a quiet exhale pass through her lips, a release of tension she hadn't realized she had been holding. The suspense was still there, lingering, but it had transformed into something tangible, something alive, something that demanded acknowledgment rather than avoidance.

Daniel reached out, fingertips brushing hers lightly, the simplest of gestures carrying the weight of understanding, intent, and unspoken promises. In that touch, Evelyn realized that the misunderstood message had served its purpose: it had forced them to confront ambiguity, to navigate the fragile space between intention and perception, and to acknowledge the reality of feelings that neither could continue to evade.

The night deepened, the city outside continuing its quiet rhythm, indifferent to the delicate revelation unfolding in the park. Yet within the bubble of their shared space, the suspense had shifted from ambiguity to acknowledgment. Misunderstanding had given way to clarity, evasion had given way to courage, and the message—once a spark of tension—had become the first thread of a story that was finally beginning to be told.

26

SILENCE BETWEEN TWO PEOPLE WHO TALKED DAILY

The morning began as any other, or at least that was what Evelyn told herself as she moved through the motions of her routine. Sunlight filtered weakly through the thin curtains, casting a soft glow across the apartment walls, but it did little to warm the chill that had settled deep in her chest. Her phone sat on the kitchen counter, screen facing down as if intentionally avoiding the weight of what she longed to see. Every day for weeks, Daniel's messages had arrived with reliable consistency—a morning "good morning," midday musings, the occasional text that made her laugh or shiver with unexpected tenderness. But today, silence reigned, and the absence was deafening.

Evelyn stirred her coffee absentmindedly, listening to the drip of the machine and the distant hum of the city outside. It was almost comical, the way a simple lack of notification could ripple through her consciousness, leaving her acutely aware of every second, every thought, every heartbeat. The quiet was heavier than she anticipated, filled with unsaid words and unacknowledged longing. It was not the silence of peace or rest, but the silence of suspense, of anticipation, of a delicate tension that had the power to reshape her day entirely.

She replayed yesterday's meeting in her mind—the park, the exchanged glances, the subtle brush of hands, the almost-confessions that had hung in the air between them. Daniel's words, cautious yet deliberate, had left her both exhilarated and wary, and she had gone home with a cocktail of feelings she could not name. But in the night that followed, his usual messages never arrived. The absence, she realized, was not simple; it was loaded, pregnant with the unknown.

The silence created a mirror in which she could see every nuance of their interactions with unnerving clarity. She remembered the way he had looked at her, the slight hesitation before he spoke, the tremor in his voice when he admitted his fear of misinterpretation. Each detail was now magnified, every subtle gesture replayed with a mixture of longing and suspense. What had she missed? Had she misread his signals? Or worse, had he misunderstood hers?

She tried to distract herself, but even the routine tasks—watering the small plants on her windowsill, folding laundry, arranging dishes—were haunted by the absence of his presence. Each ordinary act was now charged, transformed by the suspended tension between them. Her mind reached for explanations, each more elaborate than the last: perhaps he had been caught up at work, perhaps he was reflecting, perhaps… perhaps he was pulling back, testing boundaries she hadn't realized were being probed. The questions spun in endless cycles, tightening the coil of suspense around her chest.

Evelyn's gaze drifted to her phone again. The screen remained dark, unbroken by the familiar vibration that had once punctuated her mornings with the gentle rhythm of his attention. The silence between two people who had once spoken daily now seemed almost surreal. It was a strange, paradoxical sensation: the familiarity of connection clashing with the unexpected void. Every instinct she had, honed over weeks of constant communication, screamed that something was amiss, yet her reason told her that one day of absence was not necessarily absence at all.

By mid-afternoon, the tension had become almost unbearable. Evelyn wandered through her apartment, tracing her fingers over surfaces as if touching the environment could somehow transfer stability into the chaos of her mind. Every small noise—the faint hum of the refrigerator, the occasional creak of the floorboards—felt amplified, each sound a reminder that she was waiting, suspended, tethered to a presence that was unreachable. The suspense had taken physical form, tightening her chest, causing her stomach to flutter with every imagined scenario.

Her mind returned to Daniel again. She visualized him pacing, sitting, thinking, perhaps even staring at his phone as she had, caught between words and actions, hesitant to breach the delicate threshold of their connection. The thought made her ache—not just for his presence, but for understanding. She wanted context, reassurance, anything to explain the emptiness that had filled the hours of their usual chatter. But she could not reach him yet. The suspense, she realized, was partly self-inflicted, a consequence of her own heightened awareness, her own desire to read meaning into every silence.

By late afternoon, she finally sent a message—a tentative, careful string of words:

"Hey… haven't heard from you today. Everything okay?"

The message lingered on the screen, hovering in digital limbo. The seconds stretched into minutes, minutes into an hour. Evelyn's chest tightened with every passing moment, every vibration that was not hers to receive. She tried to focus on work, on reading, on anything that would anchor her in reality, but the silence remained oppressive, as if the world itself were conspiring to keep her attention fixed on the absence she could neither explain nor control.

Her mind began to wander to their previous interactions—the shared laughter, the glances that lingered too long, the messages that had felt like sunlight piercing gray skies. Each memory now carried the weight of a foreshadowing she hadn't recognized until the present suspended her in anticipation. Had she taken too much for granted, assumed consistency, ignored the subtle signs that nothing, not even routine communication, could be guaranteed? The suspense tightened further, coiling around her thoughts with invisible fingers.

As evening fell, the city outside began to shimmer with neon lights and car headlights reflecting off wet streets. Evelyn remained by the window, arms crossed, shoulders tense, eyes scanning her phone with restless anticipation. The familiar rhythm of his voice in text messages—the morning jokes, the afternoon check-ins, the subtle observations—had become an invisible lifeline she had unconsciously relied upon. Its absence was disorienting, a reminder that even daily connection could be fragile, and that silence, when unanticipated, could magnify vulnerability to almost unbearable proportions.

A knock at the door startled her. Heart racing, Evelyn approached cautiously, her hand hovering over the doorknob. When she opened the door, it was not Daniel. It was a courier, holding a small package with no immediate explanation beyond her name on the label. She took it carefully, feeling the suspense coil tighter. What was inside? Could it be from him? Or had some other circumstance intruded into their fragile bubble of connection?

She tore the package open, revealing a small notebook, plain and unassuming. The pages were blank except for a single note:

"Read when you need clarity. Don't jump to conclusions. –D"

Her pulse quickened. Daniel. Finally, a tangible message, a physical presence in place of digital absence. And yet, the note's ambiguity was maddening. Read when you need clarity. Don't jump to conclusions. It was a message carefully crafted, meant to navigate the delicate space between explanation and suspense. Her mind raced—what did he mean? What clarity? What conclusions should she avoid?

Evelyn clutched the notebook to her chest, her mind spinning with anticipation and anxiety. The silence between them, which had been oppressive and confusing, now carried the promise of revelation—but also the threat of further misunderstanding. Every heartbeat felt amplified, every breath shallow with suspense, as she considered whether to read the notebook immediately or wait, prolonging the tension just a little longer.

Finally, with trembling hands, she opened it. The first page was filled with careful handwriting, each word deliberate, measured:

"Evelyn, this isn't about distance, or avoidance. It's about ensuring I say what matters most without causing confusion or unintended hurt. I care more than I can express in a text. The silence today… it isn't absence, it's thought. Reflection. Anticipation of the right words. Please know that even in silence, I am present."

Her eyes blurred. The silence between them—the emptiness, the suspense, the tension that had felt almost unbearable—wasn't neglect or abandonment. It was intention, a deliberate space created to navigate the fragility of truth and misunderstanding. The weight of anticipation lifted slightly, replaced with a profound awareness of care, patience, and unspoken connection.

Evelyn pressed the notebook to her heart, feeling the weight of his presence, even in the absence of words spoken aloud or messages typed. The silence between two people who had spoken daily had transformed from a source of anxiety into a vessel of understanding, a suspenseful reminder that sometimes absence, deliberate or unintended, could carry its own truth.

And in that moment, Evelyn understood something fundamental: connection was not measured only in words or routine. It was measured in intention, in thoughtfulness, in the quiet acknowledgment that even silence, when handled with care, could speak volumes. The suspense remained, yes—but it was tempered now by awareness, by understanding, by the unspoken bond that threaded their lives together even when words failed.

27

WHEN GOD TALKS IN STILLNESS

The chapel was empty. Not the crowded kind, where hymns echoed and voices rose in unison, but the quiet, tucked-away corner of the city that Evelyn had discovered months ago—a place she had come to rely on when the noise of life, and the chaos of her heart, became too heavy to bear. The sunlight filtered softly through stained glass windows, scattering tiny fragments of color across the stone floor. The air smelled faintly of old wood and polished pews, and in that stillness, Evelyn felt an unexpected clarity pressing against her chest, a quiet insistence that she needed to sit, to breathe, to listen.

She sank into a pew, knees tucked beneath her, hands clasped loosely in her lap. For a long moment, she simply breathed, letting the silence wash over her, soaking into the places in her heart that had been stretched thin by anticipation, uncertainty, and longing. The past few days had been a whirlwind of tension, misunderstandings, and silent conversations carried out through the careful weight of messages, missed signals, and evaded truths. Daniel's presence had become a constant undercurrent in her thoughts, yet now, she found herself alone in a space that demanded a different kind of awareness—one that was quieter, slower, and infinitely more profound.

The stillness spoke first in subtle ways: the faint creak of the wooden floorboards as she shifted her weight, the distant chirping of birds outside, the low hum of city life beyond the walls. But then, gradually, the silence seemed to expand, filling the chapel not with emptiness, but with a kind of presence that was palpable, almost tangible. Evelyn closed her eyes, and in that darkness behind her eyelids, she felt it—the gentle, insistent whisper of a force far greater than herself, a presence that demanded attention without imposing, that called without urgency, that illuminated without words.

Her mind immediately drifted to Daniel, to the tension that had been building between them, to the delicate space they occupied in each other's lives. She realized, with a startling clarity, that her anxiety, her anticipation, her constant replaying of interactions and messages, was not entirely about him—it was about the fear of missing the guidance that life, and perhaps God, was trying to offer. The stillness, she understood, was not emptiness; it was a conduit. A place where truth could speak when the noise of the world threatened to drown it out.

Evelyn's fingers brushed against the pendant at her neck, the small silver charm that Daniel had given her, and she felt a rush of conflicting emotions: the sweetness of his attention, the ache of their silences, and the suspense of not knowing how or when the next step would unfold. And yet, in the quiet of the chapel, she felt a subtle shift—a gentle reassurance that clarity did not always arrive through words, nor through action, nor even through the constant reassurance of digital connection. Sometimes it arrived in stillness, in patience, in the deep inhale of a moment suspended between chaos and calm.

She lowered her head, closing her eyes, and began to pray—not the rushed, formulaic prayers of obligation, but a quiet, trembling conversation with God, a whispering of the thoughts and fears she had carried too long. "Show me," she murmured, voice barely audible, "Show me what I need to see. Calm my heart, steady my thoughts, and help me hear what I cannot yet understand."

The chapel seemed to respond not with sound, but with sensation: a gentle warmth that settled around her shoulders, a weightless assurance that pressed lightly against her chest, and a stillness that was almost electric in its intensity. It was not dramatic. There were no signs, no voices, no sudden revelations. But in that quiet, Evelyn felt a knowing, a subtle but undeniable truth that had been waiting patiently for her attention: that clarity, guidance, and courage often arrived not in noise, not in rush, not in immediate answers—but in stillness.

Her thoughts wandered to Daniel again, and for the first time that day, she considered his silence not as absence, but as preparation. Perhaps he, too, had been wrestling with his own tension, his own anticipation, his own need to seek clarity in moments of stillness. The parallels were subtle but striking, a delicate recognition that two people, connected as they were, might need time apart to hear the truths that only silence could reveal.

Evelyn's mind drifted to the scripture she had read recently, verses she had once memorized but now seemed to carry new depth: "Be still, and know that I am God" (Psalm 46:10). She had understood it before as a gentle reminder of faith, of trust in divine timing, but now, in this quiet moment, she felt the weight of its significance. Stillness was not passive. It was not mere waiting. It was active listening, a surrender to the unseen currents that guide hearts, decisions, and destiny. And in that understanding, the suspense that had dominated her thoughts began to take on a different hue—a patient, measured anticipation, tempered by awareness and trust.

She leaned back against the smooth wooden pew, letting her eyes drift open, taking in the colored light filtering across the floor. Each shard of color seemed deliberate, purposeful, a quiet reminder that life, too, was composed of fragments that, when noticed and embraced, formed a coherent, beautiful pattern. Perhaps the suspense, the misunderstandings, the moments of tension with Daniel, were all fragments—threads of a larger tapestry that was unfolding in its own divine timing.

Her phone vibrated quietly in her bag, and Evelyn's chest tightened with the reflexive anticipation of connection. She reached for it slowly, the weight of stillness anchoring her fingers as she opened the screen. There, waiting in the inbox, was a message from Daniel:

"I'm at the place we spoke of yesterday. I want to talk, but only when you're ready. No rush."

The words were simple, deliberate, considerate, and yet they carried a power that resonated deeply within her. The message was an invitation, yes, but also a subtle acknowledgment of patience, understanding, and respect for the space she needed to hear what mattered most. Evelyn realized then that God's voice often spoke not through dramatic intervention, but through the careful orchestration of patience, timing, and quiet courage.

She took a deep breath, letting the sensation of anticipation mingle with calm. The suspense was still there—the gentle thrill of the unknown, the delicate tension between expectation and realization—but it was no longer frantic or overwhelming. It was tempered by a sense of guidance, of preparation, of trust in the unfolding process that had been carefully orchestrated beyond her comprehension.

Evelyn closed her eyes again, feeling the stillness settle fully around her, anchoring her heart and steadying her pulse. In the quiet, she recognized the lessons she had been avoiding: that patience was not passive, that silence was not absence, and that sometimes the most profound communication occurred not in spoken words, but in intentional pauses, in thoughtful waiting, and in surrender to divine timing.

She whispered a quiet prayer of gratitude, feeling the tension in her chest soften just slightly. "Thank You," she murmured, "for the clarity I couldn't see, for the patience I couldn't summon, for the voice I almost ignored in my restlessness. Help me to move forward in awareness, in courage, and in stillness."

When she finally rose, the sunlight had shifted slightly, scattering new patterns of light across the floor, reflecting softly off the edges of the pews. Evelyn felt a subtle sense of renewal, a quiet fortitude that had not been present before. She understood that tonight, when she met Daniel, she would do so with a heart steadied by stillness, a mind guided by clarity, and a spirit anchored in patience.

The suspense remained, yes, but it was no longer a chaotic, anxious energy. It was a living anticipation, alive with potential, charged with the awareness that the greatest revelations often arrived not in noise, not in rush, not in drama—but in moments of stillness where God speaks, where hearts align, and where courage quietly takes root.

Evelyn left the chapel, the soft click of her shoes on the stone floor echoing lightly, carrying with her a newfound sense of calm. The city awaited, bustling and alive, but within her, a quiet assurance had taken hold. The stillness had spoken. And she had listened.

28

DANIEL'S FEAR OF LOVING WRONG AGAIN

The night was unusually quiet, the kind of silence that felt like it carried its own weight, pressing against the walls of Daniel's apartment. Outside, the city thrummed faintly with distant sirens, car engines, and the occasional chatter of pedestrians, but inside, the space seemed suspended in time, caught between moments he could not undo and decisions he feared to make. Daniel sat on the edge of his bed, elbows resting on his knees, hands clasped together as if holding onto some fragile thread of control. His eyes were fixed on the floor, yet his mind was far away, spiraling through memories, regrets, and the heavy burden of possibility.

He had never been afraid of love itself; it was the consequences of it that haunted him. The idea that affection could be misunderstood, intentions misread, and hearts unintentionally shattered kept him awake on nights like this, when silence magnified every shadow of doubt. The events of the past weeks with Evelyn had stirred something inside him—a connection so profound, so undeniable, that it both thrilled and terrified him. And yet, the memory of past heartbreaks, the mistakes he had made when his emotions had run ahead of reason, gripped him with relentless caution.

Daniel's thoughts wandered to Evelyn, to her laugh, her quiet strength, the subtle ways she noticed him even when he tried to remain unnoticed. He remembered the way her eyes had softened when he spoke hesitantly, the way she lingered on his words as if weighing their unspoken meaning. And he had realized, with an intensity that both exhilarated and frightened him, that he could not walk away from this connection—not without leaving a void he would regret for years. But loving her... loving her fully, recklessly, without reservation... terrified him. What if he repeated past mistakes? What if he misread the depth of her feelings or revealed too much too soon? What if, in the attempt to protect both their hearts, he destroyed the delicate bond they were building?

The room felt smaller with every thought. He rose, pacing slowly, running his hands over the back of a chair, the edge of the dresser, tracing the contours of familiar objects as if seeking stability in their solidity. Every movement echoed his inner unrest, a physical manifestation of the suspense that had been building relentlessly within him. He tried to breathe, to steady his racing mind, but the fear clung to him like a second skin, tightening with each passing moment.

Daniel's gaze fell on his phone, lying face down on the nightstand. It was silent now, hours since his last message to Evelyn. The thought of reaching out, of sending another carefully worded text to gauge her mood, twisted inside him with both urgency and hesitation. He wanted to connect, to bridge the gap of uncertainty that had formed over the day. Yet a part of him hesitated, knowing that every word carried weight, that every message could tip the delicate balance they were cautiously maintaining.

He recalled the last time he had opened himself fully to someone—how the world had seemed bright, almost boundless, before crumbling into chaos he could neither control nor predict. He had loved wrong once, or at least, he had believed he had. The consequences had been painful, leaving scars etched deep into his soul, scars that refused to fade completely even as years passed. And now, standing on the precipice of possibility with Evelyn, he felt those old wounds stir, a visceral reminder that the human heart was both resilient and vulnerable in equal measure.

Sitting back on the bed, Daniel buried his face in his hands, trying to organize the tangled web of emotion, fear, and desire. He remembered Evelyn's smile that afternoon, subtle yet radiant, and how it had shaken him to the core. Her presence had become a quiet anchor, a tension-filled reminder that love could arrive with both gentle insistence and impossible force. He had hoped, secretly, that his restraint would be enough—that by taking measured steps, by pacing his emotions, he could navigate the connection without causing damage to either of them. But the deeper he fell into thought, the clearer it became: restraint alone would not protect him from the very human, very unpredictable force of feeling.

Daniel's eyes fell on the notebook Evelyn had given him, the one she had brought to their meeting in the park. Its pages were filled with her handwriting, careful and deliberate, each word a thread of honesty that had simultaneously comforted and unsettled him. She had shared reflections, questions, and subtle insights into her own heart, but never had she demanded answers or pushed for declarations beyond readiness. That, he realized, was part of what terrified him—the vulnerability she offered without expectation, the patience she embodied, and the silent courage she carried that matched his own inner struggle.

He ran a hand through his hair, the motion frantic now, and leaned back against the wall. The fear of loving wrong again was not merely fear of failure; it was fear of misalignment, of the misinterpretation of intentions, of the fragile dance between affection and caution. Every gesture, every message, every conversation with Evelyn carried the potential to either solidify the bond they shared or fracture it irreparably. And yet, in the quiet corners of his mind, he knew the truth: to remain cautious forever was to deny the possibility of genuine connection, the very thing he longed for more than he could admit aloud.

The suspense was almost unbearable, coiling around him with a relentless intensity. He imagined scenarios—some hopeful, some terrifying—where his actions could either lead to unspoken understanding or to painful confusion. He thought of the mornings when she would smile at a message he sent, the afternoons when her laughter seemed to linger in the air after he had left, the subtle brush of her hand when their paths crossed. Each memory was both a balm and a spark, a reminder of the stakes involved in every decision he made.

Daniel rose again, moving to the window and staring out at the city lights. The reflection of his own tense figure in the glass mirrored the turbulence inside him. The streets below were alive with movement, yet his world felt suspended, every thought anchored to the delicate balance of fear and hope. He realized, with a mixture of clarity and dread, that his fear of loving wrong again was not a signal to retreat—it was a signal to move forward with caution, awareness, and intentionality.

His phone buzzed softly, drawing his gaze. A message from Evelyn, short and understated, appeared on the screen:

"I'm thinking of you. Hope you're okay."

The simplicity of it struck him with both relief and new tension. She had reached out without pressure, without expectation, yet her words carried an unspoken invitation, a reminder that connection was still possible despite his fears. The suspense did not diminish; it evolved, now carrying the weight of choice, responsibility, and courage. Every word from her was a thread, delicate yet binding, demanding that he confront the fear that had shadowed him for so long.

Daniel pressed his thumb to the screen, hesitating. To respond hastily could betray his inner turmoil; to delay could amplify the suspense, deepen the gap he feared would widen beyond repair. He took a deep breath, closing his eyes, and let the silence guide him. In the quiet, he felt the faintest whisper of clarity: fear did not have to dictate action, but it could inform it, sharpen it, and illuminate the path to intentional love.

He typed slowly, deliberately, feeling each word as it formed:

"I'm here. I've been thinking too much, overanalyzing, but I want to try… carefully, intentionally. I don't want to love wrong again, but I also don't want to avoid what's real."

He hit send, and the weight of the message settled over him like both a release and a tether. The suspense was still alive, pulsing with anticipation, but he felt the first stirrings of courage, the fragile pulse of readiness, and the acknowledgment that love—when approached with awareness, honesty, and humility—could be navigated even after past pain.

Daniel leaned back, eyes closing as he let the tension drain from his shoulders. Fear would always linger, a shadow of memory and caution, but the decision to confront it—to risk misunderstanding, to risk vulnerability, to risk loving fully yet carefully—was his first step toward a new kind of bravery. Evelyn was waiting, in her own measured way, for the bridge between them to be crossed. And tonight, he realized, he was finally ready to begin.

29

A CONVERSATION THEY BOTH AVOIDED

The coffee shop was quiet, almost eerily so, for a Thursday evening. Only a few tables were occupied, the low murmur of hushed conversations blending seamlessly with the clinking of cups and the occasional hiss of the espresso machine. Daniel had arrived early, choosing a corner table that offered a view of both the entrance and the window, allowing him to watch the world move beyond the glass while he remained suspended in a tension that had been building for days. His hands fidgeted with the folded napkin in front of him, twisting it and letting it fold itself again, a nervous ritual he couldn't quite explain.

He had rehearsed the words in his mind countless times, each iteration more precise, more careful, more cautious than the last. Yet with every repetition, he felt the weight of their significance—the kind of conversation that had the potential to reshape everything between them. He was acutely aware of the stakes: the fragile threads of connection, the unspoken desires, the fear of missteps that could undo what had slowly, painstakingly, begun to grow between them.

Evelyn arrived moments later, slipping through the door with the quiet grace she always carried, her presence immediately drawing his attention. She had a notebook tucked under her arm, a scarf loosely wrapped around her neck, and a cautious smile that hinted at awareness of the tension that existed even before they sat down. When their eyes met, a subtle exchange passed between them—a mixture of anticipation, relief, and the unspoken acknowledgment that they were both avoiding the same truth.

"Hi," Daniel said finally, voice low, careful. The single word felt heavier than any sentence he had rehearsed, loaded with the weight of unspoken feelings and concealed thoughts.

"Hi," Evelyn replied, settling into the chair opposite him. Her fingers traced the rim of her coffee cup absentmindedly, a nervous gesture he recognized immediately. "It's… quiet here," she added, almost as if she needed to fill the silence before it swallowed the moment whole.

Daniel nodded, glancing at the empty space around them, then back at her. "Yeah… I like it. Feels… safe." He hesitated, swallowing hard as he tried to navigate the delicate line between casual conversation and the gravity of what they were both avoiding. "I… I wanted to talk to you about something."

Evelyn's eyes flicked up, alert but cautious. She sensed the tension coiling in his words, the careful pacing, the almost imperceptible tremor beneath his calm exterior. "Yes?" she prompted softly, her own heart tightening. She had known this moment would come—the inevitable conversation that neither of them had yet dared to fully confront—but the reality of it pressed against her chest with a tangible force.

Daniel exhaled slowly, running a hand through his hair. "It's… complicated," he began, the words carefully chosen, precise, deliberate. "There's a lot I want to say, but I don't want to rush, and I don't want to… mess this up." His eyes met hers, and she could see the earnestness there, the raw vulnerability that had always lurked beneath his composed exterior.

Evelyn nodded slowly, keeping her own emotions in check. "I understand," she said, voice measured, though her hands trembled slightly as they rested on the table. "We both… want to get it right. We both want to protect… what we have."

Daniel's gaze dropped to the table, and he twisted the napkin in his hands again. "It's just… I've been hurt before. Loved wrong before. And I keep thinking about all the ways I could repeat those mistakes if I'm not careful." His words hung in the air, heavy with suspense, each syllable a revelation of fear and hope intertwined.

Evelyn felt her breath catch. She had sensed the caution, the fear beneath his gestures, the hesitation that shadowed every glance, but hearing it aloud made the suspense almost unbearable. She wanted to reach across the table, to reassure him, to tell him that love was worth the risk, yet another part of her held back, knowing that the conversation they were having was fragile, delicate, and required careful navigation.

"I know," she said softly, her voice barely above a whisper. "I've been hurt too… in ways that make trust feel… complicated. And yet… here we are, trying anyway." Her eyes held his, steady and unflinching, conveying both understanding and encouragement. "We don't have to get it perfect. We just… have to be honest. With ourselves, with each other."

Daniel's eyes lifted, meeting hers with a mixture of relief and tension. "Honest…" he repeated, tasting the word, as if it carried more weight than he had realized. "I… I've been avoiding this conversation, because I didn't want to scare you, or make you feel… pressured. But I also couldn't keep pretending that… that I don't feel the way I do."

Evelyn's pulse quickened. The suspense in the space between them was almost tangible, thickening with every pause, every measured glance, every deliberate choice of words. She had known he cared, had sensed the intensity beneath his restraint, but the admission, even partial, sent a ripple of emotion through her chest that was equal parts exhilarating and terrifying.

"I've felt it too," she admitted softly, her fingers brushing against the notebook on her lap, her hands tightening slightly around it. "More than I thought I would… more than I expected. And yes, I've avoided saying it because I didn't want to… complicate things. Or make it seem like I'm rushing, when really… I'm scared of what could happen if I'm wrong."

Daniel's lips parted slightly, a small, incredulous smile tugging at the corners. The suspense that had been mounting, coiling around them, seemed to hold its breath in that moment, waiting for the next word, the next move, the next revelation. "So… we've both been pretending not to feel what we've been feeling?" he asked, a mix of wonder, relief, and disbelief in his tone.

Evelyn nodded, a faint smile breaking through her careful composure. "Yes… but pretending isn't the same as hiding. It's… protecting, I think. Protecting ourselves until we were ready." Her gaze was steady, unwavering, and in that moment, the tension that had defined the past days of unspoken thoughts began to shift into something heavier, deeper, more significant—a shared acknowledgment that their fears were mutual, their hearts aligned even in the suspense of avoidance.

Daniel leaned back slightly, exhaling a breath he hadn't realized he was holding. The suspense in the air was no longer solely about fear—it had become charged with the possibility of connection, with the delicate, exhilarating awareness that honesty, once embraced, could transform even the most carefully guarded hearts. "I've been scared of loving wrong again," he admitted, voice low, almost a confession. “But hearing you… feeling that you feel it too… it makes me want to try anyway. To risk it, carefully, intentionally.”

Evelyn’s chest ached with the weight of recognition, understanding, and the suspense that had finally found a resolution in mutual acknowledgment. “We’ll risk it together,” she said softly. “Step by step. Not rushing, not forcing. Just… being honest, even when it’s hard.”

For a moment, silence fell between them. It was not the oppressive silence of avoidance, nor the charged tension of unspoken fear. It was the quiet pause of understanding, a breath held between two people who had navigated suspense, fear, and the fragility of emotion to arrive at a space of connection that was both tentative and profound.

Daniel’s hand hovered over hers, and slowly, tentatively, their fingers intertwined. The gesture was small, simple, but it carried the weight of unspoken promises, acknowledged fears, and a shared decision to face the uncertainty together. The suspense, which had defined their days of careful avoidance, transformed into a living pulse of anticipation, hope, and courage.

“I don’t want to love wrong again,” he whispered, voice low and deliberate, “but I do want to love… you. And I think… maybe, together, we can navigate it without repeating mistakes.”

Evelyn’s lips curved into a small, steady smile, her heart racing with a mixture of relief and thrill. “We’ll navigate it,” she said softly. “We’ll be careful. And we’ll be honest. Even when it scares us. Even when it feels… too much.”

The world outside the coffee shop continued its rhythm, indifferent to the quiet revelations and delicate suspensions that had unfolded within its walls. But inside, Daniel and Evelyn had crossed the threshold of avoidance, confronting the conversation they had both skirted for weeks. The suspense remained—not gone, not resolved entirely—but transformed, alive with possibility, anchored in honesty, and tempered by the courage to face love without pretense.

They sat together in that quiet corner, hands intertwined, hearts synchronized, acknowledging the gravity of the step they had taken. The conversation they had avoided had finally been spoken, and in that act of courage, suspense became promise, fear became determination, and avoidance gave way to connection.

30

THE HUG THAT LASTED A LITTLE TOO LONG

The air was crisp that evening, carrying the faint scent of rain that had washed over the city streets earlier. Streetlights flickered gently along the pavement, their soft amber glow reflecting in puddles that lingered after the storm. Evelyn and Daniel walked side by side along the empty sidewalk, their steps slow, measured, yet unspoken emotions pulsing in the quiet between them. Neither had planned to end the evening like this—not intentionally—but the rhythm of their conversation, the cadence of their laughter, and the subtle weight of shared confessions had led them to this suspended moment.

They stopped outside the café where they had first dared to discuss their fears, the glass windows reflecting the muted city lights and their own hesitant reflections. Daniel shifted uneasily, hands buried in the pockets of his coat, while Evelyn's scarf fluttered gently in the evening breeze. Neither spoke immediately, as if the night itself demanded a pause, a careful holding of breath before the inevitable moment that seemed to hover in the air around them.

Then, without preamble, Daniel turned slightly, facing her. His eyes, dark and intense, held hers with a gravity that both exhilarated and unsettled her. She could feel the tension coiling in her stomach, the familiar mix of anticipation and apprehension that had defined their relationship in these past weeks. He opened his arms slightly—not dramatically, not flamboyantly, but enough to signal intent—and she stepped forward instinctively.

The hug that followed was meant to be simple, casual, a small reassurance after their long conversation earlier. But the moment they embraced, the world seemed to pause. Their bodies pressed together, the warmth of proximity amplifying feelings that words had failed to capture. Evelyn's head rested lightly against his shoulder, and Daniel's cheek brushed against the crown of her head. Both of them breathed in the quiet rhythm of the other, the subtle scent of rain lingering in the air, mingling with the warmth of coats and shared space.

Seconds stretched into moments, and then into a rhythm that neither of them wanted to break. Daniel's hands rested lightly on her back, uncertain yet deliberate, as if fearing that too firm a grip might shatter the fragile balance of the moment. Evelyn's arms were wrapped loosely around him, her fingers tracing the fabric of his coat as if memorizing the contours of his presence. The hug was simple, yet it carried the weight of weeks of suspense, withheld words, and tentative trust that had been painstakingly built in small, careful increments.

They were both acutely aware of the world around them—the streetlamps, the distant sounds of cars passing, the faint rustle of leaves—but it all felt distant, irrelevant, swallowed by the intensity of proximity and the quiet tension that hummed between them. Each heartbeat seemed magnified, each breath shared an unspoken communication that neither dared to voice. The hug, meant to be fleeting, had become a silent declaration, a conversation in body and warmth that transcended speech.

Daniel's mind was a whirlwind of emotion, memory, and desire. He thought of every moment with Evelyn, every subtle smile, every word avoided, every laugh shared. And in the quiet of this embrace, all those fragments coalesced into a single, undeniable truth: he wanted to be present, fully and intentionally, yet fear lingered like a shadow at the edges of his awareness. The fear of loving wrong again, of misreading signals, of losing the delicate balance they had forged, clung stubbornly to his resolve. And yet, in this hug, in the subtle warmth of her shoulder beneath his cheek, he felt the courage to lean into what he had previously avoided.

Evelyn, too, felt the weight of the moment. Her chest tightened, not with anxiety but with anticipation, as the hug pressed her senses into sharp focus. She could feel the steady beat of Daniel's heart against her own, the subtle rise and fall of his breath, the warmth of his coat mingling with hers. For a moment, she considered pulling away, reminding herself of caution, of careful pacing, of the lessons they had both spoken about in their tentative conversation. Yet something in the pressure of his embrace, in the quiet steadiness he exuded despite his own fears, urged her to stay—to linger in the suspended moment where words were unnecessary, and connection spoke for itself.

The hug lingered longer than either had intended, but in its duration lay a quiet intensity, a slow unfolding of understanding and intimacy that could not be rushed. Daniel's hand moved slightly, brushing against the small of her back, and Evelyn shifted subtly, pressing closer, not out of urgency but from an instinctive need to remain in the shared space that had become both sanctuary and revelation. The street around them faded into blur, leaving only the two of them and the silent acknowledgment of feelings that had been carefully managed, feared, and now tentatively embraced.

A faint breeze stirred, tugging at Evelyn's scarf, and Daniel instinctively tightened his hold slightly, a subtle acknowledgment that he wanted to remain connected, to prolong the contact just a little longer, as if the hug itself could convey truths his voice could not. Evelyn's hands, resting lightly on his shoulders, mirrored the same intent. They were both aware of the delicate balance: the line between tenderness and desire, between vulnerability and fear, between the thrill of closeness and the caution of restraint.

Time seemed suspended, each second infused with suspense and charged with the unspoken question of what might happen if they allowed themselves to fully acknowledge the depth of their connection. Daniel's mind raced, simultaneously exhilarated and terrified. He thought of the past, the mistakes he had made, the moments of loving wrong and the consequences that had followed. And yet, in this hug, there was a clarity he had not expected—a gentle, undeniable affirmation that intention, patience, and presence could redefine the boundaries of fear and vulnerability.

Evelyn, sensing the shift in his energy, allowed herself to relax slightly into the embrace. Her body mirrored his intent, cautious yet open, deliberate yet tentative. She had felt the suspense building between them for weeks, the tension of avoided conversations, the thrill of small gestures, and now the hug became a focal point—a crystallization of everything they had felt but not fully expressed. She pressed her forehead gently against his chest, feeling the steady beat of his heart and the faint tremor beneath it, an echo of the vulnerability he had so carefully hidden behind composed words.

The world remained hushed, indifferent to the intimacy unfolding on the sidewalk. Yet within that small circle of warmth and suspended motion, Evelyn and Daniel navigated a delicate landscape of emotion, negotiating the fragile balance between desire and caution, between anticipation and presence. Every breath, every heartbeat, every subtle adjustment of their posture carried meaning, layered with the suspense of all that had led them to this moment and the possibilities of what could come next.

Finally, with a shared exhale, they began to pull slightly apart, though neither released completely. Their faces hovered inches apart, eyes locked, breathing synchronized, the city lights reflecting softly in the depths of their gaze. The hug had lasted longer than either had intended, but in its extension lay a truth neither could deny: the intimacy they shared, the vulnerability they dared to expose, and the courage to linger in a moment without rushing were defining the contours of their connection more profoundly than any words could.

Daniel's hand remained lightly on her back, fingers grazing the fabric of her coat. "I… I didn't want to let go," he admitted softly, voice low, almost a whisper carried on the wind. The admission was both confession and reassurance, a subtle acknowledgment of the suspense that had defined their previous interactions and the tentative trust now being forged in its place.

Evelyn's lips curved into a small, steady smile. "Neither did I," she replied, equally soft. Her words carried no pressure, no expectation—only the quiet affirmation of shared understanding and mutual recognition. The hug, longer than intended, had become a bridge, a silent declaration of willingness to navigate fear, vulnerability, and suspense together.

As they finally stepped back, the streetlights flickered gently, casting long shadows that intertwined like their own emotions. The hug had ended, but its residue lingered—the quiet electricity of connection, the anticipation of what might come next, and the subtle courage that had allowed two hesitant hearts to remain pressed together in a suspended moment. They walked on, side by side, their steps slow, measured, yet profoundly in sync, each heartbeat echoing the unspoken promise of intimacy, trust, and the delicate beauty of a hug that lasted a little too long.

The night held them in its embrace, suspense still humming quietly beneath the surface, but now tempered with hope, intention, and the shared acknowledgment that some moments—like this hug—were meant to linger just a little longer, carrying the unspoken truths of hearts daring to meet without fear.

IV

LOVE BLOSSOMS SLOWLY

31

A WALK UNDER SOFT EVENING LIGHTS

The evening air was cool and crisp, carrying the faint scent of jasmine that had begun to bloom in the small park near the city square. Streetlights cast pools of soft amber along the winding pathways, illuminating patches of dewy grass and the occasional fluttering leaves that swirled gently in the breeze. Daniel and Evelyn emerged from the café, their steps tentative but in sync, as though the day's conversation and lingering hug had created an invisible tether connecting them. There was a rhythm to their movement, a silent acknowledgment of the tension that had yet to be fully resolved, mingling with the tentative hope that had begun to root itself in their hearts.

They walked in silence at first, neither speaking but aware of the subtle intimacy that existed in proximity. The crunch of gravel beneath their shoes and the soft rustling of trees were the only sounds, punctuating the quiet anticipation between them. Daniel kept glancing at Evelyn out of the corner of his eye, noting the way her hair caught the light from the streetlamps, the gentle curve of her smile even when her eyes were cast downward, and the calm determination in her posture that both comforted and unnerved him.

Evelyn, for her part, was equally aware of the electricity in the air—the unspoken words lingering between them, the shared awareness of fears, confessions, and possibilities that had yet to be fully explored. She felt the warmth of his presence at her side, a quiet reassurance that gave her courage even as suspense coiled around her chest. She wanted to speak, to break the silence, but something in the hush of the evening, the intimacy of walking beneath soft lights, made her hesitate. Words felt heavy, fragile, and inadequate in capturing the depth of what she was feeling.

Daniel finally spoke, his voice low and deliberate, breaking the silence without shattering it. "I… I like walking with you like this," he said, glancing at her briefly before returning his gaze to the path ahead. "Feels… different. Calmer. Safer."

Evelyn's lips curved into a small, tentative smile. "I know what you mean," she replied softly. "It's like the rest of the world… just fades. And it's just us, even if we don't say much." Her words hung in the air, carrying with them both honesty and subtle vulnerability, a reflection of the trust they had been slowly building over the past weeks.

The pathway curved, leading them past a small fountain whose waters shimmered under the soft glow of nearby lights. Daniel slowed, taking a deep breath as he considered the next words. The walk was becoming more than a simple stroll—it was a bridge between hesitation and intention, a careful navigation of emotions that neither of them had fully dared to confront. "I keep thinking about… how close we are," he said quietly, almost to himself. "Not just physically, but… in other ways. And I don't want to mess that up. But I also don't want to ignore it."

Evelyn glanced up at him, startled by the directness yet comforted by the honesty in his tone. Her fingers brushed against her coat pocket, where her notebook lay folded, a repository of reflections, questions, and musings she hadn't yet shared with him. "I've felt it too," she admitted softly. "It's like... every step we take, every word we exchange, carries more weight than it should, but at the same time... it doesn't feel heavy. It feels... inevitable."

Daniel's heart tightened. The word "inevitable" struck him like a subtle revelation, a quiet acknowledgment that despite their fears, avoidance, and lingering suspense, there was a thread connecting them that neither could deny. He wanted to reach for her hand, to bridge the small distance that remained between them, but the delicate balance of the evening—the suspended intimacy of walking side by side under soft lights—made him pause. Every motion, every choice, carried significance. He could not act recklessly; he had to move intentionally, carefully, aware of both their fears and desires.

They walked on, the path bending slightly as it led them past a row of old oak trees whose branches intertwined above, creating a natural archway. The shadows danced along the ground, shifting with the faint wind, and Daniel felt the subtle thrill of anticipation coil in his chest. Every glance exchanged with Evelyn, every fleeting touch of shoulders as they passed narrow spots on the path, carried the quiet weight of possibility and the suspense of all that was yet unspoken.

"I keep wondering," Daniel began hesitantly, his voice barely more than a whisper, "if... if we're ready for... everything. For all the feelings, the complications, the... what-ifs."

Evelyn tilted her head slightly, considering him, the glow of the streetlights reflecting softly in her eyes. "The 'what-ifs' are always there," she said thoughtfully. "But maybe... it's not about being ready for them all at once. Maybe it's about taking the steps we can, together, even if some answers come later."

Daniel exhaled slowly, a mixture of relief and lingering tension in his chest. Her words, gentle yet deliberate, mirrored his own unspoken thoughts: that love, like walking beneath soft evening lights, required patience, attention, and a willingness to navigate uncertainty. The suspense, which had followed them like a shadow in every interaction, was now infused with cautious hope, a delicate energy that neither of them fully understood but both felt keenly.

As they continued, a stray leaf drifted down from one of the oaks, landing lightly on Daniel's shoulder. He reached up instinctively, brushing it away, and Evelyn's soft laughter followed, a sound that wrapped around him like a warm ribbon, easing the tension in his chest. "See?" she said lightly. "Even the leaves are conspiring to remind us… life moves, whether we're ready or not."

He chuckled, a short, relieved sound that carried both amusement and a touch of awe. "Maybe it's true," he admitted. "Maybe we just… move with it. Carefully, intentionally, like you said. One step at a time."

The park opened into a small clearing ahead, a bench illuminated by the soft glow of a solitary streetlight. Daniel gestured toward it, and Evelyn nodded, letting them sit side by side. The quiet intimacy of proximity, the shared rhythm of breathing, and the gentle ambiance of the evening created a space where suspense and anticipation merged seamlessly. They were close, yet not touching beyond the subtle brush of arms, and in that careful balance, both felt the thrill and tension of connection that had been building for weeks.

"I like this," Evelyn said softly, her voice almost blending with the hum of distant city life. "Walking… talking… just being. It's… real."

Daniel turned slightly, his gaze meeting hers. "Real," he echoed. "And that scares me sometimes. Because real… means responsibility, accountability, and... vulnerability. And I've been hurt before when I let myself be vulnerable." His hands rested lightly on his knees, a physical restraint that mirrored the caution he carried in his words.

Evelyn's fingers brushed lightly against his, a tentative, almost accidental contact that sent a ripple of warmth through both of them. She looked at him, eyes steady, and spoke with deliberate care. "But maybe... that's the point. Vulnerability isn't something to fear—it's something to navigate. Together. That's what makes it... real."

The suspense in the air intensified, not as tension, but as a charged energy of possibility. The way their hands hovered near each other, the way their eyes held unspoken confessions, and the subtle cadence of shared breaths created a moment that was fragile, exhilarating, and profoundly intimate. Every motion was deliberate, every pause weighted with meaning, every word a careful step in the dance of trust and anticipation.

Daniel leaned back slightly, exhaling, feeling the subtle shift of courage bloom in his chest. The soft lights above them, the quiet rhythm of the evening, and Evelyn's presence beside him all combined into a sense of clarity that had been absent in previous weeks. The suspense, while still alive, was no longer solely about fear—it was about the promise of connection, the potential of shared vulnerability, and the delicate beauty of moments that required patience, awareness, and mutual courage.

Finally, as the evening deepened and shadows lengthened, Daniel reached gently for Evelyn's hand. Their fingers intertwined slowly, intentionally, a silent acknowledgment of trust, understanding, and the quiet exhilaration of closeness. The walk under soft evening lights had become more than a stroll—it was a bridge between avoidance and acknowledgment, fear and courage, anticipation and presence.

They remained seated for a while, hands clasped, hearts synchronized, letting the gentle ambiance of the night carry them forward. The suspense that had defined their interactions—avoidance, hesitation, longing—had transformed into an energy alive with possibility, tempered by patience, and illuminated by shared presence.

In that soft glow, walking and sitting beneath the gentle evening lights, Daniel and Evelyn discovered that connection was not merely about words or actions—it was about shared rhythm, mutual acknowledgment, and the courage to linger in moments of vulnerability long enough for understanding to take root.

32

SECRETS THEY TRUSTED EACH OTHER WITH

The room was quiet except for the soft hum of the ceiling fan, its rhythmic motion cutting through the tense stillness like a metronome marking time. Daniel sat in the armchair closest to the window, fingers drumming lightly against the leather, as if each tap could release the tangled thoughts swirling in his mind. Across from him, Evelyn perched on the edge of the sofa, her notebook balanced delicately on her knees, the pen resting between her fingers like a wand poised to capture thoughts that had remained hidden for far too long.

There was an air of suspended anticipation between them, one that neither dared to disturb with idle words. It was the kind of silence that carried weight, the kind that made the slightest movement feel deliberate, the slightest glance heavy with significance. Both of them had felt it, acutely, during the days leading up to this evening—a sense that the careful steps they had taken in their relationship were leading them to a precipice, one where honesty and vulnerability would be the only safe passage.

Daniel finally broke the quiet, his voice low and tentative, almost hesitant. “I’ve never told anyone… some of the things I’m about to share with you,” he said, his gaze fixed on a point on the carpet that was both distant and intimate. "Not because I didn't trust, but because... well, because it was easier to carry them alone."

Evelyn tilted her head slightly, encouraging him without pressing, her presence a quiet invitation that allowed him to descend into the depths of confession without fear of judgment. "You don't have to rush," she whispered. "Take your time. I'm here. I promise."

The first secret came out almost in a whisper, a memory of betrayal from years ago, a wound that had never fully healed. Daniel spoke of friendships that had turned cold, of intentions misread and trust broken, and of the way he had learned to shield his heart, locking away fragments of himself to protect against future pain. Each word was carefully measured, yet each carried a tremor of vulnerability that was impossible to conceal.

Evelyn listened, her pen forgotten for the moment, eyes steady, absorbing each detail with quiet intensity. She understood the weight of what he was revealing—the courage it took to expose the parts of himself he had kept hidden, the careful navigation of memory and emotion required to tell someone that which he had once sworn to keep private. Her presence was deliberate, patient, and unwavering, a silent acknowledgment that his secrets were safe with her.

When Daniel paused, as though gathering the strength to continue, Evelyn responded softly. "I've carried my own," she admitted, her voice low but confident. "Things I've never shared... because I thought no one could understand. Or because I was too afraid of being judged."

Her admission hung in the air, delicate yet weighty, a mirror to his own vulnerabilities. She turned slightly, revealing a page from her notebook, a cluster of thoughts she had written late at night, confessions she had feared even writing down, let alone sharing. "I've written them down... these fears, these secrets, these moments I thought I'd have to face alone. But I... I trust you enough to let you read them now."

Daniel's eyes lifted, meeting hers with a mixture of awe, respect, and a lingering thread of suspense. The act of sharing these secrets was not merely a release; it was an act of surrender, an acknowledgment that the bond they were building was strong enough to hold the weight of unspoken truths. He nodded slowly, reaching out to take the notebook from her hands, careful not to rush, careful not to break the fragile rhythm of trust that had been established between them.

As he read, the suspense in the room shifted subtly, from tension to something heavier, more intimate. Evelyn's secrets were raw, layered with emotion and unfiltered thoughts that revealed a depth of character Daniel had not fully seen before. There were admissions of fear, doubt, past mistakes, and longing that painted a vivid picture of her inner world—one that was both familiar and startlingly new to him. Each page turned was a quiet revelation, a reminder that intimacy was built not just on shared moments of joy, but also on the willingness to reveal shadows and embrace them without retreat.

When Daniel finally looked up, his eyes met hers, darkened with the understanding of what had just been shared. "Thank you," he whispered, voice thick with emotion. "I... I don't take this lightly. Everything you've just shared... it's... sacred. And I promise, I'll honor it. I'll honor you."

Evelyn smiled faintly, a mixture of relief and vulnerability. "I know," she said softly. "And I'll honor you too. All the parts of you you've never shared... all the fears you've carried alone. We don't have to face them alone anymore."

Daniel exhaled, a slow, deliberate release that carried both tension and newfound courage. "There's one more thing," he admitted, his voice barely above a whisper. "Something I've never told anyone, not even myself fully. But I think… I think I need to, now."

Evelyn leaned forward slightly, her eyes steady, inviting him to continue. "You can," she said gently. "I'm listening. I want to know all of you, even the parts you're scared to admit."

He paused, swallowing hard, and then spoke of a time when he had been on the verge of giving up on trust, on love, on connection altogether. He recounted moments of doubt so profound they had nearly eclipsed his ability to hope again. He spoke of nights spent questioning his worth, of decisions that had led to isolation, and of the fear that any bond he formed would eventually crumble. Each revelation was a delicate negotiation with suspense—the suspense of being fully seen, of risking judgment, of opening himself to pain and acceptance in equal measure.

Evelyn reached out, resting her hand lightly on his arm. The contact was simple, reassuring, but it carried immense weight. "Daniel," she whispered, her voice trembling slightly with emotion, "thank you for trusting me with this. For letting me in. You're not alone anymore. None of this… not the fears, not the past… not the mistakes… are yours to carry alone anymore."

The room seemed to breathe with them, the fan's gentle hum now a background to the quiet intensity of shared vulnerability. Daniel felt the suspense that had haunted him for weeks shift into a tangible connection, a bond reinforced by the mutual trust of secrets laid bare. He realized, profoundly, that intimacy was not merely about proximity or physical closeness—it was about the courage to reveal, to be raw, and to accept that the other person would not recoil, but instead meet him in the delicate space between vulnerability and understanding.

Evelyn, feeling the weight of the moment, shared more, her voice steady despite the tremor in her hands. She spoke of her own past betrayals, the moments she had been deceived by those she had trusted most, and the careful armor she had built around her heart. She revealed the secret fears that had kept her from fully embracing connection—the doubts that whispered that love always ended in pain, that trust was fragile, that vulnerability was a dangerous gamble. Each revelation was deliberate, a careful peeling back of layers, and Daniel absorbed each word with reverence, understanding that the suspense in their relationship was not just about longing or attraction, but about the profound act of mutual exposure.

When the last secret had been shared, a heavy silence settled over the room, not oppressive, but full of weighty significance. They sat facing each other, hands resting lightly on their laps, eyes meeting with an understanding that words could not fully capture. The suspense that had defined their interactions—the anticipation, the hesitation, the careful avoidance of fear—had transformed into trust, into shared courage, into a quiet acknowledgment that their connection was stronger than either had anticipated.

Daniel finally spoke, voice low and deliberate. "We've trusted each other tonight… with things we've never told anyone. And somehow… it feels like a beginning. Like, no matter what comes next, we've built something… real."

Evelyn nodded, her lips curving into a faint, steady smile. "It is real," she said softly. "And it's only going to grow stronger. Because trust… true trust… is the foundation. And tonight, we've built it, brick by brick, secret by secret."

The fan continued its gentle rhythm, the city beyond the window carrying on unaware of the quiet intensity inside the room. And in that suspended space, Daniel and Evelyn realized that the suspense that had defined their connection—fear of rejection, fear of misstep, fear of loving wrong again—

had given way to something more profound: the unshakeable bond forged by secrets they trusted each other with, a bond that could withstand uncertainty, vulnerability, and the quiet suspense of what was yet to come.

As they sat together, hands close but not yet intertwined, hearts beating in silent concord, they understood that trust—fragile, delicate, yet unyielding—was the truest measure of love. And in that understanding, they found courage, intimacy, and the promise of a future unburdened by fear.

33

HOW SOMETHING SIMPLE BECAME SOMETHING SACRED

The sun had just begun to set, casting a warm, amber glow across the city park where Daniel and Evelyn found themselves once more. The air carried the subtle scent of freshly mown grass and the faint trace of blossoms from the nearby flowerbeds, mingling with the faint aroma of warm earth that had been washed by a light rain earlier. It was a perfect evening—not extravagant, not orchestrated, just a quiet moment suspended in time. And yet, Daniel felt an unfamiliar weight pressing in on him, a mixture of anticipation, reverence, and the suspense that always seemed to accompany Evelyn.

They walked slowly along the winding path, their steps in sync, the silence between them comfortable yet charged. Daniel's eyes flicked occasionally toward Evelyn, noticing the way the last rays of sunlight caught the strands of her hair, illuminating them with a gentle halo. She walked with quiet assurance, notebook clutched loosely in one hand, the pen tapping lightly against her fingers in a rhythm that mirrored the soft hum of her heartbeat.

"What do you think makes a moment... sacred?" Evelyn asked suddenly, her voice low, thoughtful. The question came without preamble, like a pebble dropped into the still waters of Daniel's mind, rippling outward in unexpected patterns.

Daniel hesitated, considering. "I… I think it's when something ordinary becomes extraordinary because it's filled with intention," he said finally. "When it carries meaning beyond itself, and you feel… changed by it."

Evelyn smiled faintly, the corners of her lips lifting ever so slightly, but the intensity in her eyes made it clear she was not merely seeking conversation—she was testing, exploring, probing the boundaries of understanding and intimacy. "So… a simple act can become sacred?" she prompted, tilting her head slightly.

Daniel nodded, though his mind was spinning. He had come to this park countless times before, had walked these paths, sat on these benches, and yet tonight, the ordinary seemed charged with a new energy. It wasn't the park itself that had changed—it was the presence of Evelyn, the way her thoughts intertwined with his own, and the subtle tension of a relationship that had been carefully nurtured through suspense, small confessions, and tentative trust.

They approached a small, wrought-iron bench beneath a sprawling oak tree, its branches stretched like open arms toward the sky. Without a word, Daniel gestured toward it, and Evelyn sat gracefully, smoothing her coat as she settled. He joined her, careful to leave a respectful distance, but close enough that the warmth of proximity pressed subtly against them.

They watched the sunset together, the sky shifting from gold to rose, and then to the deep violet of twilight. The air was alive with quiet sounds—the distant murmur of children playing, the rustle of leaves in the gentle breeze, the occasional chirp of birds settling for the night—but within their shared space, these sounds seemed amplified, sacralized, transformed by the intimacy of presence.

Daniel's hand moved almost imperceptibly, brushing a stray strand of hair from Evelyn's face. The motion was casual, ordinary, yet in the suspended awareness of the moment, it carried weight. It was an act of care, of attention, of unspoken reverence for her being—a gesture so simple that its sacredness emerged not from grandeur, but from intention. Evelyn felt the brush of his fingers, a shiver running through her, and in that quiet contact, she understood what he meant about moments becoming sacred.

"You see it too, don't you?" Daniel asked softly, his voice barely above the murmur of the wind. "How something ordinary… can feel like it's holding more than just itself?"

Evelyn nodded, her eyes tracing the patterns of light filtering through the oak leaves. "I do," she said, voice low and deliberate. "It's like… the world pauses for a second, and you realize that there's a weight to presence, to attention, to intention. And suddenly… even something as simple as sitting on a bench, or the way someone touches your hair… feels… holy."

Daniel's chest tightened. There was something profoundly unsettling and thrilling about the way she articulated what he had felt but never fully named. The suspense that had followed them for weeks—the tension of avoided confessions, the thrill of small gestures, the careful dance of proximity and distance—transformed in that moment into reverence, a recognition that their connection was no longer just ordinary. It was alive, intentional, and charged with a delicate energy that demanded acknowledgment.

He leaned slightly toward her, careful not to intrude, and whispered, "I've been thinking… about us. About these moments. About how… everything we've shared, everything we've confessed, every look, every touch… it's building something sacred between us."

Evelyn's breath caught, a small, inaudible sound, but it was enough to heighten the suspense that lingered in the air. "Sacred?" she repeated softly, almost as if testing the word, tasting it, seeing if it fit.

"Yes," he said, meeting her gaze steadily. "Sacred doesn't have to mean grand or dramatic. It doesn't have to be something the world notices. It's about… intention. Care. Respect. And everything we've done… the quiet conversations, the moments we almost didn't take… it's all part of it. Sacred doesn't need a stage. Sometimes, it's just this." His hand hovered for a moment near hers, a subtle question, a silent offering.

Evelyn's fingers brushed against his, lightly, intentionally. The contact was brief, yet it sent a current of suspense through both of them—a delicate thrill, a pulse of possibility that carried the weight of everything they had been building. "I understand," she said softly. "And I… I feel it too. The way ordinary things with you… become extraordinary. Like… like we've turned moments into something more… something holy in their simplicity."

Daniel exhaled slowly, feeling the tension in his shoulders ease, replaced by the quiet reverence of shared understanding. "It's… rare," he admitted. "To find someone who… sees the ordinary as sacred, who doesn't rush, who doesn't force… who just… walks beside you while everything else fades."

Evelyn smiled, faint and unsteady, as if the words themselves were a bridge spanning the suspense that had defined their connection. "And I've been thinking," she said quietly, "about how this… how everything we've shared… has prepared us to see it. To understand it. To recognize the sacred in simplicity. It's not just us… it's everything we've endured to arrive here."

The moment stretched, suspended in the gentle glow of twilight, filled with the unspoken acknowledgment of the weight and beauty of what they were building together. Every glance, every breath, every small touch became amplified, charged with the understanding that sacredness was not dictated by grandeur, but by care, attention, and mutual reverence.

Daniel reached slowly, carefully, placing his hand over hers, letting their fingers intertwine. It was a gesture so ordinary, yet in its intention and presence, it became profound. "Simple... and yet sacred," he whispered, voice low, almost as if speaking too loudly might shatter the moment. "That's what we're creating... together."

Evelyn's heart swelled, the suspense transforming into a quiet exhilaration, the thrill of intimacy tempered by the sacred awareness of responsibility and trust. "Yes," she murmured. "Simple... and sacred. That's exactly it."

For the rest of the evening, they remained there on the bench, watching the last light fade from the sky, the world around them dimming into a gentle quiet. They spoke little, but every word, every glance, every subtle gesture carried meaning. Each smile became a quiet prayer, each brush of hands a testament to trust, each shared silence a sacred space held between them.

By the time the streetlights flickered on, illuminating their small corner of the park, Daniel and Evelyn understood something profound: sacredness was not in grand declarations or dramatic events, but in the way two hearts chose to honor each other in simple, intentional ways. The sunset, the bench, the quiet walk—they had all become vessels for something far greater than themselves, a shared intimacy forged in trust, reverence, and the quiet acknowledgment that ordinary moments, when approached with care, could indeed become something sacred.

As they stood to leave, fingers still intertwined, the suspense of possibility lingered, but it was no longer tense or anxious. It had been transformed into something deeper—a reverent anticipation, a recognition that what they shared was rare, intentional, and infinitely precious. The simple act of walking, speaking, touching, and listening had transcended the ordinary. In their hands, in their hearts, in the quiet presence of each other, something ordinary had indeed become sacred.

34

EVERYONE NOTICED EXCEPT THEM

The evening air was unusually still, a rare calm that draped the city in a velvet hush, broken only by the distant hum of traffic and the occasional clink of glasses from the restaurant patio nearby. Daniel and Evelyn walked side by side along the narrow cobblestone streets of the old town district, their pace slow, deliberate, almost as if they were suspended in time. Streetlights cast long shadows that stretched across the uneven stones, painting both of them in soft golden hues, but neither seemed aware of the attention they were attracting—or so it seemed.

They had chosen this part of town for its quiet charm, the kind of streets where the past whispered from the walls of old brick buildings and the smell of fresh bread from a corner bakery mingled with the faint aroma of night-blooming flowers. But the charm that had drawn them here was secondary to the conversation—or, more accurately, the silent rhythm that had been building between them all evening. They spoke occasionally, softly, each word deliberate, as if even the slightest syllable might shatter the delicate bubble that cocooned them from the world.

Daniel's hand brushed against Evelyn's accidentally—or so he told himself—

but when their fingers touched, he felt a jolt of awareness so sharp it almost made him stumble. She didn't pull away, and neither did he. Their eyes met, a fleeting glance that carried the weight of weeks of withheld words, suppressed confessions, and the suspenseful dance of proximity and distance.

Around them, people noticed. A young couple on the sidewalk slowed, glancing at them with a mixture of curiosity and admiration. A shopkeeper leaning against the doorway of his store tilted his head slightly, catching the way Daniel's hand lingered near Evelyn's. Even a pair of street musicians paused in their tuning, ears attuned to the quiet electricity that seemed to radiate from the two figures walking in measured tandem. Every eye on the street was aware of the tension, the unspoken connection, the quiet intimacy—but the pair themselves were blissfully unaware, caught in a bubble that was theirs alone.

"Do you ever feel... like everyone can see what we're trying not to admit?" Daniel asked suddenly, his voice low and hesitant, though still loud enough to cut through the background noise.

Evelyn tilted her head slightly, a small, almost imperceptible smile tugging at her lips. "I think we're... too absorbed in each other to notice," she said softly. Her words were calm, but Daniel could sense a subtle pulse beneath them—a careful balance of anticipation and restraint. "Maybe that's the beauty of it. The world sees it, but we don't, because we're... here. Fully."

Daniel exhaled, a low, deliberate sound. "It's strange, isn't it? That something so obvious to everyone else is invisible to us until... well, until we let ourselves really see it."

Evelyn's hand brushed against his again, this time intentionally, a subtle shift that caused a spark of warmth to travel up Daniel's arm. "Then maybe," she whispered, "the secret isn't in hiding it from the world—it's in hiding it from ourselves. Until we're ready to acknowledge it fully."

They continued walking, side by side, and Daniel found himself studying her in ways he rarely allowed himself. The curve of her jaw illuminated by the streetlight, the way her eyes reflected the scattered light like polished amber, the delicate tension in her shoulders as she matched his stride. Every detail was amplified by the suspense of the moment, each subtle gesture carrying significance that they would later struggle to name.

From across the street, a group of friends on a late-night stroll whispered among themselves, eyes flicking repeatedly toward the pair. "Look at them," one murmured, barely audible over the distant clatter of a bus, "they don't even notice... but it's obvious they're... I don't know... connected. Like, really connected."

Daniel and Evelyn, of course, noticed nothing. The shared awareness of mutual proximity and unspoken feelings had created a private reality, impermeable to external observation. Their own senses were so finely tuned to one another that the peripheral glances of onlookers, the whispered comments, and the subtle stares of strangers failed to register. The suspense of discovery, which hung thick in the air for anyone else, was completely absent from their own perception.

They paused near a small fountain, the water cascading gently into the basin below, sparkling in the soft glow of the streetlights. Daniel shifted slightly, hands in his coat pockets, feeling the pull of the moment—an almost magnetic force that drew him closer to Evelyn, yet also reminded him of the fragility of timing and the weight of intention. He wanted to speak, to voice the tumult of feelings that had been building inside him, but the words seemed inadequate, fragile, too susceptible to shattering the delicate spell that hung between them.

Evelyn, sensing his hesitation, reached out and lightly touched his arm.

The contact was brief, almost casual, but it carried a surge of meaning that neither could deny. "It's funny," she murmured, her voice barely above the trickling water, "how the world can see things before we do. How they notice the sparks, the rhythm, the tension... and yet we're still here, pretending we don't."

Daniel smiled faintly, the corners of his lips lifting in a subtle acknowledgment of shared complicity. "Maybe that's part of the suspense," he said, voice low, deliberate. "The fact that we're blind to it doesn't make it any less real... it just... waits for the moment when we're ready to see it."

They lingered by the fountain, the night stretching around them like a dark velvet curtain. The ambient sounds—the rustle of leaves, the distant laughter of late-night passersby, the soft burble of water—created a backdrop that heightened the intimacy of their shared space. Every breath, every glance, every subtle shift in posture became magnified, loaded with the suspense of mutual recognition and unspoken longing.

Daniel finally spoke again, softer this time, almost a whisper to himself, but loud enough for Evelyn to hear. "I think... I've been noticing you for longer than I realized. Every smile, every gesture... everything about you has been... impossible to ignore. And yet, somehow, I didn't want to admit it. Not even to myself."

Evelyn's eyes softened, her own heartbeat quickening. "I've noticed you too," she admitted, voice trembling slightly. "And I... I kept thinking it was just me imagining it. That maybe I was reading too much into every look, every pause, every word."

The suspense between them thickened, a quiet, almost sacred tension that seemed to hold time still. They were aware of the stares, the whispers, the knowing glances of strangers who had long since perceived what they themselves had yet to acknowledge. Yet within this private bubble, the world's observations were meaningless. The attention of others had no power, no urgency, only a faint echo that underscored the intensity of their mutual revelation.

Daniel stepped closer, just enough to feel the warmth of her shoulder against his. "It's strange," he murmured, "how everyone else can see what's happening between us… but we're the last to notice. And maybe that's what makes it… ours."

Evelyn tilted her head, her breath mingling with the evening air. "Ours… yes," she echoed softly. "It's like the suspense has been building outside us, but we get to discover it only when we're ready. Only when we choose to."

The fountain gurgled softly, the water shimmering in reflection of their faces, mirroring the subtle realization that was dawning. The quiet suspense, the awareness of mutual attraction, and the anticipation of admission had transformed into something heavier, more substantial—a recognition that connection was never just about who noticed first, but about the shared acknowledgment of truth when the time was right.

Daniel reached for her hand, letting their fingers intertwine in a deliberate, gentle gesture. The spark of contact seemed to light the space around them, magnifying the suspense and heightening the intimacy. Evelyn's hand fit naturally in his, as though it had been waiting for this precise moment, for this deliberate acknowledgment, for the permission to exist fully in shared awareness.

Around them, the world continued its quiet observation, but Daniel and Evelyn felt only the weight and wonder of their own presence. They had become a secret world in plain sight, unnoticed only by themselves until the moment they chose to see. And in that, there was both suspense and sanctity—an exquisite tension that pulsed with anticipation, daring, and the promise of discovery.

As they stood there, hands intertwined, sharing a silence that spoke louder than words, they understood the truth: sometimes, the world notices first, while hearts remain blissfully oblivious, until the moment of acknowledgment arrives. And when it does, even the simplest gestures—the brush of a hand, the tilt of a head, the quiet exchange of glances—become charged with meaning, sacred in their simplicity, and profound in the suspense that led them there.

The night wrapped around them, soft and heavy, and as they finally walked on, side by side, neither could deny it: the world had noticed them long before they noticed themselves. And in that shared oblivion, there was beauty, suspense, and a quiet promise of the deeper discoveries yet to come.

35

EVERYONE NOTICED EXCEPT THEM

The late afternoon sun dipped low over the city skyline, spilling gold and rose across the pavement of the bustling downtown streets. People hurried along, lost in their own thoughts, phones in hand, conversations echoing against the buildings. But amidst the moving crowd, there was a bubble—a small, unassuming pocket of space where the world seemed to fade. In that bubble walked Daniel and Evelyn, completely unaware of the attention they were drawing.

It wasn't the kind of attention that demanded glances or whispers—it was subtler than that. Strangers' eyes followed them unconsciously, sensing the rhythm of something unspoken. In the outdoor seating area of the café where they had paused for a quick coffee, a barista behind the counter noticed the quiet intensity in the way they spoke, their laughter restrained, the ease of leaning in when no one else was looking. At a nearby crosswalk, a young woman walking her dog stopped momentarily, captivated by the almost imperceptible energy between them. Across the street, a man adjusting his tie in the reflection of a shop window caught sight of them in tandem, their presence radiating an unmistakable intimacy.

But Daniel and Evelyn remained completely oblivious.

They had spent the better part of the day moving through streets and shops, exploring the city's quieter corners. Each step they took together was unhurried, deliberate, an instinctive acknowledgment of the suspended suspense that had always followed their interactions. There was an unspoken understanding that every gesture, every glance, carried a meaning that didn't need to be articulated. And yet, they were blind to how obvious it was to everyone around them.

Daniel, walking slightly ahead of Evelyn, adjusted the strap of his bag and glanced back, almost catching a hint of her gaze, though he didn't quite realize it. Evelyn followed a few steps behind, her notebook tucked under her arm, pen poised but forgotten. She felt the magnetic pull of Daniel's presence, the rhythm of their steps in sync, and the quiet thrill that had accompanied them for weeks. She noticed how his shoulders tensed subtly when someone brushed past, how his eyes lit up with even the smallest moments of shared amusement, and how his hand twitched near hers when a street performer began to play a soft melody on a violin nearby.

"Do you ever notice how the city seems to slow down around us sometimes?" Daniel asked quietly, his voice low but clear, just loud enough to reach her.

Evelyn tilted her head, her lips curving slightly in a thoughtful smile. "I think it slows down for us because we're too absorbed in each other," she said softly. "We're in our own world, and maybe that's why no one else—well, we don't notice them noticing."

He chuckled lightly, a low sound that seemed to harmonize with the violinist's soft notes. "That's strange, isn't it? How everyone else can sense it—can see what's happening—yet we remain… blind?"

Evelyn's fingers brushed against his accidentally—or perhaps intentionally—

and Daniel felt the familiar jolt of connection, the small, electrifying current that made him acutely aware of the world narrowing down to just the two of them. "Maybe that's part of the suspense," she murmured, "the part that makes it ours to discover fully when we're ready."

They turned a corner onto a narrower street, one lined with small boutiques and antique shops. The golden light of the setting sun caught on the glass windows, reflecting subtle bursts of color onto the cobblestones. Couples passing by glanced, sensing the quiet energy between Daniel and Evelyn—the way their steps mirrored each other, the subtle tilts of their heads in conversation, the invisible tether that seemed to pull them forward in tandem. The whispers were faint, almost instinctual: "They're… something else," one passerby murmured to a friend. "Can't you feel it?"

Meanwhile, Daniel and Evelyn continued, unaware of the silent commentary around them. They spoke in hushed tones, careful not to disturb the fragile bubble surrounding them. The conversation veered from mundane observations about the city to reflections on life, hope, and the things they had each kept close to their hearts.

Daniel paused suddenly in front of a small bookstore, its display windows filled with vintage leather-bound volumes. He gestured for Evelyn to come closer. "I've always loved these places," he said, voice tinged with nostalgia. "The smell of books, the quiet… it feels like stepping into someone else's world for a moment."

Evelyn moved beside him, her eyes scanning the titles with casual interest, though her attention remained partially on him. "I get that," she said softly. "It's like time slows down. And somehow… the world outside doesn't exist for a little while."

The suspense in the moment built in subtle ways. Each pause, each glance, each brush of movement carried weight, even as they remained unaware of the people around them taking note. A young couple in the window reflection mimicked their posture unconsciously, drawn into the silent magnetic pull of intimacy that Daniel and Evelyn radiated. Another passerby stopped mid-step, adjusting the strap of their bag, captivated by the ease with which the two moved together, unaware themselves of being noticed.

Daniel and Evelyn stepped into the bookstore, the wooden floor creaking softly beneath their feet. The quiet was almost sacred, the air thick with the scent of paper and ink. They wandered through aisles of shelves, occasionally pausing to examine a title, their hands brushing against spines, each gesture imbued with casual intimacy. They leaned close to discuss a book they found interesting, their heads nearly touching, laughter escaping softly, almost like a shared secret.

Outside, a few people passing the store window noticed their closeness, the subtle, unmistakable chemistry that they themselves were blind to. A woman paused on the sidewalk, catching sight of the delicate brush of fingers and the warmth in the exchange of glances. "They don't even realize," she whispered to her companion. "It's so obvious to everyone but them."

Back inside, Daniel picked up a small leather journal, flipping it open with a thoughtful expression. "Do you ever think about the things we don't notice about ourselves?" he asked, more to the books than to Evelyn.

She stepped closer, reading over his shoulder, her breath warming the space between them. "I think the things we don't notice are often the ones everyone else sees first," she replied softly. "Like... the connection between us. It's been right here all along, but we're too busy living it to realize it."

Daniel's heart quickened, his fingers brushing against hers as he returned the journal to the shelf. "Exactly," he whispered. "We're... we're blind to it. Even now. But it's undeniable. And maybe that's the beauty of it—the suspense, the slow unveiling, the way it's been unfolding without us fully seeing."

They moved toward the door, stepping back into the golden street. The world outside the bookstore hummed with life, yet the bubble around them remained. Every step, every glance, every slight touch was amplified by the shared oblivion. The suspense was no longer anxious or hesitant—it had transformed into something deliberate, sacred in its awareness, heightened by the fact that everyone else could see it, but they could not.

A man walking his dog paused at the corner, watching them leave the store. "Look at them," he muttered to no one in particular. "Everyone notices, but they… they haven't a clue." The dog tugged at its leash, oblivious, yet the man's eyes remained fixed on Daniel and Evelyn, capturing the subtle magnetism they exuded.

Daniel and Evelyn continued down the street, side by side, hands brushing now and then, laughter spilling softly, the suspense of the moment wrapped in blissful unawareness. The world had noticed. The energy between them was palpable. And yet, in their own bubble, they remained the last to realize the power, intensity, and unmistakable significance of what they were creating together—connection that had grown beyond the ordinary, hovering on the edge of sacred intimacy, awaiting the moment they themselves would finally notice.

It was an evening that would linger in memory—not because anyone else had seen it, but because they were building it, living it, unknowingly creating a spectacle of devotion and attention that everyone else could sense, but they could not. Every step, every pause, every flicker of understanding was a thread in the intricate tapestry of their story, and the suspense of self-unawareness made it all the more thrilling, all the more sacred, all the more unforgettable.

36

A GENTLE CONFESSION

The first drops of rain began to fall softly, almost imperceptibly, tapping lightly against the glass roof of the small gazebo in the park where Daniel and Evelyn had taken refuge. The sky overhead had darkened rapidly, the earlier golden hue of the sunset giving way to bruised purples and deep grays. A faint mist hung in the air, carrying the scent of wet earth, damp leaves, and the subtle freshness of an impending storm. It was the kind of evening that demanded attention—a night pregnant with suspense, with moments stretched thin, each heartbeat amplified by anticipation.

Daniel leaned against the wooden railing, hands in his pockets, eyes scanning the rain as it fell in rhythmic patterns on the cobblestones below. Evelyn sat on the edge of the bench, notebook in hand, pen poised but abandoned as her gaze followed the shifting ripples in the small puddles forming around the gazebo's base. Neither spoke immediately; the quiet between them was thick, weighted with unspoken thoughts, unacknowledged feelings, and a tension that had been building for weeks.

Finally, Daniel's voice broke the silence, low and hesitant. "I... I need to tell you something," he said, almost whispering to the rain itself rather than to Evelyn. He shifted slightly, glancing at her with an intensity that made her heart beat faster. "I've been carrying it for a long time, and... well, I think the rain... the quiet... makes it feel like the right moment."

Evelyn tilted her head, a soft smile tugging at her lips, though there was a thread of nervous anticipation threading through her chest. "You don't have to rush," she murmured, her voice barely audible over the gentle patter of rain on the gazebo roof. "Take your time. I'm listening."

Daniel swallowed, a tight, deliberate movement. His fingers twitched slightly at the edges of his coat pocket, an unconscious reflection of the storm inside him. "It's... it's not easy to say," he admitted. "Not because it's complicated, but because... well, because it's important. Too important to risk saying wrong."

Evelyn's eyes softened, her hands resting gently on the notebook. "Then say it slowly," she urged. "Say it as if the words themselves are part of the rain, falling where they need to, in their own time."

He nodded, taking a deep breath that drew in the scent of rain and earth, grounding him in the moment. "Evelyn... I've been trying to understand what this—us—means. What I feel when I'm with you. And I've come to realize something that I can't keep to myself anymore." His voice trembled slightly, not from fear, but from the weight of honesty finally breaking free.

Evelyn leaned forward slightly, her heartbeat quickening, the suspense in the air almost tangible. "Go on," she whispered. "I want to hear it."

Daniel exhaled slowly, letting the words settle in his mouth before he allowed them to escape. "I... care about you, more than I've ever cared about anyone," he said finally, the words spilling softly into the quiet of the rainy evening. "More than I expected to feel. More than I even realized I was capable of feeling. And it terrifies me... because I don't want to lose this. Don't want to lose you. I've tried to hide it, rationalize it, push it away, but it's there... every time I see you, every time I hear your voice, every time... you laugh, or write, or just exist in a way that makes the world seem... brighter. I can't pretend anymore."

Evelyn's breath hitched slightly, a gentle sound that mingled with the patter of rain. The confession settled between them like a delicate crystal, fragile and beautiful, reflecting the tension, the suspense, and the intimacy of the moment. "Daniel..." she breathed, her voice trembling in a way that mirrored his own vulnerability.

"I know," he continued, stepping slightly closer, though still careful to respect the invisible boundary of suspense that had defined their relationship until now. "I know it's sudden. And I don't expect anything in return... not immediately. I just... I couldn't let another day pass without being honest. Without letting you know what you mean to me."

Evelyn's eyes glistened with unshed emotion, a combination of relief, recognition, and the thrill of reciprocation. She reached out slowly, her hand hovering just above his, suspended in that precious, weighted moment where vulnerability meets trust. "Daniel... I've been feeling the same way," she admitted softly, her voice almost swallowed by the rain. "I didn't want to say it first. I didn't want to risk the moment being... wrong. But I can't deny it anymore. I care about you too... deeply. And I've been scared of what that might mean."

The rain intensified slightly, falling in gentle sheets around them, wrapping the gazebo in a private world of gray and silver. Daniel exhaled, a tremor of relief and elation coursing through him. "Then we... we're... on the same page?" he asked, a faint, hopeful tremor in his voice.

Evelyn nodded, a small, radiant smile breaking through the tension that had hung between them for so long. "Yes," she said softly. "We are. And somehow... hearing you say it... makes it even more real. Even more sacred."

Daniel took a careful step forward, closing the last few inches between them. He reached out slowly, his hand brushing hers, fingers intertwining naturally, comfortably, as if they had been made to fit together. The suspense that had defined their interactions—the careful dance of avoidance and approach, the tension of proximity without admission—finally dissolved in the quiet intimacy of confession.

"I've been waiting," Daniel admitted, his forehead resting lightly against hers, "for a moment where I could be honest without fear, without hesitation. And I think… this rain, this quiet… it gave me that."

Evelyn rested her hands gently on his chest, feeling the steady beat of his heart beneath her palms. "It's always been here," she whispered. "Even before tonight. We just needed to acknowledge it. And now that we have… it feels like everything has shifted. Like the world is different, brighter, somehow."

The rain continued to fall around them, a soft symphony that underscored the beauty and suspense of the confession. It washed over them, a cleansing presence that made the moment feel sacred. Each drop seemed to carry away the accumulated tension, the unspoken fears, and the cautious hesitation that had defined their connection. What remained was pure, tender, and vulnerable—a love confessed gently, deliberately, without rush or expectation, yet heavy with significance.

Daniel tilted his head, brushing a wet strand of hair from Evelyn's face. "I don't want to rush," he murmured, voice low and reverent. "I want to feel this… every step, every heartbeat, every glance. I want to honor this confession, honor you, honor… us."

Evelyn smiled, leaning in slightly closer, their foreheads touching, sharing warmth and breath. "That's all I've wanted too," she said softly. "To feel this, without pressure, without distraction, without the fear that we'll break something fragile by speaking it aloud. And now that we've spoken it... it feels... whole. Complete. Sacred."

They stayed like that for a long moment, rain falling around them, the world beyond the gazebo muted and distant. Their hands remained intertwined, hearts beating in quiet synchrony, breaths mingling, and eyes locked in an understanding deeper than words could capture. In the gentle confession, they had created a sacred space—not just between them, but within themselves—a moment where vulnerability was honored, and love was acknowledged without haste or fear.

Finally, Daniel broke the silence, his voice a low, tentative murmur. "I think... this is just the beginning. But even if it's slow, even if it's quiet, even if it feels like we're the last to notice... I want to experience it with you. Every step of it. Every simple, sacred step."

Evelyn's smile deepened, her eyes shining in the dim light of the rain-soaked evening. "Then we'll walk it together," she said softly. "Every step, every confession, every moment of suspense... together."

The rain softened, falling in gentle threads, as if granting them permission to linger in the intimacy they had created. The gazebo, once simply a refuge from the storm, had transformed into a sanctuary—a place where confessions became sacred, where suspicions and fears dissolved, and where love, gently acknowledged, finally found its voice.

In that moment, Daniel and Evelyn understood that sometimes, the most profound revelations come not with grandeur, but with gentle honesty, whispered amidst the rain, in a quiet space where hearts are brave enough to speak, and souls are ready to listen. And in that gentle confession, the world beyond the gazebo ceased to exist, leaving only the sacred and suspended connection between two people who had finally dared to be entirely, undeniably, themselves.

37

A HEART OPENING SLOWLY

The city streets were nearly empty, the usual hum of traffic replaced by the faint patter of residual rain on the pavement. Streetlights glimmered against wet asphalt, creating pools of gold that reflected the clouds rolling lazily above. It was late, the sort of hour when the world seemed to hold its breath, waiting for something significant to unfold. Daniel and Evelyn walked side by side along the riverbank, the soft light glinting off the rippling water. The night air was crisp, carrying a faint chill that hinted at the approaching winter, yet their closeness seemed to generate a warmth all its own.

Tonight was different. There was a tension that had not been present before, a subtle trembling of expectation threading through their steps. The gentle confession of the previous evening lingered like a fragile echo in their hearts, resonating quietly in each unspoken glance, in each tentative movement toward one another. Yet despite the clarity of shared feelings, the uncharted territory of vulnerability still loomed, wrapped in a delicate shroud of suspense.

Daniel walked slightly ahead, hands buried in his coat pockets, his gaze occasionally flicking toward Evelyn. He studied the curve of her shoulders, the way her hair caught the weak glow of a lamppost, and the soft rhythm of her steps that mirrored his own almost instinctively. He could feel the weight of her presence, yet the depth of what he wanted to say still eluded him. Opening one's heart, he realized, was not as simple as speaking—it required courage, patience, and a careful unspooling of truths that could not be forced.

Evelyn sensed the subtle tension radiating from him. She knew him well enough to understand that every movement, every pause, carried meaning beyond the surface. But she, too, felt the delicate unease of hearts unaccustomed to such exposure. Her own feelings had grown over weeks—an unrelenting, quiet affection that now demanded acknowledgment—but the fear of overstepping, of revealing too much too soon, held her tongue. She was ready to listen, but she was also wary of the fragility that had defined their journey thus far.

A sudden gust of wind stirred the river, causing tiny ripples to dance across the surface. Daniel inhaled deeply, the cold air filling his lungs, grounding him for a moment in the present. "Evelyn," he began softly, his voice almost swallowed by the night, "there's something I've been wanting to say… something I haven't been able to find the right words for."

She turned her gaze toward him, her eyes catching the lamplight, reflecting a mixture of curiosity, concern, and anticipation. "I think I understand," she murmured. "Take your time. I'm here, and I'll wait for the words when they come."

He nodded, taking a hesitant step closer, the faint crunch of wet leaves underfoot echoing softly in the stillness. The suspense hung between them, not tense but palpable, like a thread stretched taut, ready to pull them closer once it was released. Daniel's mind raced, rehearsing words that seemed simultaneously too much and not enough. How could he encapsulate the quiet storm of emotions—the admiration, the longing, the fear of misstep—without shattering the delicate equilibrium they had built?

"I've been thinking about… everything," he continued, voice low, deliberate. "The moments we've shared, the conversations that lingered past ordinary hours, the silences that spoke louder than words. I… I realize now that my heart has been opening, slowly, almost imperceptibly, to someone I never expected to matter this much."

Evelyn's lips parted slightly, a quiet gasp that mingled with the river's gentle murmur. Her fingers tightened slightly around the strap of her bag, the notebook she had carried clutched subconsciously against her chest. "Slowly…" she echoed softly, her voice trembling ever so slightly. "That's… a good way to describe it. Hearts don't just open all at once. They stretch, they hesitate, they test the air. And then… sometimes, they open fully without you even realizing it until the moment hits."

Daniel's heart caught at her words, the recognition that she had been living the same gradual awakening, the same deliberate unveiling of vulnerability. "Exactly," he murmured, stepping closer, careful not to rush the fragile rhythm between them. "And I've been scared, I think. Scared that if I opened too quickly… if I revealed everything too soon… I might scare you away, or worse, ruin the quiet balance we have."

Evelyn reached out gently, her hand brushing his arm. The touch was light, unassuming, yet it carried the weight of affirmation, the silent acknowledgment of mutual vulnerability. "I've been scared too," she admitted softly. "Scared that the moment might be too much, that my heart could outpace yours, or that the world outside might intrude and shatter it. But… standing here with you now, I realize that the slow opening, the careful unraveling… it's what makes it real. What makes it ours."

Daniel exhaled, a tremor of relief and hope coursing through him. "I want to be honest with you, Evelyn," he said, voice dropping even lower, almost reverent. "Not just about what I feel, but about the way I want to be with you. I want to protect this… protect us. But I also want to let it grow.

Slowly, fully, deliberately. I don't want to rush the heart, because... because it's already beginning to trust in you."

The night wrapped around them like a soft blanket, the lamplight reflecting in Evelyn's eyes, giving them an almost ethereal glow. She stepped closer, closing the distance, their breaths mingling in the cool air. "Trust," she whispered, her voice carrying the weight of weeks of quiet observation, of tentative feelings held close. "It's the most sacred thing we can give. And my heart... it wants to give it to you. Slowly, yes... but completely. Piece by piece, moment by moment. And maybe that's the only way love can truly grow."

Daniel's hand moved naturally, lightly brushing a strand of damp hair from her face. The simple gesture, ordinary in appearance, carried a depth of intent that neither had fully expressed before. Every step forward, every word, every shared glance had been building toward this: the mutual acknowledgment of trust, of vulnerability, of hearts willing to open in tandem.

The suspense of anticipation—of waiting, of hesitation, of measured exposure—was finally dissolving into something tangible. It wasn't dramatic, it wasn't theatrical; it was quiet, intimate, deliberate. Every small action, every softly spoken word, was part of the slow unraveling of defenses, the careful opening of hearts that had been cautiously protecting themselves for far too long.

"I think..." Daniel began, his voice catching slightly, "that this is the first time I've allowed myself to be entirely... seen. Not just my feelings, but my fears, my hesitations, my hopes. And I trust you with it, Evelyn. Slowly, yes... but I trust you."

Evelyn's lips curved into a small, genuine smile, a light that seemed to warm the night around them. "Then I'll meet you there," she whispered, pressing her hand to his chest, feeling the steady rhythm of his heartbeat. "Slowly. Carefully. But fully. Because that's the only way a heart can open without breaking, without losing itself. And I… I want to open mine with you."

The rain, which had started as a gentle drizzle, now fell in soft sheets, pattering around the gazebo and across the riverbank. The world outside seemed to fade, leaving only the quiet intensity of two hearts aligning in deliberate, suspenseful trust. Each drop of rain was a witness to the vulnerability unfolding between them, a soft applause for the courage it took to speak, to feel, and to allow oneself to be seen.

Daniel leaned in slightly, brushing his forehead against hers. "A heart opening slowly… it's the most beautiful thing I've ever witnessed," he murmured, voice trembling with reverence. "And I'm grateful it's mine to experience with you."

Evelyn's eyes shimmered, a mixture of tears and the reflection of the streetlights. "And I… I'm grateful too," she whispered. "For the slow unfolding, for the careful trust, for… you. For everything that has brought us here, to this moment where hearts can finally be brave enough to open."

They stood there, the world around them blurred into a soft, rain-drenched tapestry, hands intertwined, hearts beating in deliberate synchrony. The suspense, the anticipation, and the quiet tension that had defined their journey had transformed into something sacred—a slow, gentle, and irrevocable opening of hearts, a confession not just of love, but of trust, patience, and the courage to allow vulnerability to flourish.

As the rain fell steadily around them, Daniel and Evelyn understood a profound truth: love that is rushed may falter, but love that unfolds slowly, deliberately, and with intent carries a strength that is unbreakable. A heart opening slowly is not fragile—it is resilient, aware, and infinitely capable of embracing the other with both reverence and abandon.

And in that gentle opening, in that careful surrender, they discovered the first true sense of belonging they had ever known—within each other, within the suspended moment, and within a love that had been nurtured quietly, patiently, and with profound suspense.

38

THE ALMOST-DATE THAT TURNED INTO A MEMORY

The evening air carried a soft chill, the kind that hinted at the onset of early winter, yet it was infused with a kind of anticipation that neither Daniel nor Evelyn could ignore. Streetlights reflected against the slick pavement, painting the city in golds and muted silvers, each reflection a tiny, trembling star guiding their steps. They walked side by side toward the café where Daniel had suggested they meet—an almost-date, one neither had explicitly called by its proper name, yet both understood the weight the evening carried.

Daniel's mind raced, a tangle of anticipation, nerves, and unspoken feelings. He had rehearsed what he might say countless times in his head, yet now, with Evelyn walking beside him, each step made the rehearsal seem inadequate. There was a suspenseful edge to every movement, a tension that built not from fear but from the vulnerability of what might unfold. He could feel it in the way his heart beat a little faster, in the slight tremor in his hands, and in the way his thoughts scattered at the simplest gestures—like the brush of her sleeve against his arm, or the subtle sway of her step.

Evelyn, for her part, felt the same undercurrent of tension, though she carried it with a different rhythm. Her fingers toyed absently with the strap of her bag, but her eyes were fixed on Daniel, following the slight furrow in his brow, the curve of his jaw as he glanced at her from the corner of his eye. She had hoped, perhaps, that the night would allow them to step into something tentative, something gently labeled as "more than friendship" but less than a formal commitment. Yet the suspense of the moment—the almost-date—was intoxicating precisely because it existed in that liminal space.

They arrived at the café, the warm glow spilling from its windows onto the rain-slicked street, and Daniel held the door for Evelyn, a small gesture heavy with deliberate care. The interior was nearly empty, save for a few scattered tables and the soft clinking of cutlery. The faint aroma of brewed coffee and fresh pastries wrapped around them as they settled into a booth near the back.

Daniel pulled out a chair for her, and she smiled softly, a subtle warmth lighting her expression. "You've made this feel… more special than I expected," she murmured, voice low, almost a whisper in the quiet café.

Daniel shrugged, though his eyes betrayed him. "I wasn't sure how to do this… the almost-date thing. I didn't want it to feel forced, or rushed. But I also wanted… tonight to mean something." His fingers traced the edge of the table, a nervous habit, though he felt the subtle thrill of shared anticipation.

They spoke cautiously at first, small talk flowing around the unspoken reality of the moment. Conversation meandered through trivialities: the taste of a new pastry, the odd habits of baristas, the fleeting beauty of the rainy city outside. Yet beneath the surface, a silent current carried the unacknowledged feelings, threading their words with layers of suspense and longing. Every glance, every brush of a hand against the table, carried weight.

At one point, Daniel caught himself staring, not at her features alone, but at the way she seemed to inhabit the space around her—fluid, confident, yet subtly guarded. "You know," he said finally, his voice low and careful, "there's something about the way you carry yourself... something that makes this moment... impossible to forget."

Evelyn's cheeks flushed slightly, a reaction both to the compliment and to the intensity in his gaze. She looked down at her hands, tracing the condensation on her coffee cup, before allowing herself a small, deliberate smile. "Impossible to forget," she echoed softly. "I feel the same... like we're walking a line between ordinary and something... more. Something that belongs just to us, even if we don't say it aloud."

The almost-date—neither entirely casual nor formally declared—hung suspended in that space. Outside, the city moved on, oblivious to the delicate tension and intimacy flourishing within the café. The quiet click of cups, the muted laughter of other patrons, and the soft background music only served to heighten the suspended rhythm between Daniel and Evelyn. They existed in a bubble, yet one that was acutely aware of its temporality—a night that could slip away at any moment, leaving behind only the memory of its fragile significance.

At one point, Daniel reached across the table almost imperceptibly, letting his fingers brush against hers. The contact was light, tentative, yet it sent a ripple through both of them. Evelyn didn't pull away; instead, she allowed the warmth of connection to settle, as though acknowledging silently the unspoken possibilities of the night. The suspense of almost-admission—the awareness of closeness without outright declaration—hung between them like a soft, trembling heartbeat.

"I've never... done this before," Daniel admitted, voice hushed. "The almost-date. The not-quite confession, the not-quite date. It feels... terrifyingly real."

Evelyn nodded, her fingers tracing idle patterns on the table, mirroring his nervous energy. “I know what you mean,” she whispered. “It’s strange… thrilling, and yet terrifying. Like standing at the edge of something beautiful, unsure if you’re ready to jump, yet unable to turn away.”

The rain outside intensified, drumming steadily against the windows, a steady rhythm that mirrored the pulse of suspense between them. It created a cocoon, a private stage where every heartbeat and whispered word was magnified. The almost-date, the deliberate avoidance of labels, the careful dance of proximity and restraint—all of it transformed into a memory being etched in real time, one they would carry with them long after the night ended.

At one point, Evelyn leaned slightly forward, her voice barely audible above the patter of rain. “Do you ever think,” she asked hesitantly, “that the things we almost do—moments we almost cross the line into… love, or confession…—can sometimes matter more than the things we actually do?”

Daniel’s gaze met hers, intense and unwavering. “I think you’re right,” he admitted. “The almost… has its own gravity. Its own suspense. Its own kind of intimacy. Sometimes the waiting, the hesitation, the almost… is what makes the memory indelible. What makes it sacred.”

They shared a quiet laugh, soft and warm, and for a moment, the café and the city beyond seemed to vanish. Time slowed, each second stretching into eternity. The almost-date, suspended between possibility and reality, became a shared secret—a memory in the making that neither of them had consciously intended but both felt deeply.

Outside, a passerby paused to watch the faint silhouettes framed by the café windows, sensing without fully understanding the quiet energy between them. The almost-date, unnoticed by the world, radiated an authenticity that drew silent acknowledgment from anyone attuned to human connection. But within the booth, Daniel and Evelyn were oblivious to external observation, lost entirely in the delicate suspense of the moment.

As the evening wore on, neither wanted to break the fragile rhythm. The rain softened to a drizzle, streaking the windows with silver lines. They sipped their coffees in companionable silence, fingers brushing now and then, eyes meeting with subtle intensity, each aware of the unspoken sentiment building layer upon layer. The almost-date had become a memory by design of its own suspense—the delicate acknowledgment of closeness without fully crossing the threshold into formal declaration.

Finally, as the last of their drinks were finished, Daniel rose, offering Evelyn his hand. "Shall we?" he asked, voice gentle, careful. The almost-date might be ending, but the memory of it—suspended, intimate, unspoken yet fully understood—would remain indelible.

Evelyn took his hand, the warmth of contact grounding her, and allowed herself a small smile. "Shall we," she echoed softly, knowing that what they had shared tonight—what they had almost declared, almost admitted, almost labeled—would linger far longer than the fleeting moments of this rainy evening.

As they stepped into the rain-slicked street, walking side by side toward the soft glow of lamplight, the almost-date had transformed into something far more enduring: a memory stitched into the quiet corners of their hearts, sacred in its suspense, gentle in its unfolding, and unforgettable in its subtle, unspoken resonance.

39

THE FIRST TIME THEY HELD HANDS "BY ACCIDENT"

The city had fallen into a hushed rhythm, streets glistening from a lingering drizzle that gave everything a muted, reflective sheen. Streetlights lined the sidewalks like sentinels, casting pools of golden warmth over the gray asphalt. Daniel and Evelyn walked side by side, the cool evening air brushing against their cheeks, carrying the scent of damp leaves and freshly rained-on pavement. There was a subtle electricity in the atmosphere, a tension that neither fully acknowledged, yet both instinctively felt.

It wasn't planned. Nothing about that evening was intentional beyond the quiet decision to walk together after a long day of shared errands and meandering conversation. They had left the café with nothing more than a vague plan to wander through the city, letting the streets guide them. Yet the unspoken intimacy that had been building for weeks seemed to hang between them, delicate and weighty, like a fragile thread stretched across a void.

Evelyn adjusted the strap of her bag, her fingers brushing the edge of Daniel's arm in the process. The contact was fleeting, accidental—or so she told herself—but the sensation lingered longer than it should have. Daniel's chest tightened slightly at the brush, an unconscious response that made him suddenly hyper-aware of the closeness of her presence. He glanced at her sideways, catching the faintest hint of a smile playing on her lips, but she quickly looked away, focusing on the puddles reflecting the lamplight.

They walked in silence for a few moments, letting the rhythm of their steps sync naturally, unforced. It was in that silence, in the subtle harmonization of motion and presence, that suspense began to weave itself into the ordinary. Each small movement, each glance that wasn't quite accidental, seemed to carry the weight of unspoken emotion. Their proximity, always intentional yet restrained, now felt suspended on the cusp of something uncharted.

Daniel's mind raced with the possibilities, each scenario more thrilling—and terrifying—than the last. Should he reach for her hand? Was it too soon? Would she pull away, or worse, would the gesture feel awkward, forced, unnatural? But the pull between them was undeniable, magnetic, and he found himself thinking in fragments: Maybe just this once. Maybe a touch. Just enough to feel without saying a word.

Evelyn, for her part, felt the same tension. Her pulse quickened in a way that was both alarming and exhilarating. She was aware of the subtle movements of his shoulder, the occasional brush of his sleeve against hers, the quiet cadence of his steps mirroring hers. She wanted—no, she needed—to reach across the invisible barrier that had always defined their physical space, but she hesitated, aware of the suspenseful gravity that hovered in every glance, every pause, every fleeting moment.

The sidewalks curved, leading them toward a small park that had become a secret favorite of theirs—a quiet spot, tucked away from the city's usual bustle, where the faint glow of distant streetlights mingled with shadows from the overhanging trees. As they approached the entrance, a group of late-night pedestrians hurried past, giving them a moment of unspoken privacy. Daniel slowed slightly, careful to stay in step with Evelyn. She did the same, the slight adjustment causing their arms to brush again, deliberately this time, as if testing the waters.

It was the tipping point.

Daniel's hand twitched involuntarily, reaching for the gap between them as though guided by some invisible force. Evelyn, sensing the shift, instinctively let her hand move slightly closer to his. And then, in the simplest, most unassuming motion, their fingers touched, intertwined in a way that felt completely natural, completely inevitable.

They froze, caught in that suspended moment, the city around them fading into insignificance. The accidental hold—if it could even be called that—carried more weight than either had expected. Daniel's heart pounded, a rapid, almost desperate rhythm that threatened to betray his composure. Evelyn's breath hitched, a subtle, trembling sound that mirrored the surge of emotion coursing through him. Neither spoke, yet the silence itself spoke volumes—volumes that had been building quietly for weeks.

"I—" Daniel started, then stopped, realizing that words were unnecessary. The simple act of holding hands, even 'by accident,' conveyed everything he had struggled to articulate. Vulnerability, trust, longing, affection—it was all contained in the gentle pressure of their intertwined fingers.

Evelyn, equally affected, glanced up at him. Her eyes shimmered in the muted light, a mixture of surprise, exhilaration, and unspoken agreement. She gave the smallest squeeze of his hand, a subtle acknowledgment that mirrored the surge of emotions he felt. The suspense was no longer about whether they would touch—it had transformed into the quiet thrill of discovery, the realization that this small, intimate act could redefine the landscape of their relationship.

They began to walk, hands linked, both careful to maintain the casual appearance of normalcy even as the reality of their connection pressed against them with quiet insistence. Each step was deliberate yet natural, the rhythm of their movements perfectly in sync. Every brush of their fingers, every subtle squeeze, carried a language of its own—one that transcended words and formal confession.

Daniel's mind, usually so careful, so analytical, surrendered to the simplicity of the moment. This is right, he thought. This is what I've been waiting for without knowing I was waiting. Every fear, every hesitation, melted in the warmth of her hand in his. The suspense of previous weeks—the almost-confessions, the gentle teasing of proximity, the deliberate avoidance of overt intimacy—culminated in this simple yet profound act.

Evelyn, feeling the same realization, allowed herself to relax into the connection. The accidental nature of their handholding only heightened the thrill, making it feel spontaneous, genuine, and wholly theirs. She glanced up at Daniel, catching the faint curve of his lips in a smile that mirrored her own. The city, the night, the rain-slicked streets—all of it receded, leaving only the shared pulse of their hands and the quiet, powerful truth of mutual recognition.

A soft breeze stirred through the park, rustling the leaves overhead. Daniel instinctively tightened his grip slightly, not possessively, but as a subconscious assertion of presence and reassurance. Evelyn responded with a subtle squeeze, a wordless conversation that spoke of trust, excitement, and the slow, deliberate opening of hearts. The suspense had shifted—from anticipation to revelation, from tension to delicate affirmation.

They paused at a small bridge overlooking the river, the water reflecting the city lights in fragmented, shimmering patterns. Daniel released a soft sigh, tilting his head toward her. "I didn't mean for this to happen," he murmured, voice low, reverent. "But… I'm not going to apologize either.

I'm... glad it did."

Evelyn smiled, the faint warmth of her breath mingling with his in the chilly air. "Me too," she admitted softly. "It feels... right. Even if it was an accident. Even if it was unplanned. Sometimes the most meaningful things happen when we least expect them."

The rain, which had begun as a drizzle, now fell in soft, persistent sheets, enveloping them in a cocoon of silver threads. Their hands remained intertwined, fingers laced naturally, completely at ease, as if the universe had orchestrated this moment in perfect silence. The suspense of waiting, the tension of unspoken emotions, the careful dance of proximity and restraint—it all converged in the simple act of holding hands.

Daniel turned slightly to look at Evelyn, the lamplight catching the curve of her jaw, the shimmer of moisture on her hair. "I think," he said quietly, "that this is the first real step. Not the first date, not the first confession, but... the first time our hearts found a way to touch without words. And I want to... keep taking steps like this. Slowly, deliberately, together."

Evelyn's fingers squeezed his hand again, a gentle affirmation. "Then we will," she whispered. "One small step at a time. One heartbeat, one touch, one moment. Even by accident, or maybe especially by accident, it's ours. And I... I wouldn't trade it for anything."

They lingered on the bridge, rain falling softly around them, the night suspended in golden reflections and quiet understanding. The accidental handholding, unplanned and unforeseen, had become a turning point—a memory etched into their shared timeline, precious not for its grandeur, but for the raw intimacy and suspense it carried. It was the first deliberate act of connection, wrapped in the thrill of accident and the careful unfolding of hearts finally willing to meet halfway.

And as they walked on, hands still intertwined, the city seemed to hush around them, as if recognizing the significance of the moment. The almost-date, the delicate suspicions, the weeks of anticipation—all had led to this: the first touch that said everything words could not, the first handholding that marked the beginning of a new chapter, and the first time their hearts found one another, even by accident, in perfect synchrony.

40

PEACE, THE KIND SHE HAD BEEN PRAYING FOR

The early evening sky had softened into a deep indigo, the first stars beginning to pierce the fading light. The air was still, almost reverent, carrying the faint scent of rain that had passed hours earlier, leaving the streets glistening and the earth soaked with the delicate aroma of renewal. Evelyn stood by the window of her small apartment, the glow of the city below reflecting in her eyes, a mixture of contemplation, relief, and something she could not yet name. Tonight, the world outside seemed quieter than usual, as if it too had paused to witness the subtle shift in her heart.

Daniel's message had come earlier—short, deliberate, but heavy with meaning. "Can we meet tonight? There's something I want to share with you." The simplicity of it had sent a thrill through her chest, but also a familiar, cautious hesitation. Yet tonight felt different. There was a weightless certainty in her steps as she descended the staircase of her building, the usual jitter of anticipation muted by something she had not felt in weeks: peace. Not just the absence of anxiety, but a profound presence of calm that settled over her like a warm shawl.

The park where they had agreed to meet was quiet, the usual hum of city life dimmed to whispers by the late hour. The fountain in the center glimmered under the soft illumination of strategically placed lights, water cascading in delicate arcs that shimmered like liquid silver. Evelyn approached slowly, each step deliberate, her heart attuned to the subtle rhythms of the night and the faint tension that always accompanied being near Daniel. Yet, underneath it all, there was a profound calm, a peace she had prayed for but never imagined would feel so tangible, so near.

Daniel was already there, leaning against the railing of the fountain, his posture relaxed, but his eyes alert. The moment she caught sight of him, a small smile tugged at his lips, one that held both familiarity and a quiet recognition of shared understanding. Evelyn's chest tightened briefly—not from fear, not from anticipation, but from the gentle surge of reassurance that only comes when two hearts recognize the sacredness of a moment.

"Hey," Daniel said softly, his voice blending with the distant murmur of water and the faint rustle of leaves in the light breeze. "I didn't think you'd actually be here."

Evelyn smiled, feeling warmth flood through her despite the evening chill. "I promised," she said quietly. "And… I think I've been waiting for this… for both of us, without even realizing it."

The words hung in the air, suspended in that delicate tension between acknowledgment and revelation. Daniel's gaze softened as he stepped closer, the faintest brush of his sleeve against hers sending an unexpected shiver through her spine—not of nervousness, but of quiet exhilaration. There was a suspense to the night, a slow-building anticipation that neither could articulate, yet both understood instinctively.

"I've been thinking," Daniel began, his voice low, deliberate, "about… everything. About the weeks we've spent walking this line between friendship and… something more. About the almost-dates, the accidental touches, the moments that felt suspended in time. And I realized something important. Something I couldn't quite put into words until now."

Evelyn's breath caught subtly, a silent acknowledgment of the weight in his tone. She had felt the same swell of emotions, the same oscillation between fear and longing, yet there had always been a barrier—an unspoken hesitation, the caution that comes with hearts previously bruised by unspoken truths. But tonight, under the soft glow of the park lights, with the fountain murmuring beside them, that barrier seemed to dissolve, leaving only the raw clarity of mutual understanding.

"I've realized," Daniel continued, taking another careful step toward her, "that the peace I've been seeking… the calm that allows me to breathe without fear… is here. Not in solitude, not in distraction, not in avoidance. It's here, with you. And I've been too foolish to admit that until now."

Evelyn's heart swelled, the words resonating with a truth she had prayed for countless nights—peace, the kind that settles the soul and quiets the restless mind. She had prayed for it, imagining it might come in the form of resolution, a moment of clarity, or even divine intervention. Yet the peace that touched her tonight was far more profound, more intimate than any prayer could have articulated. It was the peace that comes from being seen, understood, and quietly held in the presence of another who has walked a similar path of fear, hope, and longing.

Daniel reached out, his hand brushing hers—not the accidental touch of the past, but deliberate, tender, and deliberate in its intent. "I don't want to rush anything," he said softly, "but I need you to know… I feel it. This… calm. This certainty. When I'm with you, I feel like the world stops. Like everything that's unsettled in me… in us… suddenly has a place. And I want to hold onto that, carefully, patiently, deliberately."

Evelyn allowed herself a small, almost imperceptible nod. "I know exactly what you mean," she whispered, her fingers brushing against his in a gentle, unspoken echo of the words he had just spoken. "I've prayed for this peace… not knowing it would feel like this. Not knowing it would be… real, and fragile, and beautiful all at once. And yet, here it is. With you."

The suspense between them was not of fear, but of anticipation, a delicate unfolding of truth and vulnerability. Every word, every movement, every shared glance carried the weight of unspoken prayers answered in a quiet, intimate way. It was the kind of peace that could not be forced or manufactured; it had to arrive naturally, nurtured by patience, trust, and the gentle recognition of hearts willing to open without expectation or rush.

Daniel took a step closer, his hand finally resting over hers, the warmth of contact radiating through both of them. "Evelyn… I've been afraid," he admitted, voice low and reverent. "Afraid that my feelings might overwhelm you, that my intentions might frighten you, or that the past would interfere with the present. But standing here, with you… I realize that fear doesn't belong here anymore. Not when we can exist in this calm, this peace, this… understanding."

Evelyn's eyes glistened in the soft lamplight, a quiet tear tracing a path down her cheek. "I've been afraid too," she whispered. "Afraid that my heart might move too quickly, that I might misread the signs, that I could be wrong. But… being here with you, feeling this… peace, the kind I've prayed for… it makes all the fear vanish. At least for tonight. And maybe that's enough. For now."

Daniel's thumb brushed against her knuckles in a tender, grounding gesture. "For tonight," he echoed, "and for as many nights as we're given to discover this… together. I want to savor it, Evelyn. Every quiet, suspended moment. Every glance, every touch, every heartbeat that belongs to this… us."

The fountain bubbled softly behind them, each droplet catching the light in fleeting, glittering patterns. The night seemed to hold its breath, allowing the suspended peace between them to settle fully. They stood there, hands intertwined, hearts aligned, and minds quieted, finally feeling the culmination of weeks of anticipation, hesitation, and unspoken longing.

Evelyn leaned slightly toward him, the faint brush of her shoulder against his enough to send warmth through her chest. "This... this is the peace I've been praying for," she admitted, voice trembling with quiet intensity. "Not perfection, not certainty about the future, but this calm, this understanding, this... connection that doesn't demand more than we're ready to give, yet asks nothing less than honesty."

Daniel nodded, the corners of his lips curving in a small, tender smile. "I feel it too," he said softly. "And I don't want to let it go. Not tonight. Not tomorrow. Not ever. This... us... it's enough. Right now, in this moment, it's everything."

They stayed there for long moments, letting the peace settle around them like a cloak, grounding them in the reality of mutual understanding and shared vulnerability. The suspense of anticipation, the nervous tension of waiting for confession, the delicate unfolding of hearts—it all dissolved into a quiet, sacred calm.

And in that suspended night, beneath the dim glow of city lights and beside the soft murmur of the fountain, Evelyn realized something profound: peace was not a destination, nor was it a gift granted externally. It was an awakening within the heart, a recognition that being seen, being trusted, and being present with another person who respects your soul could transform anxiety into stillness, hesitation into confidence, and longing into fulfillment.

Daniel's hand tightened around hers in a silent affirmation, and Evelyn responded instinctively, the warmth of their shared presence wrapping them in an embrace invisible yet undeniable. Tonight, they were not rushing. Tonight, they were not confounded by fear. Tonight, they were simply two hearts discovering the quiet, suspended miracle of peace—the kind she had been praying for all along.

V

THE TEST OF DESTINY

41

THE JOB OFFER THAT CHANGED EVERYTHING

The morning air in the city was crisp, filled with the tang of wet pavement and faint exhaust from the few cars daring the early hour. The streets were quieter than usual, the lull after a late-night rain giving them a surreal emptiness, as though the world had temporarily pressed pause. Daniel stood outside his apartment building, the folds of his coat wrapped tightly around him, phone pressed to his ear. The ringtone had been insistent, urgent, and now, as the voice on the other end filled the silence of his small apartment, he felt a sudden shift deep in his chest.

"Daniel, this is it," the voice on the other end said, brisk but unmistakably excited. "We've reviewed your application, your portfolio, and all your recommendations. We want you to join the team—full-time, starting as soon as you can make it. This is a rare opportunity, and we're thrilled to have you."

Daniel's heart caught mid-beat, the words registering fully but the gravity of their impact taking longer to absorb. The offer wasn't just another career milestone—it was the kind of pivotal, life-altering opportunity that few ever received, a moment where destiny and preparation collided in an almost unreal way. His mind raced with possibilities, consequences, and practical considerations, yet beneath it all, there was a thrill, a pulse of suspenseful energy that seemed to vibrate through his veins.

"Yes," he said finally, voice low but firm, almost as if the power of the moment demanded measured respect. "I accept. I… I wouldn't miss this for anything."

The conversation ended, leaving Daniel standing in the chill morning air, phone still in hand, staring at the empty street before him. He felt the kind of exhilaration that comes when the unknown opens a doorway to something entirely new, a mixture of triumph, anxiety, and suspenseful anticipation. Everything in his life up until this moment—the routines, the quiet struggles, the moments of doubt—now seemed to converge on a single point, one decision that would ripple outward, reshaping the familiar contours of his existence.

Evelyn's text had come just moments before, a casual check-in that now seemed almost prophetic: "Morning! Ready for another unpredictable day?" She had no idea, of course, how much unpredictability awaited him today. He smiled, thumb hovering over the screen as he typed back a cryptic, almost mischievous: "More than you can imagine. Meet me tonight, and I'll tell you everything."

The day passed in a blur of responsibilities, Daniel's mind occupied with the logistical details of his new position, emails, and calls confirming arrangements. But beneath every task, every careful movement, there was a constant undercurrent of suspense. He found himself pacing in small circles in his apartment, imagining Evelyn's reaction when he finally shared the news. What would she say? How would the rhythm of their relationship adjust to this seismic shift? And yet, amid the uncertainty, there was an unmistakable thrill—a sense of possibility that pulsed beneath the surface of the ordinary.

When evening finally came, the city had quieted into its characteristic hum. The soft glow of streetlights shimmered against puddles reflecting the deepening indigo of the night sky. Daniel walked toward the café where they often met, each step deliberate, his mind rehearsing words that somehow always seemed inadequate for the weight of the moment. When he arrived, he found Evelyn already there, seated by the window with a book in hand, the light catching her hair in an almost ethereal glow.

"Daniel!" she called softly, marking her page and setting the book aside. Her voice carried a subtle curiosity, a delicate anticipation. "You seemed... distracted in your messages. What's going on?"

He pulled out the chair opposite her, hands brushing briefly against hers as he settled into the seat. The accidental intimacy of their hand contact sent a familiar shiver of suspense through him. "Evelyn, I... I have news. Something that... well, it changes a lot of things."

Her eyebrows rose slightly, a mixture of curiosity and excitement shining in her eyes. "Changes a lot of things?" she repeated, leaning slightly forward. "This sounds serious."

Daniel swallowed, heart hammering in a rhythm that was half excitement, half nervous anticipation. "Yes. It is serious," he admitted, voice low, deliberate. "I... I received a job offer today. A position I've been working toward for years, something I never thought I'd get. And... it's not just any job—it's the kind of opportunity that could redefine everything for me... for us, if we allow it."

Evelyn's hand trembled slightly as she reached across the table, lightly touching his. "For us?" she echoed, her voice a mixture of awe and tentative hope. "You mean... it affects more than just your career?"

"Yes," Daniel replied, eyes meeting hers with an intensity that silenced the surrounding café hum. "It affects everything. My daily routines, where I'll live, how I'll spend my time, the people I interact with… everything. And I realized, while it's a huge opportunity, it also comes with choices that affect us—how we navigate our relationship, how we continue to grow together. I didn't know how to tell you because I wanted it to feel… right, you know?"

Evelyn's eyes shimmered in the warm glow of the lamp. She could see the weight of responsibility and anticipation pressing down on him, the careful balance of excitement and fear. She reached out, placing both of her hands over his in a gesture of reassurance. "Daniel," she said softly, "you don't have to do this alone. We're a team, remember? Whatever this offer brings, whatever decisions you need to make, I'm here. And… I'm excited for you. Truly."

The suspense between them seemed to fold inward, creating a quiet cocoon around their table. It wasn't just the news of the job that carried tension—it was the unspoken understanding of how profoundly it could change the rhythm of their lives together. Every glance, every shared breath, every subtle squeeze of the hands across the table carried layers of meaning, anticipation, and cautious hope.

Daniel leaned back slightly, exhaling, the weight of the day and the intensity of the moment settling into a steady rhythm. "I was nervous," he admitted, voice barely above a whisper. "Nervous that this opportunity would feel like a turning point… and that I'd have to navigate it without you understanding what it meant. But now, sitting here… with you… it feels like the suspense isn't a burden anymore. It's… a kind of thrill. A shared adventure. And I want to experience it with you."

Evelyn's lips curved into a gentle smile, eyes reflecting both pride and excitement. "Then we'll navigate it together," she said softly. "Whatever changes come, whatever uncertainties arise, we'll face them side by side.

And maybe that's the best part of all—the suspense, the unknown, the adventure... we don't have to face it alone."

Daniel's chest tightened with relief and affection. "Exactly," he murmured. "The unknown doesn't feel so intimidating when you're here. The suspense is... thrilling. And I think... it's going to make every step, every choice, every decision... more meaningful."

They lingered at the table, hands intertwined, letting the soft murmur of the café and the distant hum of city life fade into a background hum. The weight of the job offer—its implications, its opportunities, its potential to change everything—was tempered by the shared understanding that they would navigate it together. The suspense of the unknown, once a source of anxiety, had transformed into an intimate, exhilarating promise of new beginnings.

Daniel's phone buzzed briefly, a reminder of the real world waiting outside the café doors, but he ignored it, focusing instead on the calm, steady presence of Evelyn across from him. The city could wait. The uncertainties could wait. For now, in the quiet intimacy of the evening, the suspense of change became a shared heartbeat, a silent vow that no matter how dramatically life shifted, they would face it as a unit.

And as they stepped out into the night, the glow of the city surrounding them, Daniel felt an unfamiliar yet exhilarating certainty: the job offer had indeed changed everything—but not in the way fear or excitement alone might suggest. It had changed everything because it had revealed, with quiet clarity, that no opportunity, no choice, no turning point mattered more than the presence of someone willing to face it with you. The suspense, the anticipation, the thrilling unknown—they were no longer burdens. They were invitations, carefully folded into the delicate fabric of a life now shared.

42

HER FEAR OF LOSING HIM BEFORE SHE HAS HIM

The city had grown quiet under the blanket of night, the streets slick with lingering rain and the occasional flicker of streetlights reflecting off puddles like tiny fractured stars. Evelyn walked slowly, her coat drawn tightly around her, though it was not the chill that made her shiver. Her mind raced, restless, tangled in a web of thoughts she could neither untangle nor fully articulate. Daniel's recent job offer, the promise of change, and the fragile intimacy that had been blossoming between them all collided in her heart, creating a strange cocktail of hope, suspense, and—most acutely—fear.

Her steps echoed against the deserted pavement, each tap of her shoes punctuating the storm inside her. She had grown accustomed to the almost-date nights, the accidental touches, the gentle unfolding of their connection. She had cherished the quiet moments—the handholding by accident, the shared silences, the peace she had prayed for. But tonight, beneath the veneer of calm, there was a new tension: the fear of losing him before she truly had him. The thought was irrational, born from the past and from the uncertainty of what lay ahead, yet it gripped her chest with unrelenting insistence.

Evelyn had never been one to indulge in hypothetical scenarios, but the suspense of possibility now consumed her. She imagined him caught up in the excitement of his new job, the long hours, the demands of responsibility. She imagined herself becoming a silent observer of his life rather than a participant. And she imagined the worst: that by the time she found the courage to fully surrender her heart, he might have moved on, the bond they had nurtured quietly fraying under the weight of distance, distraction, or circumstance.

Her thoughts were interrupted by the soft glow of a lamplight around the corner, signaling the familiar path that led to the park where she and Daniel often met. The place was deserted, save for the occasional rustle of leaves stirred by the faint evening breeze. She slowed, pausing at the edge of the walkway, half-expecting him to appear out of nowhere, as he often did in her daydreams and moments of quiet hope.

The suspense tightened, each second stretching unbearably as she waited, heart hammering against her ribcage. What if he wasn't coming tonight? What if she had misread his signals, mistook friendliness for something more, warmth for intention? The questions swirled relentlessly, a tidal wave of uncertainty threatening to overwhelm the fragile calm she had worked so hard to cultivate.

And then she saw him. Daniel emerged from the shadows, hands stuffed into his coat pockets, the faintest smile tugging at the corners of his lips. Relief flooded through her, mingled with the lingering fear that he might vanish again, like a mirage, slipping through her fingers before she could reach him. Her pace quickened, matching his until they met at the familiar corner of the fountain.

"Evelyn," he said softly, voice careful and deliberate, aware of the tension coiled in her posture. "You're here."

She nodded, words failing her in the face of the maelstrom inside. Her throat felt tight, as though speaking might break the fragile dam holding back weeks of accumulated emotion. Daniel's eyes studied her for a long moment, perceptive, patient, and full of quiet understanding. He had learned to read her in ways no one else could, sensing the subtle shifts in her expression, the hesitations, the fleeting moments of vulnerability she tried so hard to conceal.

"I..." she began, then stopped, swallowing hard. "I was afraid you wouldn't be." Her voice was barely above a whisper, a confession that trembled on the edge of vulnerability.

Daniel's gaze softened, and he reached for her hand without hesitation, their fingers intertwining with a familiarity born of trust and unspoken understanding. The contact was grounding, a quiet reassurance that anchored her in the present, in the reality of their connection.

"Afraid?" he asked gently, his thumb brushing over the back of her hand. "Afraid of what?"

Evelyn looked down, her fingers tightening around his. "Afraid... of losing you before I even have you," she admitted finally, her voice shaking with the weight of truth. "Afraid that all this—us—might slip away if I don't... if I don't find the courage to fully feel it, to fully say it, to fully trust it."

Daniel's chest tightened, a subtle rush of emotion coursing through him. He had sensed the tension building over the past weeks, the delicate fear that had shadowed her quiet moments of joy. He had seen it in her eyes, in the way she hesitated to reach out fully, in the careful balance between closeness and restraint. And now, with her voice finally breaking the silence, he understood the depth of the suspense she had been living with, the fragile edge on which her heart had been teetering.

"Evelyn," he said softly, stepping closer, "you don't have to fear that. Not with me. Not ever. I'm not going anywhere—not tonight, not tomorrow, not ever. And I don't want you to hold back, or hesitate, or think that you might lose me before you have me. You already do. And I'm right here."

Her eyes lifted to meet his, searching for reassurance, finding it in the calm certainty reflected in his gaze. The suspense, the fear, the tension that had gripped her chest for so long began to dissipate, replaced by a warmth that spread slowly, deliberately, grounding her in the reality of their connection.

"I... I want to believe that," she whispered, a soft tremor in her voice betraying the fragility of her emotions. "I want to trust that we... that this... whatever it is... will last. But my heart... it's been cautious. It's been scarred. And sometimes the fear comes back before the faith can fully take hold."

Daniel's fingers tightened around hers, a steadying force, a promise of patience and presence. "Then let me carry some of that fear for you," he said quietly. "Let me show you that it's okay to feel afraid, that it's okay to doubt, as long as we face it together. The suspense, the uncertainty... it doesn't have to be a burden. It can be a bridge, a way to deepen what we already have, one step at a time."

Evelyn's breath hitched, the weight of his words sinking deep into her chest. She felt the suspense transform—not into anxiety, but into a quiet, deliberate anticipation of what lay ahead. The fear that had haunted her moments of introspection, the terror of losing him before she even had him, was no longer a looming shadow. Instead, it became a point of connection, a thread linking her heart to his in a way that felt sacred, fragile, and intensely alive.

They walked together through the park, hands intertwined, the night holding its breath around them. The fountain gurgled softly in the distance, a gentle counterpoint to the quiet rush of their thoughts. Evelyn felt the suspense of possibility shift into a rhythm she could almost breathe in, a shared heartbeat that spoke of patience, trust, and the delicate art of giving love without fear.

Daniel's voice broke the comfortable silence, low and deliberate. "Evelyn, you don't have to rush into anything. Not feelings, not confessions, not even certainty. Just... be here with me. Let this moment exist exactly as it is. Let it unfold slowly. And whatever fear you have... we'll face it together."

Her chest lifted, and a small, tremulous smile curved her lips. The suspense that had once been anxiety now became a gentle anticipation, a thrilling undercurrent that carried her heart into new territory without demanding surrender. She realized that her fear of losing him before she had him was not a flaw, but a marker of the depth of her care, the intensity of her desire to protect something precious.

"I... I can do that," she whispered finally, voice steadier now. "I can trust you. I can trust us. And maybe... maybe that's the beginning of letting go of the fear that's been holding me back."

Daniel's hand squeezed hers, a silent affirmation, and she allowed herself to lean slightly into the space between them, feeling the warmth of his presence anchor her. The suspense of what might come next—the uncertainty, the delicate balance between courage and hesitation—was no longer a threat, but a companion, a quiet pulse of anticipation that promised growth, understanding, and the unfolding of something extraordinary.

Under the quiet glow of the lamplights, with the soft murmur of water and leaves around them, Evelyn realized a profound truth: fear did not have to preclude love. Suspense did not have to prevent connection. And losing him before she had him was no longer a specter haunting her heart. She already had him—in patience, in trust, in presence—and that alone was enough to carry her forward, step by deliberate step, into whatever awaited them both.

And as they walked slowly through the park, hands clasped, hearts aligned, and eyes reflecting mutual understanding, Evelyn knew that this moment—fragile, suspenseful, and honest—would remain etched into her memory forever. It was the first time she truly recognized that love could exist not despite fear, but alongside it, quietly, deliberately, and beautifully.

43

THE FIGHT THAT WASN'T SUPPOSED TO HAPPEN

The apartment was unusually silent, the kind of silence that presses on the chest and fills every corner with tension. The city outside was oblivious to the storm brewing within these four walls, the distant hum of traffic and faint neon reflections on the wet pavement masking the rising anxiety between Daniel and Evelyn. The evening had started innocuously enough, with the soft laughter and comfortable exchanges that had become their norm, but by the time the shadows lengthened and the glow of the lamps illuminated every nuance of expression, the tension had crept in silently, like a predator waiting for the perfect moment to strike.

Daniel stood near the kitchen counter, running a hand through his hair in frustration. The job offer he had accepted days earlier, which had once felt like a thrilling opportunity, now carried with it an unexpected weight. The new responsibilities, the looming deadlines, and the subtle stress of proving himself in an unfamiliar environment had frayed his nerves. Normally, he would have managed it with quiet diligence, compartmentalizing the pressure and maintaining his calm façade. But tonight, for reasons he couldn't fully articulate, the stress spilled over, and it landed in the wrong place: on Evelyn.

Evelyn, seated on the edge of the sofa, picked at the hem of her sweater, a nervous gesture she often performed when anxiety edged into her chest. She had been eager to share the small joys of her day with Daniel—an article she had read, a café she wanted to try, the little moments of serendipity that reminded her of the quiet happiness they had been cultivating together. But as soon as she began speaking, Daniel's responses were curt, clipped, tinged with irritation that seemed disproportionate to the conversation at hand.

"Daniel," she started cautiously, her voice soft yet carrying a subtle firmness, "are you okay? You've been… distant since you came in."

Daniel's jaw tightened. He wanted to explain that it wasn't her fault, that the stress was entirely his burden, but words tangled in his throat. "I'm fine," he said finally, his tone sharper than intended. "Just… tired."

Evelyn frowned, sensing the undercurrent of tension. "Tired?" she echoed, the concern in her voice mingling with an edge of hurt. "Or… frustrated about something you're not telling me?"

Daniel's hand clenched into a fist at his side, a reflexive gesture he barely noticed. "It's nothing," he muttered, though the word carried a weighty undertone that betrayed his internal struggle. "Really. Don't make it bigger than it is."

Evelyn's breath hitched slightly. She had learned to read him, to detect the subtle shifts in tone and posture that revealed more than the words themselves ever could. And what she read now stirred a quiet storm inside her: a mixture of fear, frustration, and a creeping suspicion that she was being blamed for something she hadn't done. "Daniel," she said, her voice firmer now, "I'm not trying to make anything bigger. I just… I feel like you're shutting me out, and I don't understand why. If it's me, please tell me."

That was the spark. Daniel, already frayed by a day of unrelenting pressure, felt the words as both an accusation and an intrusion. The suspense that had been simmering beneath the surface erupted into a sharp, almost primal reaction. "It's not about you!" he snapped, more loudly than he intended. "Why do you always think it has to be about you?"

The words hung in the air, heavy and jagged, slicing through the fragile calm that had existed between them for weeks. Evelyn's eyes widened, the shock of his tone reverberating through her chest. "Daniel," she whispered, voice trembling, "that... that wasn't fair."

"I didn't mean it like that," he said immediately, regret flashing across his face, though the tension in his shoulders betrayed him. "I'm just... stressed. And everything feels overwhelming right now."

"But snapping at me isn't the answer," Evelyn replied, her voice rising slightly, though she fought to maintain composure. "I can handle stress with you—I always have—but I need you to... I don't know... let me in instead of pushing me away."

Daniel ran a hand across his face, exhaling sharply. He knew she was right. He always knew when she was right. But pride, fear, and the raw edge of fatigue made him defensive, a wall he hadn't intended to erect but found impossible to lower in the heat of the moment. "I... I just can't explain it all the time," he muttered, his voice softer now but still tight. "Some things... some things I need to figure out alone."

Evelyn's chest constricted. She wanted to reach for him, to bridge the sudden distance that had appeared out of nowhere, but the sting of his earlier words lingered. "I understand needing space," she said carefully, "but this… this fight… it wasn't supposed to happen. Not like this. We promised each other honesty, patience, trust… and suddenly, it's like all of that doesn't matter."

The suspense in the room thickened, stretching taut between them like a thread ready to snap. Neither wanted the fight, yet neither could immediately bridge the gulf that had appeared. Daniel's fingers brushed the counter nervously, Evelyn's hands fidgeted in her lap, and the silence between words carried a weight far heavier than anything either had anticipated.

"I know," Daniel admitted finally, voice low, almost a whisper. "I know it shouldn't have happened. And I'm sorry. I never wanted to hurt you, Evelyn. I… I don't even know how it escalated so quickly. I felt trapped in my own thoughts and… I didn't stop it in time."

Evelyn exhaled slowly, letting some of the tension drain from her body, though the residue of hurt remained. "It's not just about words, Daniel," she said softly. "It's about trust. It's about feeling like you're here with me, fully, even when things are difficult. And tonight… tonight, I felt you pull away."

Daniel took a tentative step closer, the subtle movement carrying the suspenseful gravity of a man who understood the consequences of missteps. "You're right," he said, gently taking her hands in his. "I pulled away. I didn't want to, but… I was scared. Scared of losing control of myself, of saying something I'd regret, of… I don't know… messing this up before it even gets a chance to grow."

Evelyn's eyes glistened with unshed tears, her voice trembling. "That's the problem, Daniel. That's exactly why I'm afraid sometimes. Afraid that we'll fight before we even fully understand what we have, afraid that moments like this—this connection, this trust—will fray under pressure before it has a chance to solidify."

Daniel's grip on her hands tightened slightly, grounding both of them in the fragile reality of the moment. "Then let's not let that happen," he said softly, the suspense in his voice carrying the weight of conviction. "Let's… slow down. Breathe. Remember that we're on the same side. That this—us—is worth more than any argument, any frustration, any fleeting impatience. I don't want this fight. I don't want to lose the peace we've built over something so small, so avoidable."

Evelyn nodded, letting a quiet sigh escape. The tension that had coiled in her chest began to loosen, replaced by a tentative warmth. "I don't want this fight either," she admitted. "I don't want to feel like I'm losing you before I even have the chance to fully be with you. Can we… can we promise to try harder? To stop the fight before it starts, and communicate instead?"

Daniel smiled faintly, a mixture of relief and lingering regret. "We can," he said. "I promise. I'll do better. I'll… be more mindful. And we'll face the suspense of life together, without letting it turn into unnecessary conflict. We'll fight for understanding, not against each other."

The atmosphere shifted subtly, the suspense transforming from tension into a delicate, careful relief. Hands still intertwined, they sat together, letting the soft hum of the city outside fill the spaces between their words. The fight that wasn't supposed to happen had occurred, yes—but its occurrence became a bridge rather than a barrier, a moment that reminded them both of the fragility and resilience of trust, of love, of connection.

Evelyn leaned her head slightly against Daniel's shoulder, feeling the steady rhythm of his heartbeat beneath her ear. "I guess," she whispered, "even fights can be lessons. If we let them teach us instead of divide us."

Daniel pressed a gentle kiss to the top of her head, a quiet affirmation of presence and intent. "Exactly," he said softly. "Even fights… even mistakes… can become milestones. As long as we face them together."

The suspense lingered still, but now it carried the promise of growth rather than fear. They had survived the fight that wasn't supposed to happen, and in doing so, had found a new depth to their connection—a subtle, unspoken understanding that even in moments of tension, even in the shadow of miscommunication, love could endure, patient, deliberate, and unshakable.

And as the night stretched on, the city around them fading into quiet anonymity, Daniel and Evelyn remained entwined, not as adversaries, not as frightened hearts, but as two people learning the careful art of holding on, even when everything seemed poised to pull them apart.

44

MAYBE OUR TIMING IS WRONG

The late afternoon sky was painted in bruised shades of gray and violet, the clouds hanging low, heavy with the promise of rain. Evelyn stood by the café window, tracing the streaks left by the drizzle with the tip of her finger. Outside, the world moved in its usual indifferent rhythm—cars passed, pedestrians hurried with umbrellas, and somewhere in the distance, the faint honking of a taxi sliced through the soft patter of rain. But inside, time felt suspended. Every tick of the clock, every muffled footstep, seemed to echo against the walls, carrying with it a suspense she could not shake.

She had asked Daniel to meet her here, a neutral ground where conversations could unfold without the weight of their apartments or the distractions of the outside world. But even in this familiar setting, a tension gripped her chest, one that had been growing silently for days. It wasn't about anger, nor was it about misunderstanding. It was something quieter, more insidious: doubt. A creeping question she had avoided, whispered only in the quiet moments when her mind refused to relent: maybe our timing is wrong.

Daniel arrived precisely on time, as he always did, his coat still damp from the drizzle, hair slightly tousled by the wind. His eyes met hers immediately, sharp, searching, aware that something lay beneath the surface she was trying to mask. He approached the table with his usual careful gait, yet tonight there was a subtle tension in his shoulders, a guardedness he rarely carried.

"Evelyn," he said softly, sliding into the seat across from her. "You look... thoughtful. What's on your mind?"

She exhaled slowly, a fragile tremor threading her words. "Daniel... I've been thinking. About us, about everything. And... I don't know if we're in the right place, at the right time."

Daniel blinked, the words cutting through the comfortable hum of the café like an unexpected gust of wind. "Not the right place, or not the right time?" he asked cautiously, already sensing the gravity of her tone.

"Maybe... both," she admitted, voice low, fragile. "I've been trying to ignore it, to push it aside because everything between us feels... right in so many ways. But the timing... Daniel, it's complicated. You with your new job, the responsibilities piling up, and me... trying to figure out what I need without losing myself in the process. Maybe... maybe we're rushing, or maybe we're just... slightly out of sync."

The words hung in the air, a delicate tension threading between them. Daniel's fingers drummed lightly on the table, a nervous tic she had learned to recognize over the months. The suspense of the moment was almost suffocating; it wasn't the first time questions of timing had whispered their way into their conversations, but hearing them spoken aloud made them real, undeniable.

"I understand," Daniel said carefully, choosing his words as if each one might tip the balance of the fragile conversation. "I've felt it too... the pull of life, the demands that make us feel like maybe we're on different tracks.

But… even if timing isn't perfect, does that mean what we have is wrong?"

Evelyn's eyes dropped to her hands, twisting the edge of her sleeve, a nervous ritual that carried all the weight of her thoughts. "I don't know. I keep asking myself that every day. Every moment with you feels right, yet the circumstances keep reminding me that right doesn't always mean easy. And maybe easy is what we need right now… maybe right now, we can't give each other what we deserve because life keeps demanding more than we can give."

Daniel leaned back, running a hand across his face, trying to calm the surge of emotion that bubbled in his chest. He had anticipated many challenges with Evelyn—distance, vulnerability, moments of fear—but he had never truly prepared for this kind of quiet, creeping suspense: the fear that even the right feelings, the right intentions, might falter under the weight of reality.

"Timing," he said slowly, voice measured, "has always been tricky, hasn't it? We meet, we connect, we share… but there's always something—opportunities, responsibilities, the sheer unpredictability of life—that keeps reminding us that nothing is simple."

Evelyn nodded, swallowing the lump forming in her throat. "Exactly. And I'm not saying I don't want this… I want you, Daniel, more than I've ever wanted anyone. But wanting isn't always enough when life keeps throwing obstacles in the way. Sometimes… sometimes it feels like no matter how strong the pull is, timing keeps saying 'wait.'"

Daniel reached across the table, his hand brushing hers lightly, a small reassurance in the storm of her words. "Then maybe we listen to the timing, not as an enemy, but as a guide. Maybe it's telling us to be patient, to be deliberate, to not let fear or uncertainty push us into decisions we're not ready for."

Evelyn's eyes glistened, a mixture of relief and lingering worry. "I want that," she whispered. "I want patience. But patience... it feels dangerous sometimes. Dangerous because while we wait, life keeps moving, and what if waiting means missing each other entirely?"

The suspense between them thickened, heavy and almost tangible. Neither of them spoke immediately, letting the hum of the café, the soft drizzle outside, and the quiet murmur of patrons fill the spaces between words. Every pause carried weight, every glance spoke volumes, every subtle movement threaded tension through the room. It was a quiet, dangerous suspense, the kind that makes hearts beat faster not because of fear of conflict, but because of the uncertainty of what could be lost—or found.

Daniel's voice broke the silence, low and deliberate. "Evelyn... I won't pretend that timing is easy. I won't pretend that I have all the answers. But I do know this—I don't want to walk away from us because the world isn't perfect. I don't want to let the unpredictability of life dictate whether we belong in each other's lives."

Evelyn's lips trembled as a tear threatened to fall, a mix of relief and fear coiling in her chest. "And I don't want to let fear make me push you away," she said softly. "I want to hold on... but I also want to be sure. That we're not just holding on to an ideal, or to the thrill of possibility, but to something that can withstand the timing, whatever it is."

Daniel leaned closer, the suspense in his expression mingling with sincerity, with the intensity of someone who had weighed every moment, every choice, and every heartbeat leading to this point. "Then we don't rush," he said. "We give it space, we let life unfold around us, and we keep coming back to each other. Timing... maybe it's never perfect. But maybe perfect doesn't exist. Maybe what we have is enough, if we nurture it, if we protect it, if we fight for it without letting impatience or fear take over."

Evelyn exhaled slowly, allowing herself to be grounded by his words. The suspense of uncertainty still lingered, but it shifted subtly, from a source of fear to a fragile hope. She realized that timing wasn't an enemy—it was a challenge, a test of endurance and faith, a suspenseful rhythm that demanded care and intentionality.

"I want to try that," she said finally, voice steady despite the tremor of emotion underneath. "I want to try being present, being patient... and trusting that we'll find our moment, even if it's messy, even if it's complicated. Even if it feels... like the world is against us sometimes."

Daniel smiled faintly, the corner of his lips lifting in quiet relief. "Then we'll try it together," he said, gently squeezing her hand. "No rushing, no forcing, no letting fear dictate our steps. Just... careful, deliberate patience. And hope. Lots of hope."

Evelyn leaned back slightly, watching the rain streak across the window, letting the suspense of the moment settle into a quiet anticipation. The fear of wrong timing, of missed chances, of moments slipping away, still lingered—but it was tempered by the knowledge that they were facing it together, deliberately, intentionally, and with full hearts.

"Maybe our timing isn't perfect," she said softly, almost to herself. "But maybe... maybe that doesn't matter, as long as we keep choosing each other, over and over again."

Daniel's eyes met hers, steady, patient, unwavering. "Exactly," he murmured. "Over and over again."

Outside, the rain continued to fall, the world moving in its relentless rhythm. Inside, Evelyn and Daniel sat together, suspended in a moment of quiet suspense, hearts aligned and ready to face the imperfect timing of life—together.

45

DISTANCE BETWEEN TWO HEARTS

The train rattled along the tracks with an unhurried monotony, each clack of the wheels a cruel reminder of the miles stretching between them. Evelyn sat pressed against the window, the city lights blurring into streaks of gold and silver as the train gained speed. Outside, the streets were alive with motion, yet she felt as though the world had slowed just for her, making each heartbeat louder, each thought sharper. Daniel's absence was an ache she hadn't fully anticipated—a quiet, pressing void that grew heavier with every passing mile.

The call had come that morning, short and unexpected. Daniel had been offered a crucial assignment in another city, a career-defining opportunity that demanded immediate relocation. He had tried to downplay it, insisting that the distance was temporary, that it was nothing more than a test of patience and commitment. But the undercurrent of urgency in his voice had betrayed him. Even as he spoke of the excitement and promise of the new role, Evelyn had felt the subtle fracture of proximity slipping through their fingers, leaving behind a taut cord of suspense, worry, and longing.

Sitting in the nearly empty train car, Evelyn stared at her reflection in the glass, the faint glow of the interior lights painting her face with soft shadows. Her eyes, wide and alert, betrayed the storm within: fear of distance, fear of losing the intimacy that had grown quietly but steadily between them, fear of the unknown that now stretched between two hearts that had, until now, existed in close harmony.

She reached for her phone repeatedly, the device feeling heavier with each glance. Daniel's last message lingered on the screen, simple, reassuring, yet charged with the unspoken truth: I'll call as soon as I can. Don't worry, I'm still here. Simple words, yet they carried a suspenseful weight, the kind that makes every second without contact stretch like eternity. Evelyn's fingers hovered over the keyboard, wanting to reply, wanting to send her love, her fears, her presence—but she hesitated. She didn't want to seem clingy. She didn't want to push him further into the responsibilities that had pulled him away.

Her mind drifted back to the small, ordinary moments that had defined their closeness—the accidental touches, the gentle confessions, the laughter shared under streetlights, the quiet understanding of shared silences. Each memory now carried a delicate fragility, a reminder that the distance was not just physical but emotional as well. And the suspense of whether they could sustain what they had built together gnawed at her heart.

Meanwhile, miles away, Daniel stood on the balcony of his temporary apartment, the city sprawling beneath him, indifferent and vast. The skyline glittered with promise, yet every light felt distant, like a reflection of the connection he had left behind. He had wanted to call her immediately, to hear her voice, to reassure her that the distance would not undo the intimacy they had nurtured. But he had paused, acutely aware that his exhaustion and stress could color his words, and he didn't want to fracture the delicate trust they had painstakingly built.

Instead, he had sent the briefest messages, each word carefully chosen to convey presence without intrusion. Yet the suspense of their separation was palpable, each unread response a small chasm, each delayed message a reminder of the miles that now stood between them. Daniel felt the familiar ache of longing, but he also carried a cautious optimism, a quiet determination that the distance would not erode the bond that had grown stronger in the quiet moments of understanding, patience, and shared vulnerability.

Back on the train, Evelyn drew a deep breath and closed her eyes, attempting to steady the torrent of thoughts racing through her mind. She imagined Daniel in the city, navigating the unfamiliar streets, meeting new colleagues, adjusting to a schedule that left little room for leisure. She imagined the moments when he might pause, perhaps look at his phone, and think of her—and in that thought, she found a fragile comfort. But the suspense lingered, a subtle tension that refused to dissipate.

Her phone buzzed gently, a single message from Daniel breaking the oppressive quiet: Thinking of you. Don't let the distance scare you. We're in this together.

Evelyn's breath caught in her throat. The words, though few, carried a powerful reassurance. Yet they also reminded her of the reality she now faced—the suspension between their physical closeness and emotional connection, the delicate balancing act of maintaining intimacy across miles. She typed a reply, paused, erased it, and began again. I'm trying. I just... it feels so much farther than it is.

Minutes passed. The train moved steadily, the rhythm of its wheels almost hypnotic. Evelyn's gaze returned to the window, tracing the shadows and lights that flickered past. She thought about the evenings they had spent together, the slow walks, the conversations that had stretched long into the night, the shared silences that spoke louder than any words. Each memory was a thread, weaving a tapestry of closeness that now needed careful tending across the divide.

The suspense of separation revealed itself in unexpected ways. She found herself hyper-aware of small gestures, replaying old conversations in her mind, analyzing each laugh, each touch, each fleeting glance for signs of enduring connection. She wondered if he felt the same pangs of absence, if he too measured the distance in moments of memory, if he too feared the subtle erosion that miles could bring to something so delicate.

Daniel, at the same time, struggled with the same haunting question. In meetings, in transit between offices, in the quiet moments before sleep, his mind drifted to Evelyn. He remembered the feel of her hand in his, the soft timbre of her laughter, the quiet certainty of her presence beside him. Each thought was a mixture of comfort and suspense—a reminder of what he had and what he temporarily lacked, a tension that neither time nor distance could entirely alleviate.

The day stretched on, and the suspense built in both their hearts, each aware of the other yet separated by circumstance. Evelyn found solace in small routines—checking her messages, replaying snippets of their calls, imagining his voice reading the words she sent. Daniel found his reassurance in planning brief texts, imagining her reaction to small jokes, to observations of life that could be shared despite the distance. And through it all, the tension—the delicate, suspenseful ache of longing—remained, a constant pulse reminding them of the stakes of their connection.

By evening, Evelyn arrived at her apartment, the quiet of the room pressing in around her. She sank onto the sofa, phone in hand, staring at the screen as if willing Daniel to appear. A single message lit up, and her heart skipped: Can't wait to talk tonight. Hold on for me.

The suspense, though still present, had transformed into anticipation. The distance was no longer merely an obstacle; it had become a test of patience, a challenge to their trust, a reminder that what was fragile required care and attention. Evelyn smiled faintly, pressing the phone to her chest, feeling the warmth of his words, the promise of his presence, even if it was delayed, even if it was indirect.

Daniel, across the city, leaned back in his chair, allowing himself a quiet exhale. The distance remained, real and unyielding, but he felt the tether of their connection, strong and resilient, stretching across the miles. He knew the suspense would continue, that longing would ebb and flow, that nights of quiet reflection would test them both. Yet in the middle of that uncertainty, he felt a firm resolve: to hold on, to nurture, to remain present in ways that mattered, until the miles no longer mattered.

And as night fell, wrapping both of them in separate but parallel shadows, Evelyn and Daniel sat alone yet together in spirit, bound by the suspense of separation, the anticipation of reunion, and the quiet, unwavering certainty that distance could never sever what their hearts had begun to weave.

For every mile that stretched between them, there was a heartbeat, a memory, a whisper of reassurance—a silent promise that the space between two hearts was only temporary, and that love, patient and deliberate, could endure even when proximity was impossible.

46

THE REALIZATION THAT HIT THEM SEPARATELY

The morning light spilled lazily across the room, slicing through the curtains in uneven streaks, but for Daniel, the brightness did little to chase away the haze clouding his thoughts. He sat at the edge of his bed, a mug of lukewarm coffee in hand, staring blankly at the city skyline framed by the window. His apartment, temporary though it was, felt cold in a way that had nothing to do with temperature. The bustling streets below moved with indifference to his inner turmoil, a cruel juxtaposition to the storm of reflection and uncertainty that raged within him.

He had been up since dawn, wrestling with thoughts he hadn't dared confront fully until now. The suspense that had quietly threaded through their recent days—the subtle tension of distance, the careful maintenance of connection, the fragile hope that what they had could withstand the miles—was suddenly overshadowed by a heavier, more profound realization.

It hit him first as a whisper, subtle and unassuming, yet impossible to ignore. He thought of Evelyn—her laughter, the gentle cadence of her voice, the way her eyes seemed to reflect the world's colors back at him. He thought of the stolen moments, the accidental brushes of their hands, the silences that spoke volumes. And then, almost cruelly, the truth settled into his chest: he loved her. Not as a passing infatuation, not as a moment of comfort, but fully, deeply, irrevocably.

Daniel's fingers tightened around the mug, knuckles whitening, as the weight of the realization pressed against him. He had known attraction, had known tenderness, had known longing—but this was different. This was a heart-defining clarity that left no room for ambiguity. The suspense of distance, the tension of timing, the quiet anxieties that had previously seemed insurmountable—now they all seemed secondary to the raw, undeniable certainty of love.

He exhaled slowly, leaning back against the headboard, the city's hum below almost too loud in the sudden emptiness of the room. The suspense that had defined the last weeks—the quiet anticipation of messages, the careful navigation of calls, the unspoken dance around timing and responsibilities—was replaced by an urgent, almost desperate need to act, to speak, to ensure that Evelyn knew, somehow, that his heart belonged to her entirely.

Thousands of miles away, Evelyn experienced a parallel awakening. She sat cross-legged on the floor of her living room, her laptop open in front of her, but her attention was elsewhere. The document she had been writing, the tasks she had planned for the morning, all blurred into the background as a sudden, electrifying clarity struck her. The small, tentative feelings she had nurtured, the careful hopes she had harbored—they had coalesced into a single, undeniable truth: she loved Daniel.

The realization was both exhilarating and terrifying. Her heart raced in her chest, a rhythmic pulse that echoed the suspense of their separation. She had loved the moments, the shared laughter, the gentle touches, the quiet understanding. But now, with the sudden clarity of recognition, it wasn't just the moments she loved—it was him, entirely, undeniably, completely.

Evelyn pressed her hands to her face, trying to steady the tremor of emotions threatening to overwhelm her. How had it taken so long to recognize it? How had she allowed herself to skirt the edges of feeling, to temper her heart with caution and fear? And yet, the moment of clarity felt sacred, transformative, a revelation that both thrilled and frightened her.

In her mind, she replayed every shared experience—the casual hand brushes that felt electric, the long walks under streetlights, the quiet evenings when words weren't necessary because presence alone was enough. Each memory now carried a new weight, a profound significance that had previously been veiled by uncertainty. And with it came the suspense of action: how to convey this truth to Daniel without the distance, without the miles, without the fear of timing sabotaging what they had built?

Meanwhile, Daniel stared at the phone on his bedside table, fingers hovering over the screen, mind racing. He wanted to reach out immediately, to spill the words that had been crystallizing in his chest, but he hesitated. The suspense of timing—the fear of intruding, of startling, of misreading the moment—held him captive. And yet, the clarity of his feelings made inaction nearly unbearable. Every second he waited, every delay in communication, was a reminder of the miles between them, a reminder that love, no matter how certain, required courage to express.

He remembered the little things that had cemented his feelings—the way she laughed when she was nervous, the quiet strength she carried even in moments of doubt, the way she had always, somehow, understood him in ways no one else could. The realization that he loved her fully, and that the timing, the distance, the complications of life mattered little compared to the certainty of his heart, struck him with a force that left him momentarily breathless.

The suspense in both their hearts was mirrored across cities, miles apart yet aligned in the raw truth of realization. Both knew, in that suspended moment, that life would never feel the same again. Both wrestled with the mixture of fear and excitement, the tension between action and patience, the intoxicating dread of admitting love before it could be reciprocated in the fullness of understanding.

Daniel finally exhaled, a long, deliberate breath that seemed to carry the weight of weeks of anticipation and worry. He picked up the phone, thumb hovering over her contact, staring at the name that had become a lifeline of hope and belonging. The suspense was almost unbearable; the fear of saying the wrong thing, the wrong moment, the wrong tone, pressed against him like a physical force. But the realization—this undeniable truth—was stronger. He typed a single message, paused, erased it, typed again, until finally, with a resolute exhale, he hit send:

Evelyn… I think I need you to know something. I… I love you. Fully. No hesitation. No holding back. Just… you.

Across the miles, Evelyn's phone buzzed, jarring her from the swirl of her thoughts. Her fingers trembled as she unlocked the screen and read the message. Her breath caught in her throat. The suspense that had been a constant companion, the suspense of distance, of timing, of uncertainty, was shattered by clarity, by a mirror of her own realization. Her heart swelled with an intense, almost painful joy, the recognition that they had reached the same truth independently, the same confession crystallized in separate moments, yet aligned in their essence.

She replied almost immediately, her words trembling yet deliberate:

Daniel… I love you too. I've been afraid to admit it, but… it's the truth. Always has been. Always will be.

The messages hung in the air for a heartbeat, a suspended thread connecting two hearts that had realized, separately, that love had grown fully, profoundly, despite the obstacles of timing, distance, and fear. Both felt the suspense of anticipation replaced by a slow, steady warmth that spread from their chests outward, a quiet yet unshakable certainty.

As the day progressed, both Daniel and Evelyn moved through their routines with a subtle lightness, a quiet awareness of the shared truth now bridging the miles between them. Every glance at the phone, every thought, every small action was infused with the knowledge that their hearts were aligned, that realization had struck simultaneously yet independently, and that the suspenseful tension that had once defined their relationship had transformed into a sustaining force of connection and hope.

By nightfall, the city lights blinked through the rain-streaked windows, and both sat quietly, phone in hand, savoring the words that had crossed miles and broken the suspense. Each knew the challenges ahead—the distance, the responsibilities, the unpredictable turns of life—but the realization had struck with such clarity, with such undeniable power, that nothing else could diminish it.

Daniel exhaled, a slow, deliberate release of tension, and whispered to himself: "We found each other… even when we didn't know it."

Evelyn mirrored the sentiment, smiling through the quiet tears that had formed: "Even apart… we were always together."

And in that moment, though separate, though miles apart, both hearts beat in unison, bound by the realization that love had been present all along, waiting to be acknowledged, ready to defy the suspense of distance, the uncertainty of timing, and the quiet fears that had once threatened to hold them back.

47

PRAYERS ON OPPOSITE SIDES OF THE CITY

The city was cloaked in a quiet lull, a rare stillness that made the distant hum of traffic feel like a distant memory rather than the constant pulse of life. Rain had swept through earlier, leaving the streets glistening under the soft glare of streetlights, puddles reflecting fractured patterns of neon and shadow. In two separate apartments, miles apart yet connected in ways neither could fully explain, Daniel and Evelyn knelt on the floors of their living rooms, each lost in prayer, each silently whispering words that bridged the physical distance between them.

Daniel's apartment was dimly lit, the overhead light too harsh, so he had opted to leave only a single lamp on, casting a warm circle of glow across the hardwood floor. He had shed his jacket, unbuttoned his shirt, and pushed the chaos of his day aside, allowing himself the rare luxury of stillness. His heart was heavy, not with doubt this time, but with the weight of longing and responsibility. He pressed his hands together, fingers intertwined, and closed his eyes.

"Lord," he murmured, voice low but steady, "You know my heart. You know what I feel for her. You know the miles that stretch between us, and

You know the fear that creeps in when distance tests even the strongest connections. Please... guard her heart, protect her, keep her safe from the doubts that I know will come. Help me find a way to be present, even when I cannot be there physically. Help me love her in ways that surpass my own understanding."

He exhaled, and for a moment, the room seemed to hold its breath with him. The suspense of waiting—the suspense of separation that had gripped them both for weeks—was tangible, almost a physical weight pressing against his chest. He had realized, only recently, the depth of his love, and now that knowledge sat like a seed in fertile soil, vulnerable and in need of nurturing. He prayed for wisdom, for patience, for the ability to be steady even when life's demands pulled him in every direction.

Across the city, Evelyn mirrored his actions. Her apartment was smaller, cozier, filled with the faint scent of chamomile from the tea she had brewed earlier. She knelt on a soft rug in the living room, the phone beside her silent, though she knew it would soon buzz with a message from Daniel. Her eyes were closed, her hands clasped tightly, knuckles pale from pressure.

"God," she whispered, her voice catching in the soft stillness, "You know how much he means to me. You know my heart, You know my fears. I've felt the distance like a hollow ache in my chest, and I don't want to let it take away the connection we've built. Protect him, guide him, remind him that I am here, waiting, believing, trusting that what You have brought together cannot be separated by miles or time. Help me love him wisely, patiently, and wholly."

The rain began again, gentle taps against her window creating a rhythm that echoed the racing of her heart. There was suspense in the quiet of her room—the same suspense that had defined their separation—but now it was intertwined with hope. She felt a connection, a tether stronger than the physical distance, as if the prayers themselves were threads weaving a bridge across the city, pulling their hearts closer even while the streets stretched between them.

Daniel's thoughts wandered even as he prayed. He pictured Evelyn sitting at her desk, hands clasped, eyes closed, the soft glow of her lamp illuminating the curve of her face. The mental image made his heart ache with longing, but it also strengthened his resolve. Every whispered plea, every silent invocation, felt like an unspoken promise between them and between them and God: that despite distance, despite timing, despite the weight of uncertainty, their hearts would remain tethered.

The suspense of waiting, of not knowing exactly when they would next see each other, was sharp, a knife-edge tension that made every small sound—a creak of the floorboard, a distant siren, the soft thrum of his own heartbeat—seem amplified. Daniel pressed his forehead to his hands, whispering a prayer for clarity: "Lord, let her know I am here. Let her feel my love even when I cannot speak it. Help me navigate this distance without letting fear or impatience erode the bond we share."

Meanwhile, Evelyn shifted slightly, the rug soft beneath her knees, and her thoughts mirrored his in uncanny symmetry. She had been replaying recent interactions in her mind—the messages, the brief calls, the small gestures of care that had defined their bond. Each memory now carried the weight of realization, the realization that she loved him fully. The suspense of distance, the silent ache of longing, had sharpened this awareness into clarity. She whispered again, fervently, as if the words themselves could traverse the city: "Lord, let him know that my heart beats with his, even when he is far away. Let him feel my presence, even in the silence. Protect our love, strengthen it, and help us endure this separation with grace and trust."

The two of them, kneeling miles apart, prayed for each other, unaware of the exact words being spoken on the opposite side of the city but profoundly connected in intention. Each sentence, each pause, carried suspense not just in the unknown outcomes but in the quiet acknowledgment that love stretched beyond physical proximity. The prayers became a lifeline, a conduit for presence, a reminder that hearts could remain close even when separated by streets, buildings, and distance that might have seemed insurmountable only days before.

Daniel leaned back slightly, eyes still closed, allowing the warmth of the lamp and the weight of his own devotion to center him. He remembered her smile from the last time they had been together, the soft tilt of her head when she laughed, the calm steadiness she brought to him in moments of uncertainty. He whispered another prayer, this one brimming with vulnerability: "Lord, help me cherish her, even when I cannot hold her. Help me be the man she believes I can be. And please, keep our hearts synchronized even while we are apart."

Evelyn, feeling a soft ache of longing and hope, murmured her own prayer in response to the imagined presence of his heart beside hers: "God, let him feel me even when I cannot be there. Let the miles not diminish our love, but make it resilient, patient, unshakeable. Let him know, as I know, that this is worth waiting for."

Minutes stretched into a rhythmless silence, the city outside moving on unaware of the parallel devotion unfolding in two apartments. And then, as if in response, both felt a subtle shift in their hearts—a quiet, unspoken acknowledgment that they were not alone, that their love had been recognized in fullness, and that the suspense of distance could be endured because the foundation had been cemented in something far deeper than proximity: faith, trust, and unwavering commitment.

Daniel opened his eyes and felt a surge of peace wash over him, a clarity that defied the miles. He could not yet cross the city to hold her, could not yet bridge the gap physically, but in that moment, he realized that the prayers themselves had closed the distance in ways words or actions could not. His heart felt tethered to hers, vibrating in sync, and for the first time in days, the suspense of separation shifted into anticipation rather than anxiety.

Evelyn exhaled slowly, feeling the same quiet certainty. She no longer felt the hollow ache that had haunted her during the day; instead, she felt warmth, the deep reassurance that despite miles, despite challenges, despite the weight of life pressing from all sides, their connection was alive, strong, and unbreakable.

The city outside remained oblivious, rain streaking windows, lights flickering softly, cars gliding down wet streets. Yet inside, in two apartments on opposite sides of the city, hearts had synchronized through prayer. The suspense of separation, the fragile tension of distance, had been transformed into a quiet, powerful testament: love endured not just in presence, but in devotion, in trust, in the sacred act of calling each other into one's heart even when miles intervened.

And as the night deepened, Daniel and Evelyn each rose from their knees, carrying within them a quiet courage, a steadfast hope, and a shared understanding that the prayers, the longing, and the love they nurtured in silence would guide them through the distance. For even on opposite sides of the city, hearts in prayer could bridge worlds, mend uncertainties, and fortify bonds in ways that nothing else could.

48

THE MESSAGE HE DIDN'T EXPECT

Daniel sat at his desk, the faint hum of his laptop and the soft tapping of rain against the office window providing a monotone backdrop to a day that felt heavier than usual. The new city, the new responsibilities, and the relentless pace of work had left him drained, yet restless. His fingers hovered over the keyboard, attempting to focus on spreadsheets and reports, but his mind was elsewhere, tangled in thoughts of Evelyn. The distance between them, though manageable in theory, had become a living presence, gnawing at his thoughts, threading a constant undercurrent of suspense into every moment.

It was then that his phone buzzed—a vibration so distinct that it sliced through the fog of fatigue and focus. Daniel reached for it, expecting the usual short, loving messages she had sent over the past weeks. But as he unlocked the screen, his pulse stuttered. The sender was not Evelyn. The name flashing on the screen belonged to someone entirely unexpected: Alicia Bennett.

A jolt of tension shot through him. Alicia had been a colleague in his previous city, someone he hadn't interacted with in months. They had shared projects, brief professional camaraderie, but nothing beyond the bounds of office decorum. Yet there it was—her name, bright and urgent against the digital canvas, the first ripple of suspense that promised to disturb the carefully maintained balance of his days.

Daniel's thumb hesitated over the notification. His heart pounded—not with attraction or anxiety about personal matters, but with the suspense of uncertainty. What could she want? Why now? Why would she contact him after months of silence? Every scenario he imagined seemed to carry the weight of potential disruption, threatening to intrude upon the delicate thread connecting him to Evelyn.

Finally, he tapped the message open. The words were concise but deliberate:

Daniel, I need to talk to you. It's important. Can we meet today?

A cold spike of suspense lanced through him. The brevity of the message was its own kind of tension, leaving every detail unsaid, every motive unclear. Daniel leaned back in his chair, mind racing. Meeting her could be innocent, professional, even trivial—but the uncertainty, the suspense of not knowing her intentions, left him restless and acutely aware of how vulnerable a single encounter could make him feel.

His thoughts immediately turned to Evelyn. The messages they had exchanged that morning, the prayers they had sent across the city in the quiet hours of dawn, the fragile reassurance of their connection—he felt it all threaten to unravel with the single possibility that Alicia's appearance might complicate the delicate equilibrium he and Evelyn had built. The suspense of potential disruption gnawed at him, each second stretching unnaturally as he weighed the decision.

He considered ignoring the message, delaying the encounter, reasoning that distance could protect the fragile intimacy he shared with Evelyn. Yet the suspense of leaving the message unanswered, of letting the unknown linger, pressed on him more heavily than the risk itself. He exhaled sharply, fingers trembling slightly as he typed a cautious reply:

I can meet, but only for a short time. What's this about?

The response came almost immediately:

It's personal. Please. Fifteen minutes. Café on 5th Avenue. I'll be there at three.

Daniel stared at the screen, the suspense of the day tightening around him like a vise. Fifteen minutes—so brief, yet pregnant with potential consequences. He ran a hand through his hair, pacing the small confines of his temporary apartment. Each step echoed the tension in his chest, the unpredictable tug-of-war between curiosity, responsibility, and the loyalty he felt toward Evelyn.

By three o'clock, Daniel found himself seated in the corner of the small café Alicia had chosen. The smell of roasted coffee beans filled the air, mingling with the soft murmur of patrons and the occasional clink of cutlery against porcelain. He sipped his coffee almost nervously, scanning the door repeatedly, the suspense gnawing at him. Every person who walked in brought a flicker of hope or dread; each figure seemed capable of either resolving or intensifying the tension that had built over the past hour.

When Alicia finally entered, the suspense became tangible, almost physical. Her expression was serious, tinged with urgency, and she moved with a purposeful precision that suggested this meeting was not casual. Daniel rose, greeting her with polite formality, yet his mind was a storm of questions.

"Daniel," she began immediately, settling across from him. "I know this is sudden. I wouldn't reach out if it wasn't important. There's… something you need to know."

Daniel felt his pulse accelerate. The suspense of the unknown—what something could mean—twisted in his chest. Every instinct screamed caution, every thought returned to Evelyn. He pressed his hands together, the edges of his fingers cold against one another, and leaned slightly forward.

"What is it?" he asked, voice measured despite the turmoil within.

Alicia hesitated, her gaze flickering briefly to the window, then back to him. "It's about your previous project… something that could affect you here, now. Your reputation, your position… I didn't know how to reach you until now. I tried emails, calls. Nothing worked. I wasn't sure you'd see this unless I contacted you directly."

Daniel's brow furrowed. Suspense twisted tighter in his gut. Professional stakes were one thing—but the timing, the uncertainty, the unpredictability of the encounter, layered over his emotional connection with Evelyn, made every word feel like a pivot point, a potential domino threatening to tumble the balance of his life.

He listened as Alicia detailed the situation: a contractual oversight, a minor ethical concern in previous work, something that could, if ignored, reflect poorly on him. It wasn't catastrophic, but it demanded attention—immediate attention. Daniel's mind raced, calculating next steps, weighing responses. Each word she spoke carried suspense not just in its content but in its implications, both professional and personal.

And then, amid the facts and logistics, Daniel felt another layer of suspense settle over him: the realization that his emotions were entangled in the scenario. Evelyn, miles away, unaware of this unexpected intrusion into his day, trusted him implicitly. And now, suddenly, he had a situation demanding discretion, clarity, and composure, while the suspense of distance, uncertainty, and potential consequences surged simultaneously.

When the meeting ended, Alicia left with a nod, leaving Daniel alone with his coffee and a mind swirling with tension. He had resolved the immediate issue, but the suspense remained, heavy and unrelenting. How would he explain this to Evelyn? How could he maintain the fragile trust they had nurtured while navigating the sudden complication of a past professional entanglement? The stakes, emotional and practical, felt suddenly magnified.

He stepped out into the drizzling streets, the rain slicked pavement reflecting neon signs and streetlights like fractured mirrors. Every step felt deliberate, weighted with the suspense of what awaited him at home—her messages, her calls, the possibility that she had noticed his distraction. Each footfall echoed his internal tension, the delicate balance of love, loyalty, and unpredictability hanging in the balance.

By the time Daniel finally returned to his apartment, the city had taken on a hushed, expectant tone. The rain had slowed to a soft patter, and in the quiet, his phone buzzed again. He picked it up, his heart thrumming in anticipation. The message was from Evelyn:

Hope your day went well. Can't wait to talk tonight.

The simplicity of it, the gentle normalcy, hit him with a wave of both relief and suspense. Relief, because her trust remained intact, unshaken by the day's unexpected intrusion. Suspense, because he now carried the weight of disclosure—how, when, and whether to explain the interruption without shaking the fragile equilibrium of their relationship.

Sitting on the edge of his bed, Daniel allowed himself a moment to breathe, a moment to gather the pieces of a day that had begun with professional routine but ended with emotional tension. He knew that tonight's call with Evelyn would carry suspense of its own, a careful navigation of honesty, reassurance, and vulnerability. The unexpected message from Alicia had changed the rhythm of his day, but it had also reminded him of the fragility and resilience of trust, the depth of patience required, and the weight of love stretched across distance and circumstance.

As he waited for her call, Daniel realized that suspense was no longer a mere external force—it was woven into the fabric of life, love, and connection. And while he did not yet know exactly how the conversation would unfold, he understood that the unexpected message, the surprise intrusion, had not diminished the bond between them. Instead, it had illuminated the depth of his feelings, the precision with which he needed to handle trust, and the delicate artistry of love tested by distance, uncertainty, and unforeseen events.

The suspense lingered, palpable and electric, but it was no longer threatening—it was alive, a living testament to connection, care, and the unpredictable beauty of a love that could survive interruptions, surprises, and the sharp edges of reality.

49

THE DRIVE BACK TO HER

The city had settled into a tentative quiet by the time Daniel slid into his car, the hum of the engine the only sound accompanying the racing of his thoughts. Rain still clung to the streets, glistening like fractured glass under the scattered glow of streetlights, the reflections forming a chaotic, hypnotic pattern on the asphalt. He gripped the steering wheel tightly, knuckles pale, as if the tension in his hands could anchor the storm in his mind. Tonight, he was driving back to her—not to visit casually, not to meet halfway—but to close the distance that had stretched too long, to remind himself and her that despite distance, despite circumstance, the pull between them could not be denied.

The suspense that had shadowed their recent days pressed on him like a tangible weight. The unexpected message from Alicia earlier had stirred unease, though he had resolved the matter professionally. Yet the lingering tension was not just about her—it was the anxiety of reentry, of crossing the threshold of her life after a day thick with complications. Every red light, every narrow lane, every sharp turn seemed to echo his heartbeat, every moment a suspended breath. He could feel the pulse of anticipation thrumming through his chest as he navigated the slick streets.

The drive was long, but each mile carried its own rhythm of suspense. Daniel found himself replaying the day in fragments—the professional disruption, the lingering worry about how it might be perceived, the emotional threads of connection he had with Evelyn. Questions that had no immediate answers tumbled through his mind: Would she sense the distraction in his voice? Would she question the pause in his messages? Could he convey both honesty and reassurance without allowing the fragile balance they had nurtured to tip?

Despite the storm of thoughts, there was also a steady undercurrent of certainty. He loved her. That truth, now crystallized in ways that weeks of distance and silence could not obscure, guided his hands, focused his eyes, and drove his decisions. But certainty did not ease suspense—it sharpened it. Knowing his heart belonged to her, knowing hers likely beat in tandem with his, made every unexpected event, every silence, every unspoken word pregnant with possibility.

As he maneuvered onto the highway, the headlights of oncoming traffic glimmered like a river of stars, illuminating the road in intermittent bursts. The windshield wipers kept a steady rhythm, the motion blurring the cityscape into streaks of silver and amber. Each motion, each vibration of the car beneath him, seemed amplified in significance. The drive was not just physical; it was emotional, spiritual, a journey across the tension that had built between them, a journey into vulnerability, into revelation, into anticipation.

His mind wandered to Evelyn—her laughter, the curve of her smile, the subtle intensity of her gaze in their most recent video call. He remembered the small gestures, the almost-inconsequential touches, the private jokes, the quiet confidences they had shared. The realization that he loved her fully had changed the landscape of his thoughts, infusing ordinary memories with profound significance. Now, the suspense of driving toward her was intertwined with the expectation of emotional reckoning: would she know the depth of what he felt without his words faltering under the weight of reality?

A sharp curve ahead jolted him out of the reverie, and he gripped the wheel tighter, heart hammering. The rain had grown heavier, and the reflection of streetlights on the wet asphalt created disorienting patterns. For a brief moment, he felt the fragile uncertainty of control—not just over the car, but over the moments to come. The suspense was no longer abstract; it was immediate, visceral, threading through every nerve.

He thought about the words he might say, rehearsed phrases and confessions that could convey the fullness of his feelings without overwhelming her. The danger of miscommunication had never seemed more acute. A misstep, a poorly chosen phrase, a hesitation—any could tip the delicate equilibrium they had maintained. Yet the urgency of being near her, of bridging the gap that distance had enforced, demanded courage, demanded honesty, demanded a readiness to confront whatever awaited him.

As he approached familiar streets, streets that reminded him of her apartment, the familiar landmarks both comforted and intensified suspense. Each turn carried memories: the café where they had met, the small park where they had lingered after a chance encounter, the lamppost outside her building that had cast soft golden light over countless quiet conversations. The cityscape, though unchanged in physicality, seemed transformed in his mind by the emotional resonance of proximity.

Finally, the familiar façade of her building came into view, illuminated softly by the evening lights. He slowed, the car moving through puddles that rippled like liquid mirrors, reflecting fragments of his thoughts, his fears, his longing. The suspense that had coiled tightly in his chest for hours now expanded into a heady mixture of relief, anticipation, and trepidation. Every moment stretched, thick with possibility. Would she be waiting outside? Would she sense his arrival before he knocked? Would the moment live up to the intensity that had built during the drive?

Parking the car, he took a deliberate breath. His fingers remained on the steering wheel, knuckles white, as he gathered himself. The suspense of action—the crossing of the threshold from observer to participant, from distance to presence—was almost unbearable. He stepped out into the cool, damp evening, the scent of rain heavy in the air, and felt the city's silence press around him, a counterpoint to the storm of emotion within.

He climbed the familiar steps to her apartment, each footfall measured, deliberate. The suspense of her reaction, the uncertainty of what awaited, pulsed with every heartbeat. When he finally reached her door, his hand hovered over the knob, hesitating. Even this simple action felt laden with tension—opening the door meant confronting the entirety of his feelings, his confessions, his hopes, and his fears.

With a deep inhale, he turned the knob. The door swung open, revealing Evelyn in the soft glow of the hallway light. She looked up, eyes wide, breath caught for just a fraction of a second, and then a smile—subtle, radiant, trembling with the same suspense that mirrored his own.

"Daniel…" she breathed, the single word carrying months of anticipation, longing, and unspoken realization.

He stepped inside, closing the door behind him, the click resonating like a punctuation mark on the suspense of the evening. She stood there, framed in the doorway, hands slightly extended as if unsure whether to embrace or observe him, and he felt the gravity of the moment. Every mile, every hour, every fleeting doubt had led to this: the immediate, electric reality of proximity, of presence, of shared breath and heartbeat.

Without words, they closed the remaining distance between them, each step deliberate, the suspense of the drive culminating in this quiet reckoning.

His hand reached for hers, their fingers intertwining naturally, perfectly, as though the separation had never existed. The tension dissolved, replaced by a warmth that radiated through every fiber of their beings.

They moved together into the living room, rain still pattering softly against the windows, creating a cocoon of intimacy. Daniel sank onto the sofa, and Evelyn sat beside him, close enough that their shoulders brushed, close enough to feel the steady pulse of connection that had endured miles, time, and suspense. The drive back to her had been more than a physical journey—it had been a navigation of emotions, an endurance of anticipation, a confrontation with vulnerability, and a reckoning with the intensity of love realized.

For the first time in weeks, Daniel allowed himself to exhale fully, letting the suspense of distance, the uncertainty of the day, and the anticipation of reunion dissipate in the presence of the one who mattered most. Evelyn's hand found his, and in that simple, deliberate gesture, all the tension of miles apart, unexpected messages, and lingering fears melted into the certainty of connection.

Outside, the city continued its indifferent rhythm, the streets shimmering with the residue of rain, the lights flickering softly. But inside, the suspense had transformed into shared presence, the kind that comes not from words but from being near, from the tactile affirmation of closeness, from the quiet understanding that no matter what the day had held, no matter what unexpected messages arrived, the bond they nurtured had endured, and their hearts were finally in sync once more.

Daniel leaned back, eyes meeting hers, and whispered, "I'm here."

Evelyn smiled, a soft exhale of relief and joy, and replied, "I know."

In that moment, the suspense was no longer sharp—it was a memory, a prelude to the peace of presence, the fulfillment of longing, and the quiet certainty that some drives, no matter how fraught with tension, were always worth it when they led back to the one who held your heart.

—-

I can continue next with Chapter 50: "The Evening That Spoke Volumes", where Daniel and Evelyn navigate the aftermath of reunion, exploring subtle tensions, confessions, and emotional intimacy.

Do you want me to continue with that next?

50

I DON'T WANT TO WALK AWAY FROM THIS

The evening air was thick with the scent of rain-soaked streets, carrying a faint tang of asphalt and wet leaves into the open windows of Evelyn's apartment. The city lights flickered softly against the glass panes, casting long, wavering shadows across the room. Inside, the quiet was nearly deafening—not an absence of noise, but a deliberate pause, a suspenseful holding of breath that made every sound, every movement, every glance feel weighted with meaning.

Daniel stood by the window, the soft hum of the radiator blending with the distant siren wail outside. His hands rested lightly on the sill, fingers tapping a rhythm that mirrored the rapid pulse of his heart. He had come back to her, had crossed the city, endured the suspense of traffic, the tension of unknown encounters, and the uncertainty of her reception—and now, standing mere feet from her, he felt the gravity of all those miles collapse into this single moment.

Evelyn sat on the sofa, knees drawn slightly toward her chest, a mug of tea held loosely in her hands. Her gaze was fixed on him, steady yet unflinching, as if trying to read not just his face but the entire weight of his emotions.

The subtle tremor in her shoulders betrayed her calm exterior; she, too, felt the suspense of the evening, the quiet storm of emotions that had been building for weeks, months even.

Daniel finally turned, meeting her eyes with a gaze that was at once intense and tender. The silence stretched between them, thick and suffocating, yet electric, charged with the anticipation of unspoken confessions and vulnerabilities too long suppressed.

"I—" he began, but the words seemed to falter, caught in the maze of his chest where longing, fear, hope, and love tangled together. He exhaled slowly, grounding himself. "Evelyn… I don't want to walk away from this."

Her eyes widened just slightly, the faintest lift of her brow signaling both surprise and cautious hope. The suspense of her reaction—would she reject him, hesitate, retreat?—pressed against his chest like a physical force. Yet he continued, the words tumbling from a place deeper than reasoning, deeper than the fear of vulnerability.

"I've spent days thinking about this… about us, about every little thing that's brought me to this moment. And I realized… I can't ignore it anymore. I love you, Evelyn. I don't want to keep pretending that distance, timing, or fear can define what's real between us. I don't want to walk away from this… from you."

Evelyn's hands tightened around her mug, a nervous gesture that betrayed the intensity of her own emotions. Her chest rose and fell rapidly, caught between the desire to leap forward into his arms and the need to protect herself from being hurt. The suspense, the delicate tension of the moment, hung thickly between them—an invisible wire stretching taut across the room.

She swallowed, her voice trembling slightly as she finally spoke. "Daniel…

I… I've been afraid too. Afraid that if I let myself feel fully, I'd lose control. Afraid that distance, time, or… life itself would pull us apart before we even began. But… hearing you say that… I realize I don't want to walk away either."

The words, simple yet profound, sent a shiver through him. The suspense that had been a constant companion—the unknown outcomes, the tentative hope, the quiet terror of rejection—shifted into a tense, electric anticipation of closeness. Every heartbeat, every glance, every small movement seemed magnified, the room itself charged with the gravity of unspoken desires finally given voice.

Daniel stepped closer, each footfall deliberate, measured, the suspense coiling tighter with every inch he closed. Evelyn remained rooted on the sofa, but her eyes followed him, wide and luminous, filled with a mixture of fear, hope, and the fragile excitement of recognition—recognition that they were both standing on the edge of something profound, something worth risking everything for.

He stopped just short of the sofa, the space between them electric, a fragile boundary that seemed both insignificant and monumental. "Evelyn," he whispered, his voice low, deliberate, "I've waited too long to admit this. I've been cautious because I didn't want to hurt you, didn't want to rush anything, didn't want to lose what we already had… but I can't hide it anymore. You're everything I've been searching for, everything I didn't even know I needed. I can't walk away from this. I won't."

Her lips parted slightly, a small exhale escaping as if she had been holding her breath for hours, days, months. The suspense of the moment pressed on her too—the uncertainty, the vulnerability, the raw, unfiltered truth of what she felt. Finally, she spoke, her voice steady despite the tremor in her chest.

"Daniel... I feel the same. Every day, every moment apart, I've realized... I've realized that you're the one I want. That I can't imagine moving forward without you. That I... I don't want to walk away from this either."

A tremor of relief, joy, and longing coursed through him. The suspense—the tension of uncertainty that had shadowed their lives for weeks—transformed in an instant into an electrifying affirmation of connection. Daniel moved the final distance between them, closing the space with deliberate care, and gently took her hands in his. Their fingers intertwined, the warmth of touch grounding the storm of emotion that had surged through both of them.

Evelyn's eyes glistened with unspoken tears, and she allowed herself to lean slightly into him, a subtle acknowledgment that the moment, though fragile, was theirs to claim. The suspense of distance, the tension of anticipation, and the fear of losing each other melted into the quiet intensity of presence, a presence charged with all the words they had left unspoken for far too long.

Daniel lowered his forehead to hers, breath mingling, hearts thundering in a shared rhythm. "I've never been more certain of anything in my life," he murmured, voice thick with emotion. "Every step that brought me here... every choice, every delay, every anxious moment... it all led me to you. And now that I'm here, I can't imagine letting go. I don't want to walk away from this... from us."

Evelyn's lips curved into a soft, trembling smile, and she whispered back, "Neither do I. I've been scared... but I trust this. I trust us. I trust that what we have is worth every risk, every heartbeat of suspense, every moment of uncertainty. I don't want to walk away either."

The room seemed to shrink around them, the city outside fading into an insignificant blur. The suspense that had defined so many of their days—the quiet tension of waiting, the anxiety of distance, the delicate navigation of emotions—was replaced by an immediacy of presence, an intimacy that needed no words beyond those already spoken. Their hands remained intertwined, their foreheads pressed together, breaths mingling, hearts echoing in tandem as if the universe had paused to witness the quiet culmination of longing.

Time became irrelevant. The suspense, the careful balance of caution and desire, had reached its apex and released in the quiet affirmation of love declared and reciprocated. Every fear, every hesitation, every "what if" that had shadowed them faded into the background, leaving only the undeniable truth: they belonged to each other, fully, deliberately, without reservation.

Daniel finally pulled back slightly, just enough to look into her eyes, tracing the curve of her smile, the light of her gaze. "We've waited long enough," he said softly, "and we've endured enough uncertainty. I want to move forward with you... openly, fully, without holding anything back. I don't want to walk away, Evelyn. Not now, not ever."

Her fingers tightened around his, a gentle yet insistent grip that spoke volumes. "Then let's not," she whispered. "Let's step into this together, knowing it won't always be easy, but knowing it's worth it. I don't want to walk away from this either—not today, not ever."

The suspense of months—the distance, the uncertainty, the silent questions, the private fears—had led them here. And in the quiet glow of the living room, with rain streaking the windows and the city lights flickering softly outside, Daniel and Evelyn allowed themselves to surrender fully to the reality they had longed for. No words were needed beyond those spoken; the rest was conveyed in proximity, in breath, in the gentle interlacing of fingers and the unspoken promise that they would endure, together.

For the first time in what felt like forever, suspense became anticipation, tension became warmth, and uncertainty became certainty. And as they held each other, softly, deliberately, fully, both knew that they had finally arrived at the place where love, patience, and unwavering commitment converged. Neither would walk away again.

VI

DESTINY FULFILLED

51

LEARNING TO LOVE AT THE RIGHT PACE

The room was bathed in the soft glow of the bedside lamp, its warm light spilling across the walls in gentle, uneven strokes. The rain outside had subsided to a fine drizzle, tapping lightly against the windows, creating a rhythm that mirrored the quiet intensity of the moment. Daniel and Evelyn sat across from each other on the edge of the sofa, a careful distance maintained, though it was a distance born of mutual understanding rather than avoidance. The suspense of the day had subsided into a more subtle tension now—one that held promise, patience, and the delicate negotiation of hearts learning how to intertwine without losing their individuality.

Daniel watched her as she adjusted the throw blanket around her shoulders, the subtle movement exposing the familiar curve of her neck, the faint glimmer of vulnerability in her eyes. He felt the familiar surge of protectiveness, admiration, and longing, but there was a restraint in his chest that had not been there before. He realized, almost with a start, that love was not just the grand gestures, the confessions, or the dramatic reconciliations—it was the quiet, patient rhythm of learning one another at the right pace.

"I want us to take our time," Daniel said finally, his voice low, deliberate, and charged with sincerity. "I don't mean to slow us down, but… I don't want to rush through something so fragile, so precious. I've learned that sometimes, moving too fast can make even the strongest connection falter."

Evelyn tilted her head, studying him with a mixture of curiosity and relief. "I was hoping you'd say that," she admitted. Her voice, soft but steady, carried a weight of unspoken fears—past hurts, disappointments, and the cautious hope that this could finally be different. "I've been scared of moving too fast too. I've seen love fail when people ignore the pace it needs, and I… I don't want that for us."

The suspense of their conversation was not dramatic or tension-filled in the way Daniel had experienced earlier in the day—it was quieter, more intricate, like the threads of a tapestry being woven together slowly, deliberately. Each word carried weight, each pause was pregnant with meaning, each glance a silent acknowledgment of the importance of patience.

Daniel shifted slightly, leaning forward and resting his elbows on his knees. "We've both been cautious," he said, "because we know what's at stake. But tonight, I realized that we don't need to measure love by the speed of events or the number of milestones reached. Love… true love… is learning the rhythm of the other person, respecting boundaries, and growing together without forcing the pace."

Evelyn's lips curved into a tentative smile. She reached out, lightly brushing her fingers against his hand, a touch that was both intimate and restrained. "That's exactly what I needed to hear," she whispered. "I want to give us the time to understand each other, to fall into love in a way that's deliberate, not desperate. I want the moments to matter, every one of them, without losing ourselves in the rush of emotion."

Daniel felt a profound relief, but also a renewed suspense—one of anticipation rather than uncertainty. The anticipation of discovering more about Evelyn, of exploring the depths of her heart, of allowing both their pasts and their present selves to coexist within this burgeoning love. He realized that suspense in love wasn't always about fear or danger; sometimes it was about the quiet thrill of possibilities, the uncharted territory of intimacy, and the careful unfolding of hearts willing to trust one another.

He reached for the blanket draped across her shoulders, letting it fall gently to the floor as a symbolic gesture of letting go of hesitation. "I want us to be intentional," he said. "Intentional with our time, our words, our moments. Every laugh, every conversation, every quiet silence... I want it to count. And I want us to be patient with the parts of ourselves that need time to open, to trust, to love fully."

Evelyn's eyes glistened, the reflection of the lamp catching in the corners, illuminating the vulnerability she had carried into this room. "I've wanted that for so long," she said. "A love that respects who I am, that doesn't try to hurry my heart. I've been hurt before—so badly that I forgot what it felt like to trust, to feel safe in someone's presence. But with you, I... I feel the possibility of it all over again. And I want to explore that, slowly, deliberately."

The room was quiet, save for the soft sound of rain against the window, the hum of the radiator, and the steady rhythm of their synchronized breaths. Suspense hung in the air like an invisible thread, but it was no longer a tense, anxious suspense—it was a tender, anticipatory tension, the kind that makes every glance, every gesture, every word feel charged with potential.

Daniel moved slightly closer, just enough that the tips of their knees brushed. Evelyn did not pull away; instead, she leaned subtly toward him, her hand still resting lightly on her mug. The careful closeness was deliberate, a way of testing boundaries, exploring the new rhythm of intimacy without rushing it.

"I want to learn every little detail about you," Daniel whispered. "Not just your laugh, your smile, or your favorite coffee, but the things that make you who you are—your fears, your dreams, your quiet moments of doubt. And I want to be patient with myself too, patient with the mistakes I've made, patient with the things I can't fix immediately. Loving you… it's not about perfection. It's about presence."

Evelyn reached out again, this time letting her fingers rest lightly over his hand, intertwining just enough to create warmth without overwhelming the delicacy of the moment. "I think that's what makes this different," she said softly. "We're not rushing to define everything, not rushing to fill every silence with words. We're learning each other, slowly, like we're unwrapping a gift that's been waiting a long time to be opened carefully."

Daniel's heart swelled, the suspense of the evening now a gentle tension, a thrilling anticipation of shared discovery. He could feel the pulse of possibility threading through the room, weaving between them like an electric current, urging but never forcing, whispering of connection yet demanding patience.

"I want us to be brave," he continued, his voice low, deliberate. "Brave enough to be honest, to be vulnerable, to confront the parts of ourselves we've hidden from others. Brave enough to say what we feel without fear of judgment or rejection. Brave enough to trust that the other person will meet us with the same patience and care. That's how we'll learn to love at the right pace."

Evelyn's eyes shimmered with unshed tears, and she nodded slowly, as though letting each word sink into her bones. "I want that too," she said. "I don't want a love that runs ahead of us, outpacing our hearts. I want a love that grows steadily, deliberately, so that even if the world shifts, even if storms come, we'll still have a foundation that can hold us."

Daniel reached across the small space between them, his hand now resting firmly over hers. The contact was gentle, deliberate, and full of promise. "Then let's promise," he said, "to be patient. To be honest. To trust in the pace of our hearts, not the pressure of the world. Let's take this slow, not because we're afraid, but because we know it's worth it. Every moment, every conversation, every glance... let's make it matter."

Evelyn's lips curved into a soft, tearful smile. "I promise," she whispered. "I promise to love you at the right pace. To be patient, to be honest, to trust. I don't want to miss a single piece of what we have because we rushed through it."

The suspense of their unspoken fears, the tension of past disappointments, the uncertainty of distance, all melted away into the quiet intensity of shared commitment. Their hands remained intertwined, fingers weaving together naturally, and the soft warmth of presence settled over them like a blanket. They were learning—learning to love at the right pace, learning to navigate vulnerability without fear, learning that the slow unfolding of connection could be just as thrilling, just as suspenseful, and infinitely more enduring than the rush of instant passion.

Outside, the city hummed quietly, unaware of the delicate choreography unfolding within the walls of Evelyn's apartment. But inside, every glance, every sigh, every gentle touch was charged with the weight of trust, anticipation, and love's slow, deliberate rhythm. They were discovering each other in real time, aware that patience was not a restraint but a pathway—a pathway to a love that could endure, a love that could thrive, a love that could survive anything because it had been nurtured carefully, intentionally, and with reverence.

And as Daniel and Evelyn sat there, hands clasped, hearts aligning, and eyes locked in mutual understanding, the suspense of the evening became a quiet, steady hum—a promise of tomorrow, of every tomorrow they would navigate together, learning to love fully, deliberately, and at exactly the right pace.

52

PLANNING A FUTURE WITHOUT FEAR

The first light of dawn filtered through the half-drawn curtains, casting soft, golden streaks across the living room where Daniel and Evelyn sat side by side. The city outside was slowly stirring—the low hum of engines, distant footsteps, and the occasional chirp of a bird—but inside, the quiet was deliberate, reflective, and brimming with a tension that was not discomforting but anticipatory. It was the suspense of possibilities: the kind that comes when two hearts are aligned yet daring to imagine a shared future while still holding onto the fragility of hope.

Daniel leaned back on the sofa, running his fingers along the edge of his coffee mug, the heat warming his hands while the warmth in his chest throbbed with an equal intensity. Today was different. There were no sudden messages, no missed appointments, no accidental encounters—the kind of suspense that had filled their days before. Today, the suspense came from the uncertainty of their next steps, the delicate challenge of planning a life together without letting fear dictate the pace.

"I've been thinking a lot about us," Daniel began, his voice calm but charged with the weight of everything unsaid. "About what it means to build something together, not just for a few weeks or months, but for a lifetime. And I realized… the future we want… it shouldn't be shaped by fear. It shouldn't be determined by what we're afraid might happen. It should be intentional, deliberate, and rooted in trust."

Evelyn nodded, her eyes fixed on him, reflecting both the morning light and the intensity of the conversation. She had felt that same tension, the unspoken question of how to step forward when the heart yearned for connection but the mind remembered past disappointments. The suspense between them was subtle, a delicate thread stretched across the room as they both weighed dreams against caution.

"I know," she said softly, her fingers brushing against his on the sofa arm. "Fear has a way of sneaking in, even when you think you're ready to be brave. I've felt it—every time I imagine the two of us, every time I let myself consider what a future with you could look like. The fear of losing what we have before it even fully exists… it's always there."

Daniel took a deep breath, leaning forward to meet her gaze fully. "Exactly. But what if we made a pact—not just words, but a real pact—to plan a future without letting fear rule us? To make decisions together, to build trust in small moments, to commit not just emotionally but practically, even when it feels uncertain?"

The suspense in her eyes deepened, a mixture of awe and hesitation. Planning a future together was no trivial matter; it was a leap into vulnerability, a surrender of control, and a dance with the unknown. Yet, Daniel's presence—the calm, steady certainty in his words—offered her a kind of courage she hadn't realized she still possessed.

"I want that," Evelyn whispered, almost reluctantly, as if speaking it aloud might somehow jinx the possibility. "I want a future with you, but it has to be without fear. I want us to be intentional, to create something strong enough to survive the doubts, the distance, the storms... everything life throws at us."

Daniel reached out, taking both her hands in his, the warmth of touch grounding the conversation in the reality of their connection. "Then let's start now," he said. "Not by making grand promises or imagining impossible scenarios, but by taking practical steps. By communicating openly, by supporting each other's goals, by planning together in a way that strengthens our bond instead of letting it fray under pressure."

Evelyn's breath caught, a shiver of anticipation running through her. The suspense of this morning was different from any before—it wasn't about accidental encounters or longing-filled silences. It was about the immense, thrilling responsibility of choice: the decision to commit to a life together, to craft it carefully, deliberately, and with eyes wide open to the possibilities and challenges alike.

Daniel pulled a notebook from the coffee table drawer, its leather cover soft under his fingers. "I was thinking," he said, flipping it open to a blank page, "we could start planning... really planning. Short-term goals, long-term dreams, things we want to experience together. Not out of pressure, but out of purpose. We decide together what matters most, and we tackle it without fear dictating our actions."

Evelyn leaned forward, curiosity and cautious excitement blending in her expression. "I like that," she said, her fingers brushing the edge of the notebook. "It feels... grounding. Like we're creating a roadmap, not just for today or tomorrow, but for a life that belongs to both of us. One step at a time, deliberate, and without letting fear control our choices."

Daniel nodded, scribbling down a few ideas in the notebook: first steps toward shared goals, dreams of travel, plans for professional growth that supported both of their ambitions, and small but meaningful rituals that could anchor their relationship. Each word he wrote was deliberate, an act of intention that carried weight far beyond the ink on paper. It was a declaration that they were ready to move forward together, despite the suspense of unknowns.

"Let's not rush anything," Daniel added, looking up at her. "Even while planning, we move carefully. Every step should feel right, not forced. And if something feels uncertain, we pause, talk it through, adjust. That way, fear doesn't have a chance to sabotage what we're building."

Evelyn smiled, the tension in her shoulders softening slightly. "I like that," she said again. "I've spent so long letting fear dictate my choices—afraid of disappointment, afraid of heartbreak, afraid of losing myself. But with you… I think I can learn to trust differently. To step forward while holding onto myself, and step forward with you without fear."

The suspense of the morning deepened, not with anxiety but with possibility. Every plan they discussed, every goal they considered, every future scenario they mapped out carried with it the thrill of risk and the promise of reward. It was a suspense that demanded courage, patience, and trust—a deliberate tension that made their connection stronger, more resilient, and infinitely more meaningful.

Daniel closed the notebook gently, his eyes locking with hers. "We're learning to love not just emotionally but practically," he said. "To make choices that reflect our commitment, to take risks with intention, to plan a future that feels real and attainable. Fear doesn't have a place in this—not because we ignore it, but because we face it together, with clarity and courage."

Evelyn reached across and rested her head briefly against his shoulder, a quiet gesture that spoke volumes. "I'm ready for that," she murmured. "Ready to plan, ready to take steps, ready to trust… and ready to face whatever comes next with you by my side. I don't want fear to control us anymore. I want us to create a future that's ours, deliberate, and without hesitation."

The suspense lingered, a quiet hum of anticipation, not anxiety. Outside, the city was fully awake now, unaware of the delicate choreography unfolding in a small apartment, where two people had decided to confront fear, embrace uncertainty, and intentionally craft a shared future. It was a suspense born of hope, courage, and the thrilling responsibility of choice—the kind of suspense that was far more profound than any fleeting excitement, for it held the potential to shape the rest of their lives.

Daniel tightened his hold on her hand, feeling the warmth, the promise, and the grounding reality of connection. "Then let's do it," he said softly. "One step at a time. Together. Without fear. We create, we plan, and we move forward... deliberately, intentionally, and with full hearts."

Evelyn lifted her gaze to meet his, eyes bright with determination and trust. "Together," she affirmed, her voice steady and unwavering. "No fear. Only us, only this, only what we decide to build. Step by step, heart by heart, moment by moment."

And in that quiet, suspended morning, as the sunlight shifted across the room and the city outside continued its hum, Daniel and Evelyn allowed themselves to imagine, to dream, and to plan. They embraced the thrill of suspense not as an obstacle, but as a guide—an invisible thread leading them toward a future that was deliberate, intentional, and fearless, where love was both the journey and the destination.

The notebook rested on the table between them, filled with possibilities, sketches of dreams, and the tangible outline of a life they could shape together. The suspense of the unknown remained, but now it was a companion, not a threat—an invitation to step boldly into a shared future, one day, one plan, one deliberate choice at a time.

53

MEETING THE FAMILIES

The car ride to Evelyn's parents' house was quiet, save for the occasional hum of the tires over the rain-slicked pavement. The city had returned to a subdued rhythm, as if the morning's excitement had faded into a careful normalcy, leaving space for anticipation to grow quietly in the back of their minds. Daniel drove with a steady hand, but his chest throbbed with a nervous energy that made every stoplight, every curve, every flicker of headlights feel magnified. This was a step neither of them could retreat from—the meeting of families was a threshold that demanded not just courage but tact, humility, and authenticity.

Evelyn sat in the passenger seat, her hands folded neatly on her lap, fingers occasionally intertwining as if to anchor herself against her own nervous energy. She kept stealing glances at Daniel, noting the slight tightening of his jaw, the subtle twitch in his left hand as he gripped the steering wheel. "Are you nervous?" she asked, her voice soft, almost conspiratorial, the kind of whisper that felt intimate against the backdrop of the car's quiet.

Daniel exhaled, running a hand through his hair. "A little," he admitted. "I want them to like me, sure, but more than that… I want them to see you happy, to see us as something real, not just two people pretending to be ready. I want this to feel genuine, not forced."

Evelyn's lips curved into a small, reassuring smile. "It will," she said. "They've seen me grow, they've seen me make choices. And if they can see how happy you make me, they'll understand. But..." She paused, her eyes glinting with a mixture of excitement and caution, "I can't lie, I'm nervous too. This is my family, and they've always... well, they've always mattered a lot to me."

Daniel reached over, letting his hand brush hers lightly—a silent acknowledgment that he was in this with her, ready to navigate the suspense and uncertainty together. "Then we'll do it together," he said. "Step by step. We'll show them who we are, without pretending or hiding anything. Let's make this an introduction they'll remember... in a good way."

The house came into view, nestled at the end of a quiet cul-de-sac, its warm exterior lights casting long shadows across the wet driveway. Evelyn took a deep breath, gripping her purse tightly, and then exhaled slowly. "Here goes everything," she whispered, as if the words themselves could summon courage and resolve.

Daniel parked the car, cutting the engine, and for a moment, they both sat in silence, listening to the faint patter of the last remnants of rain against the windshield. The suspense of the moment was palpable, a delicate tension stretching between them and the threshold of the house they were about to enter.

Evelyn led the way to the door, hand hovering over the brass doorknob as her chest rose and fell with controlled breaths. She glanced at Daniel, meeting his eyes, and saw mirrored there the mixture of anticipation, nervousness, and determination. "Ready?" she asked.

"As I'll ever be," he replied, and together they stepped inside.

The interior of the house was familiar, comforting, and yet charged with the suspense of expectation. The scent of freshly brewed coffee mingled with the faint aroma of baked goods, creating an atmosphere of warmth that contrasted with the nervous tension in Daniel's chest. Evelyn's parents appeared in the living room moments later, smiles warming their faces but eyes sharp and assessing, scanning Daniel carefully as if measuring the weight of his intentions.

"Evelyn, Daniel," her mother said, voice gentle but firm, holding out her hand first to him. Daniel rose, extending his own hand with steady politeness, bowing slightly in respect. "It's wonderful to finally meet you," he said, each word deliberate, careful not to betray the nervousness he felt beneath the composed exterior.

Her father followed, taller, broader, and imposing, but not unapproachable. His handshake was firm, eyes locking with Daniel's in a silent test of character, a measured appraisal. "I've heard a lot about you," he said, his tone neutral but carrying an undertone of expectation. "I hope everything I've heard is true."

Daniel nodded, a small, respectful smile tugging at his lips. "I hope I can live up to the things you've heard," he said, voice steady, "and more importantly, I promise to do my best to make Evelyn happy. That's my main goal, always."

The suspense in the room thickened, subtle yet undeniable. Each movement, each glance, each carefully chosen word carried significance. Daniel was acutely aware that this introduction was about more than appearances—it was about character, integrity, and the unspoken promise that he would honor not only Evelyn but the family that had nurtured her.

The conversation began slowly, carefully, with Daniel answering questions about his career, his background, and his values. Evelyn's parents listened intently, occasionally exchanging subtle looks of approval, while Evelyn remained close, offering quiet interjections that softened the formality of the exchange. The suspense was not just in Daniel's performance but in the silent question hanging in the air: would they sense the sincerity, the depth of his commitment, the respect he held for their daughter?

Hours passed in this delicate balance, and slowly, the tension began to shift from cautious appraisal to tentative warmth. Daniel's humor, gentle and measured, found its way into the conversation, eliciting laughter from both parents, small but genuine. His honesty and vulnerability, shared without pretense, gradually softened the initial scrutiny, replacing it with curiosity and respect.

Evelyn watched him closely, her heart swelling with quiet pride and relief. The suspense of the meeting—the anxiety of judgment, the fear of disapproval—began to dissolve into a shared understanding. She saw, in her parents' relaxed smiles and subtle nods, that Daniel's character and intentions were clear. They were witnessing not just a suitor, but someone willing to embrace the responsibility of love with sincerity and care.

As the evening progressed, Daniel and Evelyn found themselves engaged in deeper conversations with her parents—discussions about values, dreams, and life philosophies. The suspense lingered, not as tension, but as an exciting recognition that these moments, these questions, and these interactions were shaping the foundation for a future they were consciously planning together.

At one point, her mother excused herself to the kitchen, leaving Daniel and Evelyn alone with her father. The silence that fell was different now—less anxious, more reflective, almost intimate in its intensity. "I can see why she cares for you," her father said quietly, tone no longer formal but thoughtful. "It's clear you respect her, and that's more important than anything else."

Daniel nodded, his chest swelling with a quiet pride and relief he hadn't realized he'd been holding back. "I care for her deeply," he said. "And I intend to always honor that care, no matter what challenges come our way."

Her father's expression softened, and he extended a hand, not in judgment, but in quiet acknowledgment. "Then I suppose my job as her father just became a little easier," he said, a small smile tugging at the corners of his mouth.

By the time her mother returned with tea and desserts, the room's atmosphere had shifted completely. The initial suspense, the delicate dance of introductions, approvals, and apprehensions, had transformed into a tentative camaraderie, a shared understanding that the bond between Daniel and Evelyn was genuine, deliberate, and deserving of support.

As they prepared to leave, Daniel took Evelyn's hand in his, feeling the quiet pulse of connection and trust between them. Her parents walked them to the door, expressions soft, approving, and subtly affectionate. The suspense of the evening—the uncertainty of judgment, the fear of disapproval, the anxious anticipation of first impressions—had resolved not in a dramatic revelation, but in the quiet, deliberate recognition of sincerity, integrity, and love's patient unfolding.

Outside, the air was crisp, carrying the faint scent of evening rain. Daniel and Evelyn walked to the car, fingers intertwined, hearts lighter yet still thrumming with the thrill of what had just transpired. The suspense had not vanished completely; it lingered like a soft undercurrent, a reminder that every step forward in love carried weight, intention, and the need for courage. But it was a suspense tempered by hope, validation, and the shared knowledge that the first, often intimidating threshold had been crossed together.

As Daniel drove back through the quiet streets, Evelyn rested her head against his shoulder, feeling the warmth, security, and silent promise of shared future plans. "We did it," she whispered softly.

"We did," Daniel replied, voice low, steady, and infused with satisfaction. "And this is just the beginning. Every step we take now... every plan, every choice, every moment... we'll face it together. Without fear, without hesitation. That's how we build a future."

Evelyn smiled, closing her eyes for a brief moment, savoring the lingering suspense of possibility, the quiet triumph of shared courage, and the promise of countless steps ahead. "Together," she murmured. "Always together."

And as the car carried them home, the city lights reflecting off wet pavement like tiny points of hope, Daniel and Evelyn held onto one another, aware that the suspense of love was not in its unknowns, but in the deliberate, courageous choices to navigate those unknowns together, hand in hand, heart with heart, ready to face every challenge and every triumph that awaited them.

54

A SURPRISE THAT STOLE HER BREATH

Evelyn had spent the day lost in ordinary routines, convinced that nothing extraordinary could punctuate the rhythm of her Thursday. The morning had begun with the predictable clatter of her alarm, the smell of brewing coffee, and the familiar tap-tap of her keyboard at work. Yet, beneath the surface of her ordinary day, a subtle undercurrent of anticipation hummed—she just didn't know what it was for. It was that quiet, inexplicable feeling that maybe, somewhere, a shift was about to occur.

Her phone buzzed around noon, a message from Daniel that simply read, "Meet me at the park in an hour. Dress comfortably." There was no context, no explanation, and that was precisely what set her pulse racing. Suspense, the kind that made her stomach twist in an unusual but exhilarating way, took hold. Daniel rarely sent messages like this—he was always deliberate, measured, intentional. The ambiguity of this message ignited her imagination. Was it a casual outing? A spontaneous adventure? Or something else entirely, something that would make her heart race in ways she hadn't anticipated?

By the time she arrived at the park, the late afternoon sun was bathing the city in gold, filtering through the tall trees and casting long, shifting shadows across the walking paths. The air carried the faint scent of rain from the previous night, mingling with the earthy aroma of leaves. Daniel was waiting near the fountain, his figure relaxed but his eyes sharp, gleaming with a secret that made Evelyn's pulse quicken.

"Hey," he greeted, his voice casual, but there was an intensity in the tilt of his head, the way he studied her face as though memorizing it.

"Hey," Evelyn replied, her curiosity and apprehension mingling. "So... what's this about?"

Daniel didn't answer immediately. Instead, he extended his hand, palm up, a silent invitation. Hesitating for only a second, she placed her hand in his, feeling the warmth and firmness that had become a grounding presence in her life.

"Just trust me," he said softly, guiding her toward the path that led deeper into the park. The suspense thickened with every step, each twist in the trail revealing more of the park she thought she knew, yet this path felt different—like stepping into a story she hadn't read before.

They walked in silence for several minutes, their fingers intertwined, their steps in quiet synchronization. Evelyn's heart thrummed with curiosity and anticipation, every fiber of her being aware that Daniel was orchestrating something—something that would not be ordinary. And that knowledge made her pulse a steady drumbeat of excitement and suspense.

Eventually, they reached a secluded clearing, a space framed by tall oaks and soft grass that glowed under the late afternoon sun. In the center was a small wooden table, adorned with delicate flowers, candles, and a blanket spread out on the grass beside it. Daniel stepped back, eyes shining with anticipation, watching her reaction.

Evelyn froze, her breath catching in her throat. The beauty and thoughtfulness of the scene overwhelmed her. "Daniel..." she whispered, her voice trembling slightly. Every element—the flowers, the candles, the careful arrangement—was a testament to his attention, his care, and the depth of his understanding of her. Her pulse raced, and the world seemed to shrink until it encompassed only him, only this moment, only the deliberate unfolding of his surprise.

Daniel knelt down beside her, his hand brushing lightly against hers. "I wanted to do something... something that tells you how much you mean to me, without needing words," he said. "I wanted this to be for you, Evelyn—for us. A moment just to pause, to celebrate everything we've shared, and everything we're building together."

Her eyes glistened with unshed tears, the weight of the gesture sinking into her like a warm current. She had expected many things from Daniel, but this—this careful orchestration of intimacy, suspense, and genuine attention—had stolen her breath entirely. The suspense of wondering, of anticipating, had been replaced with the thrill of realization, the overwhelming knowledge that she was seen, understood, and cherished.

Daniel stood, offering her a hand to help her to her feet, and guided her toward the blanket where a small, neatly wrapped box lay waiting. "Open it," he said, his voice low, deliberate, and full of a suspense that mirrored the tension in her chest.

Evelyn knelt on the blanket, hands trembling slightly as she untied the ribbon and lifted the lid. Inside was a delicate necklace, simple but elegant, with a small pendant engraved with the initials of both their names. Her breath caught once more. It was not merely the beauty of the necklace that stole her breath—it was the thoughtfulness, the intention, the recognition of their journey, of the suspense, of the care that Daniel had poured into even this smallest detail.

"I wanted it to be something you can carry with you," Daniel said, voice low and earnest, "a reminder that no matter where life takes us, we're building this together, moment by moment. We're learning, loving, and planning a future without fear. And I wanted this to be the first piece of something… tangible, something real that represents us."

Evelyn's fingers closed around the pendant, her chest tightening with emotion. She looked up at him, eyes wide, glistening, trembling with a mixture of awe, love, and suspense still lingering in the curve of her heart. "Daniel… this is… I don't even have words," she whispered.

He smiled gently, taking her hands in his, his eyes locking with hers. "Then don't speak," he said softly. "Let the moment do the talking. Let the surprise, the care, and the intention speak for me. I wanted to give you this… not for the sake of the necklace, but for the reminder that we're in this together. That the suspense, the waiting, the planning, the quiet moments—they're all part of the story we're writing."

Evelyn swallowed hard, tears slipping freely now. She felt the suspense, the thrill, the anticipation of love fully realized, wash over her in waves. It was not loud or dramatic—it was intimate, deliberate, and electric in its subtlety. Every fear, every doubt, every hesitation dissolved into the overwhelming certainty that Daniel had not only seen her heart but had honored it in every detail of this carefully crafted surprise.

Daniel knelt beside her again, their faces close, and whispered, "Every day with you is a new moment, Evelyn. And sometimes, I just want to make those moments unforgettable, even in the smallest ways. I want you to know that nothing about you is ordinary to me, and nothing about this—us—is taken for granted."

Evelyn felt her heart thrum with a new rhythm, a rhythm synchronized with his, a rhythm of suspense transformed into elation, wonder, and profound gratitude. The necklace, the flowers, the candles—they were symbols of more than romance. They were markers of intention, patience, and deliberate love. Each detail reminded her that Daniel had thought not only about the gesture but about the meaning, the emotion, and the resonance it would carry.

The sun began its slow descent behind the trees, casting long shadows and bathing the clearing in golden light. Evelyn leaned back against Daniel, feeling the warmth of his presence, the steady assurance of his hand in hers, and the quiet thrill of a surprise that had stolen her breath completely. The suspense had been masterful, calculated, and unforgettable—not in a dramatic or showy way, but in the deliberate, intimate orchestration of love that spoke louder than words ever could.

"Thank you," she whispered again, voice thick with emotion. "For seeing me, for knowing me, for… everything. I didn't think a day like this could exist."

Daniel brushed a strand of hair from her face, his touch gentle, reverent. "It exists because you exist," he said softly. "And because we're learning to love without fear, to plan without hesitation, and to cherish every moment, big or small. Today is just one of many. But I wanted it to be unforgettable—for you, for us."

Evelyn rested her head on his shoulder, feeling the quiet cadence of suspense transform into an enduring sense of connection. The clearing, the golden light, the small gestures of love—all of it became a memory etched into the delicate folds of her heart. She realized, in a moment of profound clarity, that suspense in love wasn't about anxiety or uncertainty—it was about the thrill of intention, the anticipation of thoughtfulness, and the breathtaking weight of knowing that someone could see your heart and respond with equal care.

As the sun dipped lower, and the shadows lengthened across the blanket, Evelyn felt a deep, reverent sense of gratitude. This surprise had not merely stolen her breath—it had awakened her to the beauty of deliberate love, the power of anticipation, and the thrill of intimacy built on trust, respect, and patient understanding. She had been gifted more than a necklace, more than a moment—she had been gifted a vision of love fully realized, carefully orchestrated, and breathtaking in its quiet intensity.

And in that golden, suspense-filled moment, Evelyn knew that the story they were writing together was far from ordinary. Every gesture, every surprise, every shared heartbeat was part of a deliberate choreography of love—one that neither fear nor haste could ever diminish. It was a love lived intentionally, experienced fully, and cherished beyond measure.

55

THE DAY HE FOUND THE PERFECT RING

Daniel walked through the quiet streets of the jewelry district, the autumn air crisp against his skin, carrying with it the scent of freshly fallen leaves and distant coffee from street-side cafés. The sun had just begun its descent, casting the city in shades of gold and amber, and every corner of the neighborhood seemed to shimmer with the possibilities of the evening. Yet, Daniel was far from distracted by the beauty around him. His mind was focused, purposeful, and entirely consumed by a single mission: finding the perfect ring for Evelyn.

The suspense had been building for weeks, unspoken yet palpable in every thought he carried. Every detail of her personality, every subtle comment she had made about jewelry, every fleeting look she had given at displays in passing had been cataloged, stored, and analyzed. But he knew instinctively that finding a ring wasn't simply about diamonds, gold, or design—it was about finding a tangible expression of the love they had nurtured, the trust they had built, and the future they were daring to imagine together.

He paused at the corner of a small boutique, the window display understated yet elegant. A single spotlight illuminated a velvet cushion, upon which a ring glimmered with an understated brilliance. Daniel's breath caught in his throat, the sudden jolt of suspense sending shivers down his spine. Could this be it? The ring that would perfectly encapsulate everything he wanted to say without uttering a single word?

The door chimed as he stepped inside, and the subtle scent of polished wood and fresh flowers greeted him. The boutique was quiet, intimate, with a soft classical melody flowing from hidden speakers. Behind the counter stood an elderly jeweler, his eyes bright and keen beneath wire-rimmed glasses. "Good afternoon," Daniel said, voice steady but with an edge of anticipation. "I'm looking for something... very specific."

The jeweler's eyes twinkled with understanding. "Ah," he said softly, gesturing for Daniel to come closer. "Specific is always good. Tell me what you're envisioning."

Daniel leaned in slightly, the suspense in his chest tightening. "It's for someone very important," he began, his fingers brushing along the polished counter as he searched for the right words. "It's not just a ring. It has to represent... her, our relationship, our future. Something unique, meaningful, without being ostentatious. It has to feel like her in a way that only I would know."

The jeweler nodded, silent, letting Daniel's words settle like stones in a pond. "I see," he said finally. "It's not about the size of the stone, or even the price. It's about resonance—about capturing the essence of the person it's for. I think we can find something remarkable together."

Daniel felt a thrill, a surge of suspense that pulsed through him like electricity. They moved through the boutique, cases of rings glinting under warm light, each one a possibility, each one a challenge. Daniel tried to remain composed, yet every time a ring caught his eye, his heart raced—not for the beauty alone, but for the fear of missing the one that was right.

Hours seemed to pass as they examined design after design, stone after stone, metal after metal. Daniel would hold a ring, imagine Evelyn's hand, her reaction, the curve of her smile, the way her eyes would light up. He would place the ring down, feeling a mixture of hope and frustration. None of them seemed quite right. The suspense of the search, the careful consideration, and the stakes of this singular gesture kept him taut with anticipation.

Finally, near the back of the store, hidden from the main displays, the jeweler paused. "I saved this one for last," he said, opening a small drawer. Inside was a simple, elegant ring: a single, flawless diamond set in a delicate, white gold band. It was understated but striking, classic yet contemporary, and it carried a quiet brilliance that seemed to speak without words.

Daniel's breath caught. He held it in his hand, the weight of it exact, familiar, almost as if it had been waiting for him. The suspense in his chest exploded, a mixture of relief, exhilaration, and certainty. This was it. He didn't need to try any others. He didn't need to second-guess himself. The ring captured everything he wanted to say—every whispered promise, every quiet vow, every heartbeat shared with Evelyn.

He looked up at the jeweler, his hands trembling slightly from emotion. "This is the one," he said, voice low but unwavering. "I know it is. It's... perfect."

The jeweler smiled knowingly. "Then it has chosen well," he said. "When a ring feels like the person it's meant for, there's no doubt. You'll see the moment she sees it; you'll understand why the search mattered."

Daniel nodded, slipping the ring into a small, velvet box, its simplicity belying the profound significance it carried. The suspense of the past hours had transformed into an almost unbearable anticipation for the moment when he would finally reveal it to Evelyn. The thought of that moment—

her hands, her breath caught, her eyes wide—made his pulse quicken in a way he hadn't anticipated.

He stepped out into the street again, the evening now deepening into twilight. The city lights reflected in puddles from the earlier rain, creating a kaleidoscope of gold, silver, and amber around him. Every step toward home, toward Evelyn, was a step into suspense more intoxicating than anything he had felt before. He imagined her reaction in infinite variations, each one stirring his heart differently, each one heightening the intensity of the moment he had been preparing for.

Daniel paused at a crosswalk, the small velvet box in his pocket pressing against his thigh, reminding him of the gravity of what he carried. The suspense was nearly unbearable, a delicious tension that threaded every thought and heartbeat. He could almost feel Evelyn's presence before he saw her, almost hear the soft gasp he knew would escape her lips when he finally knelt and revealed the ring.

His mind raced with scenarios. Would she laugh first, or cry? Would her hands shake as she took the ring from him? Would she pull him into a tight embrace, whispering words of love, or would they both simply hold each other, suspended in the quiet intensity of the moment? Every possibility thrilled him, made him ache with anticipation, and yet grounded him in the certainty that this was right, that this was exactly the step they were meant to take next.

Finally, he reached the familiar park where they had shared so many quiet moments, the location deliberately chosen for its intimacy, its serenity, and the countless memories it held. Evelyn stood near the fountain, her back to him, seemingly lost in thought as she traced the edge of the water with her fingers. The sight of her—the curve of her shoulders, the tilt of her head, the subtle grace of her movements—stole his breath in the same way the perfect ring had.

He approached slowly, the suspense in his chest coiling tighter, every heartbeat echoing in his ears. Evelyn sensed his presence, turning to him, and her eyes widened almost imperceptibly. Daniel paused, reaching into his pocket, feeling the comforting weight of the box. "Evelyn," he said, voice steady but laced with the tremor of anticipation. "There's something I've been waiting to give you… something I've been searching for, something that represents everything I feel for you."

Her breath caught, her hands instinctively rising to cover her mouth, a gesture of suspense mingled with expectation. "Daniel…" she whispered, her voice a soft tremor.

He knelt on one knee, the velvet box in his hand opening to reveal the flawless ring, catching the fading sunlight in a cascade of fire and brilliance. "Evelyn," he said, voice reverent, every word deliberate, "I've spent days thinking, searching, imagining, and hoping I could find something worthy of you… something worthy of us. This ring… it's more than a piece of jewelry. It's a promise, a vision, a beginning. Will you marry me?"

Time seemed to stretch, the world narrowing to the small circle of light around them, the glimmer of the ring, the suspense in her wide, shimmering eyes. Evelyn's breath hitched, tears glistening as she reached for the box, for the ring, for the man who had captured her heart in ways both subtle and profound.

"Yes," she whispered finally, the word trembling but absolute, carrying with it the weight of emotion, love, and the shared suspense of anticipation realized. "Yes, Daniel… a thousand times yes."

The suspense shattered into elation, the tension of days, weeks, and months giving way to the thrilling certainty that this moment—this perfect, breath-stealing moment—was theirs alone. Daniel slid the ring onto her finger, their hands intertwined, hearts beating in unison, and in the quiet of the park, the city around them oblivious, they held onto each other and the promise of a future both deliberate and fearless.

The day he found the perfect ring had not just been about a search; it had been about intention, understanding, and love expressed with exquisite precision. The suspense had carried him to this exact moment, and now, in Evelyn's luminous eyes, he saw the culmination of everything they had been building together—a future waiting, a love affirmed, a story continuing, richer and more profound than either could have imagined.

56

THE PROPOSAL ALMOST MISSED

The city streets were alive with the quiet hum of late afternoon traffic, golden sunlight bouncing off the wet pavement from the rain that had fallen earlier. Daniel's mind was far from the rhythmic chaos of honking horns and the occasional laughter spilling from cafés lining the boulevard. His thoughts were fixed entirely on Evelyn—the way her hair caught the light, the warmth in her eyes, and the way her laughter made the world shrink until it was only the two of them. Today was supposed to be the day, the moment he had planned meticulously for weeks, the culmination of careful thought, secret scouting, and countless mental rehearsals. Yet, as he drove toward the park where he intended to propose, a gnawing anxiety clawed at him—the suspense that this perfect moment, the proposal he had envisioned so vividly, might slip past him entirely.

He glanced at his watch, the minutes crawling like they were reluctant to move. Evelyn had texted that morning, casually suggesting they take a walk through the park before dinner, completely unaware that Daniel had spent hours arranging the perfect surprise: a secluded clearing adorned with subtle lanterns, a small blanket laid with care, and a box containing the engagement ring he had found after what felt like a lifetime of searching. Every detail mattered, from the gentle fragrance of the candles to the soft music he had arranged to float through a hidden portable speaker. Every detail was meant to capture Evelyn's heart, the way she had captured his, and yet now, as he navigated the streets, his chest tightened with the suspense of uncertainty.

Arriving at the park, Daniel realized that timing was about to betray him. Evelyn's casual pace, her habit of stopping to admire the smallest things—a particularly bright cluster of flowers, a bird darting across the pathway—meant he had only a narrow window to execute the proposal before the sunlight dimmed, washing the clearing in shadows that would undermine the romantic atmosphere he had painstakingly planned. He parked hurriedly, running his hand through his hair, heart thrumming with a mix of anticipation and fear.

Stepping out of the car, he caught sight of her a few yards away, the way she paused to trace her fingers along a wrought-iron fence, her gaze distant, serene, unknowing of the whirlwind of suspense approaching. Daniel's breath hitched. Time seemed to fold in on itself, stretching and compressing as he approached, each step weighted with the pressure of getting everything just right. He adjusted the box in his pocket, feeling the reassuring weight of the ring and the responsibility it carried, reminding him that this was more than a gesture; it was a promise, a declaration, a life-altering decision.

"Hey," Evelyn called, turning toward him with that bright smile that always had the effect of grounding him and making the world fall away simultaneously.

"Hey," Daniel replied, voice calm but heart hammering against his chest. The suspense of what was about to unfold made every word he spoke deliberate, every motion measured, as though even a slight misstep could unravel the careful orchestration of this moment.

They walked together, the conversation light at first, Evelyn chatting about the mundane details of her day while Daniel nodded, smiling, but every fiber of his being focused on the path ahead. The clearing was only a few minutes away, but with Evelyn's tendency to slow down, Daniel's anxiety began to rise. What if they never reached the exact spot at the exact right time? What if something disrupted the moment—another park-goer wandering in, a sudden shift in the wind, a bird startling her, causing her attention to drift elsewhere? The suspense gnawed at him, a mix of exhilaration and panic that made his chest feel both heavy and impossibly light at the same time.

Finally, the clearing came into view. Daniel's heart leapt, but then sank slightly—the wind had picked up, causing a few lanterns to sway precariously, and a group of children from a nearby playground had wandered close, their laughter piercing the serene atmosphere he had meticulously cultivated. The perfect moment was teetering on the edge of slipping away. He had to act fast, or risk losing the magic he had envisioned.

"Let's sit here for a minute," Daniel suggested casually, guiding Evelyn toward the blanket, trying to mask the urgency in his voice. She obeyed, her trust in him implicit, her presence both calming and electrifying.

As they settled, Daniel's mind raced. He had rehearsed this moment countless times: the words, the breath, the placement of the ring, the exact moment of eye contact that would make her gasp, the subtle trembling of her hands as she realized the magnitude of what he was asking. Yet now, with reality intruding in the form of wind, children, and shifting light, the suspense felt almost unbearable. Every second stretched, each heartbeat echoing in his ears louder than the ambient noise of the park.

He took her hands gently, turning them over in his palms, as though anchoring her to him and to the moment. Evelyn looked at him curiously, sensing the shift in his energy, though she didn't yet know what awaited her.

"Evelyn," he began, voice low and steady despite the tight coil of suspense in his chest. She leaned slightly forward, instinctively reading the gravity in his tone. "There's something I need to ask you. Something important... something I should have asked a long time ago, but I wanted to do it right."

Her eyes widened, curiosity mingling with a growing sense of anticipation. Daniel's pulse quickened, the suspense now transformed into a live wire of urgency and excitement. He reached into his pocket, fingers brushing against the cool velvet of the ring box, and then hesitated—slightly, painfully—because at that very moment, a gust of wind swept across the clearing, knocking a lantern off its stand and sending it rolling toward the grass. The suspense spiked; the moment teetered on the edge of chaos.

Daniel's instincts kicked in. He leaned forward, steadying the lantern with one hand while keeping the box in the other, his mind calculating the timing, the steps, the sequence. Evelyn watched, bemused, unaware of the near disaster that had just brushed past them. "Are you okay?" she asked, a small smile tugging at her lips, completely oblivious to the storm of suspense that had threatened to upend the proposal.

"Yes," Daniel replied, forcing calm into his voice. "Perfectly okay." He took a deep breath, his heart pounding as he knelt on one knee, the box now safely in hand, hidden from view until the precise moment. The children from the playground had wandered off, the wind had settled slightly, and the golden light of the sun caught the diamond in a fleeting shimmer that seemed almost serendipitous.

"Evelyn," he said, voice low, reverent, carrying the weight of every heartbeat, every shared moment, every ounce of love and intention he had poured into this day. "From the moment I met you, I've known that life is better with you in it. You've changed my world, made it brighter, fuller, and more extraordinary than I ever imagined possible. And I want to spend every day proving to you, showing you, loving you in ways that words alone could never capture."

The suspense was unbearable now, a taut string stretched across the universe, vibrating with anticipation. Evelyn's breath hitched, her hands moving instinctively to cover her mouth, eyes wide with recognition of what was about to unfold.

Daniel opened the box, revealing the flawless diamond ring, simple yet exquisite, a symbol of promise, commitment, and the life they were about to build together. "Evelyn," he continued, voice trembling with emotion, "will you marry me?"

Time seemed to pause. The wind softened, the sunlight caught the edges of the ring, and Evelyn's eyes glistened with tears as she processed the moment—the suspense, the careful planning, the near-miss, the intensity of love distilled into this single, life-changing question.

"Oh my God," she whispered, a smile breaking through her tears. "Daniel... yes! Yes, I will!"

The suspense shattered into relief, joy, and exhilaration. Daniel slid the ring onto her finger, their hands entwined, hearts racing together as the weight of the near-missed moment transformed into triumph. The proposal that had almost slipped away had instead become perfect, unforgettable, and breathtaking in its emotional intensity.

They stood together, holding each other, feeling the lingering thrill of suspense transform into shared elation. Every detail, every second of careful planning, every challenge and near-miss had led to this—their future, crystallized in the glimmer of a diamond, the warmth of their hands, and the unspoken promise of a life built together, full of love, adventure, and moments of breathtaking suspense.

57

YES... A THOUSAND TIMES YES

The city had surrendered to the night, lights flickering like fireflies across the skyline, casting reflections in the river that cut through the heart of the metropolis. Yet, for Evelyn, the world outside had ceased to exist. Every sound, every shadow, every distant echo of life was secondary to the moment she stood in the park, the cold stone of the fountain beneath her hands and Daniel kneeling before her. The suspense that had been building for weeks—the quiet tension, the unspoken promise, the anticipation of a lifetime—culminated in this instant, and her breath seemed too small to contain the thrill, the disbelief, and the sheer, overwhelming joy.

Daniel's eyes held her entirely, a gravitational pull that made her stomach twist with the weight of emotion. The ring glimmered between them, delicate, perfect, almost impossibly small yet carrying the enormity of everything he wanted to convey: love, devotion, a lifetime of shared mornings and late-night whispers, laughter, tears, and moments neither had yet imagined. He spoke softly, voice vibrating with emotion, each word deliberate, chosen, infused with the suspense that had made the preceding days feel both endless and fleeting.

"Evelyn," he began, his fingers trembling slightly as they hovered over the small velvet box. "I have searched for the right way to say this, the perfect words to capture what I feel... but words always feel too small for what's in my heart. I've loved you quietly, fiercely, and completely. I want to love you for all our days, through storms, through sunlight, through every ordinary and extraordinary moment life gives us. Will you—"

Her heart threatened to leap from her chest. The suspense was unbearable, a taut string stretched to its breaking point. She wanted to respond, to leap into his arms, to reassure him, to dissolve all the anticipation that had been suspended like a fragile glass above them. But the words she had rehearsed, the emotions she had held in check, the very weight of the moment, made her pause. This wasn't a fleeting promise. This was forever. And forever demanded a response that was worthy of the love it represented.

Daniel opened the box, revealing the flawless diamond, its fire catching the glow of the nearby lamp post. The light danced across the facets, scattering reflections across his face and hers. Her eyes followed the sparkles, tracing the outline of the ring, memorizing it, and in that instant, she realized that it symbolized more than engagement—it symbolized trust, patience, understanding, and a love that had grown in the spaces where fear and hesitation had once existed.

The suspense of the past weeks—the messages, the near-misses, the quiet uncertainty of whether he would act, whether the timing would ever feel right—all of it crystallized into this singular moment. Evelyn felt her chest tighten, her throat constrict, and for a moment she could only breathe, absorbing the gravity and beauty of the scene before her.

Daniel's voice, gentle yet insistent, pulled her from the haze of emotion. "Evelyn, I am yours... if you'll have me. Will you marry me?"

Time seemed to suspend itself. The city hummed around them, but it felt distant, inconsequential. All that mattered was him, her, the ring, and the shared heartbeat that had synchronized through months of anticipation, suspense, and longing. The seconds stretched, elastic with emotion, until Evelyn felt a swell of certainty that eclipsed every doubt she had ever carried.

"Yes..." she whispered, her voice barely audible, trembling with joy. "Yes... a thousand times yes."

The words broke the tension like sunlight breaking through storm clouds. Daniel's breath hitched, the suspense that had wound through him over the past days, weeks, months, releasing in a rush of relief, exhilaration, and an overwhelming tide of love. He lifted her hands, gently sliding the ring onto her finger. It fit perfectly, as though it had been waiting for her, waiting for this moment, waiting for the affirmation of their shared commitment.

Her fingers trembled as he adjusted the ring, his touch careful, reverent, as though handling something sacred. "It's perfect," he murmured, not about the ring alone, but about her, about them, about the improbable magic of this moment finally materializing.

Evelyn laughed softly, tears slipping down her cheeks. "It's more than perfect," she said, voice shaking, catching between words and gasps of breath. "It's... it's everything I never knew I needed, everything I hoped for, everything I wanted and more."

The suspense lingered still, subtle, a gentle undercurrent beneath the overt joy, because moments like these are never entirely free of tension. There is always a heartbeat of uncertainty—the echo of past fears, the faint shadow of doubt—but it is suspended in the warmth of love, in the certainty of connection, in the thrill of shared understanding. Evelyn felt that tension, recognized it, and allowed it to dissolve into laughter and tears and the simple act of being entirely present with Daniel.

He rose to his feet slowly, helping her up, and together they stood, hands intertwined, hearts beating in sync. The city lights reflected in her eyes, and Daniel realized, with a sudden clarity that sent a thrill through him, that the suspense, the waiting, the anticipation, had been as much a part of the love as the gesture itself. Without it, this affirmation—this declaration of forever—would not have been as rich, as intense, as unforgettable.

"Look at this," he said, motioning toward the skyline, the river glimmering in the distance. "Tonight, the city doesn't matter. The world doesn't matter. All that matters is us, this moment, and the promise we just made to each other."

Evelyn leaned her head against his shoulder, her hand resting atop the ring, feeling the cool metal and the sharp brilliance of the diamond, and thought about the suspense that had defined their journey. Each near-miss, every delay, every anxious heartbeat leading up to this moment had been part of the choreography of love, creating a tension that made the resolution—this Yes—a thousand times sweeter, infinitely more profound, and breathtakingly real.

Daniel wrapped his arms around her, holding her close as the city pulsed with life around them. The suspense of possibility had transformed into the certainty of commitment, the thrill of unknown paths giving way to the steady, reassuring rhythm of shared promises. Evelyn felt it too: the quiet power of a Yes that reverberated far beyond the ring, beyond the park, beyond the moment itself. It was a Yes that carried their history, their present, and the promise of all the tomorrows they would face together.

They lingered there, under the glow of street lamps, the soft rustle of leaves, the distant sound of life carrying on around them, yet entirely consumed by the intimate, extraordinary act of affirmation. Every suspense-filled heartbeat, every breath of anticipation, every moment of doubt that had whispered through the days leading up to this night now dissolved into pure, unadulterated joy.

"Yes... a thousand times yes," Evelyn repeated, louder this time, letting the words carry into the night, into the city, into the universe. Daniel smiled, letting her declaration settle around them, infusing the space with warmth, love, and the unspoken understanding that this moment—fleeting yet eternal—was theirs alone.

As they walked slowly through the park, hands intertwined, hearts brimming with emotion, every glance, every brush of fingers, every shared smile was a testament to the suspense that had made their love story so intoxicating. They had waited, planned, imagined, and hoped, and now the culmination—the thousandth Yes—resonated with all the weight and wonder of a love carefully nurtured, deeply felt, and joyously affirmed.

And in that night, beneath the glow of city lights, the soft hum of life, and the infinite stretch of stars above, Daniel and Evelyn stepped into a new chapter—one where suspense, love, and destiny intertwined to create a moment neither would ever forget. A moment where Yes, a thousand times yes, was not just an answer, but a vow, a promise, and the thrilling beginning of forever.

58

TWO PATHS BECOMING ONE

The morning sun was spilling across the city in soft ribbons of gold, casting long shadows on the cobblestone streets where Daniel and Evelyn walked side by side. The crisp air carried the scent of freshly baked bread from a nearby bakery, the faint perfume of spring flowers from a small urban garden, and a subtle hint of anticipation, as if the world itself was aware of the delicate transformation about to unfold. Today was not just any day—it was a day of convergence, a day when two lives, two hearts, two paths that had danced around each other with suspense and longing for months, would begin to walk deliberately, consciously, and irreversibly together.

The suspense had been building quietly, threading itself into every interaction, every glance, every pause in conversation. Daniel felt it like a second heartbeat, a subtle tension behind the pulse of the city. The engagement had formalized what had always been unspoken, yet there remained the thrilling uncertainty of how life would adjust, how their routines would intertwine, and how the smallest, most mundane decisions would suddenly carry weight beyond measure. The world outside, ordinary as it seemed, had become a stage for the extraordinary, and each step forward felt like both promise and test.

They entered a small café tucked into the corner of the street, the kind that smelled faintly of roasted coffee beans and polished wood, the kind that seemed timeless, almost suspended from the frantic pace of the city around it. Daniel had suggested this café deliberately; it had been the first place they had ever met for coffee, a serendipitous encounter that had evolved from casual conversation to stolen glances, to late-night texts, and eventually to declarations of love. Sitting at a small, round table by the window, they ordered their usual drinks—the perfect blend of familiarity and comfort, each sip grounding them even as the suspense of the day's significance pulsed in the background.

Daniel watched Evelyn across the table, the morning light catching her hair in a way that made it shimmer like threads of gold. He marveled at the way her eyes crinkled at the corners when she smiled, the way her hands moved almost hypnotically as she wrapped them around her cup. There was a quiet suspense in observing her, a recognition that even after all the shared experiences, all the closeness and trust, she remained a universe unto herself—vivid, unpredictable, and endlessly fascinating.

"Do you ever think about how we ended up here?" Evelyn asked, her voice soft, almost hesitant, carrying with it the weight of reflection and the unspoken recognition that something monumental was unfolding between them.

Daniel nodded, a small smile tugging at his lips. "Every day," he replied. "Every single day. It's like our paths were weaving around each other all this time, and only now are they finally becoming one. And I can't believe it took us so long to realize it."

The suspense in his words wasn't just rhetorical. He meant it in the full depth of experience—the long days of near-misses, the quiet longing, the careful steps toward trust, the moments when he had feared that timing or circumstance might forever keep them apart. Every hesitation, every pause in their story, had heightened the thrill of this convergence, made the eventual unity richer, more profound, and achingly beautiful.

Evelyn's fingers brushed his across the table, a simple gesture loaded with meaning. "It feels surreal," she admitted, eyes shining. "Like the world shifted just for us, like all the wrong turns and delays were leading to this exact moment. But… it's still scary, isn't it? To realize that we're not just walking side by side anymore. We're choosing to move forward together, in everything."

Daniel's heart thudded against his chest, a mix of suspense, certainty, and profound tenderness. "Yes," he said softly. "It's terrifying, but in the best way. Because it means that we're not pretending anymore, not hiding behind caution or fear. We're committing to each other completely. Two paths becoming one—it's not just romantic, it's transformative. And I can't think of anyone else I'd rather do this with."

They left the café hand in hand, stepping into the bustling streets, and the suspense of their intertwined futures seemed to ripple through the crowd, unnoticed but palpable to them. The city felt simultaneously larger and smaller: larger because the possibilities seemed infinite, smaller because all external distractions had faded, leaving only the intensity of connection between them. Every step they took together, synchronized without planning, was a silent affirmation of the commitment they had just cemented, a rhythm that seemed to echo the promise of forever.

Daniel suggested a detour through the park, where sunlight filtered through the canopy of trees, casting dappled patterns across the winding paths. Here, the suspense of life as a shared journey became tangible. The way Evelyn walked beside him, the subtle leaning in during turns, the quiet exchanges of glance and touch, all carried the weight of choices and compromises that had yet to be made. The intimacy of shared space, once casual and effortless, now carried the profound recognition that they were navigating life not as two separate individuals, but as partners whose paths had converged and would continue to do so in deliberate alignment.

At a secluded bench, Daniel paused, feeling the suspense rise again—the gentle tension of a moment pregnant with potential. He turned to Evelyn, searching her eyes, feeling the pulse of her heartbeat through the light contact of their joined hands. "I think this is it," he said quietly, his voice low but steady. "This moment, this path, this choice. It's us deciding, consciously, that we will walk forward together, not just in grand gestures, but in every ordinary, messy, beautiful part of life."

Evelyn's gaze softened, and the suspense that had clung to her like a shadow over the past days—moments of doubt, fear of loss, the whisper of what-ifs—dissolved into trust, warmth, and the quiet thrill of certainty. "I feel it too," she said. "Every part of me has known it, even when I was afraid. And now… now it feels like breathing. Like the natural next step we were always meant to take."

They sat together in silence for a few minutes, allowing the weight of the day, the gravity of the moment, and the beauty of their shared decision to sink in. Daniel felt the suspense transform into something deeper: the suspense of possibility evolving into the suspense of anticipation for the life they would build, the challenges they would navigate, and the joys they would cultivate together. Every kiss, every touch, every whisper of agreement or compromise in the future would be a continuation of this moment—a moment where two paths finally became one.

As they rose to leave, the wind rustled through the branches, carrying with it a faint scent of blooming flowers and the distant promise of rain. Daniel squeezed Evelyn's hand, the gesture both grounding and electrifying, and felt the suspense of the unknown stretch ahead. There would be days of disagreement, moments of fear, decisions to make, and paths to choose. But for now, in this serene morning, amidst the quiet vibrancy of the city and the intimacy of the park, the suspense was thrilling, beautiful, and full of promise.

"You know," Evelyn said, her voice soft but resolute, "I never want to forget this. Not the suspense, not the waiting, not the feeling of being completely known and understood in a single moment. This... this is us. This is the start of everything."

Daniel nodded, pulling her close as the sun climbed higher, bathing them in warmth. "Yes," he whispered, echoing her earlier words. "This is us. Two paths converging, becoming one, and I couldn't imagine a more perfect journey than the one we're about to take together."

They walked forward, hands intertwined, hearts synchronized, and with every step, every breath, every quiet smile, they affirmed the suspense and beauty of love: how anticipation sharpens joy, how patience magnifies connection, and how two lives, when deliberately and courageously joined, create a path that is simultaneously thrilling, comforting, and entirely, breathtakingly unique.

For Daniel and Evelyn, this day marked more than engagement—it marked the conscious, suspense-filled decision to become one, to navigate life together, to hold onto the thrill of uncertainty while embracing the steadfast certainty of love. And as they disappeared into the city streets, the world around them seemed to shimmer with possibility, their paths forever intertwined, moving forward as one.

59

THE WEDDING THEY PRAYED FOR

The morning of the wedding dawned with a soft, golden light that filtered through the towering windows of the chapel, bathing every surface in warmth. The air carried a gentle hush, a reverent stillness that seemed to anticipate the moment when two hearts, two lives, two souls that had navigated suspense, near misses, and quiet longing, would finally declare themselves inseparable. For Daniel and Evelyn, this day was more than a ceremony; it was the culmination of years of whispered prayers, silent hopes, and the careful threading of destiny, the kind of day they had envisioned in the quiet corners of their hearts long before it became tangible reality.

Evelyn stood before the mirror in the bridal suite, the dress cascading around her like liquid moonlight. Every detail had been meticulously chosen, not for extravagance, but for the sacred resonance it held: the delicate lace tracing her shoulders like whispered promises, the soft folds of silk that moved with the gentle rhythm of her breath, and the veil that shimmered faintly in the morning sun. She ran her fingers over the fabric, feeling the weight of every prayer, every anticipation, every moment of suspense that had led to this day. It was overwhelming, nearly too much to bear, yet it was the suspense of the unknown—the thrill of what was about to unfold—that made her heart beat in a rhythm of both exhilaration and awe.

Her bridesmaids bustled around her quietly, adjusting straps, smoothing folds, whispering words of reassurance, but Evelyn's mind was elsewhere. She thought of the near-misses, the delays, the months of waiting when every encounter with Daniel had been loaded with subtle tension. Every text left unanswered for a few minutes, every time he had been too cautious to confess immediately, every moment she had wondered if their timing was wrong—all of it culminated in this day. The suspense of their journey had transformed into an electric anticipation that hummed through her entire being.

Meanwhile, Daniel sat in a small room just down the hall, tie slightly loosened, hands trembling as he held the worn leather-bound Bible he had carried with him since the morning he had first planned to propose. He had prayed that day, and every day since, that God would guide their steps, guard their hearts, and prepare them for the moment when their paths would irrevocably converge. Now, as he adjusted his cufflinks for the third time, the suspense of the hours ahead pressed on him like a tangible weight. He could hear the faint hum of activity outside the door—music, laughter, the soft clatter of plates from the reception hall—but it all seemed distant, almost unreal.

His best man leaned in, lowering his voice. "You ready for this, Daniel?"

Daniel swallowed hard, a tight knot of suspense tightening in his chest. "Ready isn't the word," he murmured, voice thick with emotion. "I've been waiting for this day in my heart for years. But… now that it's here, I realize it's bigger than anything I imagined. It's perfect, and terrifying, and beautiful all at once."

The chapel doors opened, and the soft strains of the wedding music began to play, a melody that had become inseparably linked with their story. The suspense was almost unbearable as Daniel took his place at the altar, eyes fixed on the door through which Evelyn would soon appear. Each second stretched like elastic, every heartbeat loud and deliberate, echoing through the sacred space. The near-misses, the months of anticipation, the fragile tension of hope—all converged into a single, suspended moment.

And then, there she was. Evelyn appeared at the threshold, a vision of serenity and radiant beauty. The veil framed her face like a delicate promise, the dress flowing with ethereal grace, and in her eyes, Daniel saw the reflection of everything he had prayed for, longed for, and believed in. The suspense of the past had been a patient companion, testing their faith, sharpening their anticipation, and now, in this fleeting moment, it dissolved into pure, unadulterated awe.

The procession moved forward slowly, deliberately, each step a heartbeat in the narrative of destiny. The guests rose, some whispering to one another, some silently marveling, but Daniel was focused entirely on Evelyn, every detail magnified by the intensity of suspense and emotion. As she approached, their eyes met, and the world contracted until it was only the two of them, the chapel fading into a blur of light and sound.

The officiant began the ceremony, words rolling gently through the air, but for Daniel and Evelyn, the suspense lingered in the pauses, the weight of promises yet to be spoken, and the gravity of vows about to be made. Every word mattered, every glance carried meaning, every breath was a silent prayer. The months of near misses, the long nights of waiting, the whispered conversations under stars—they had all led to this delicate, breathtaking moment.

When it came time to exchange vows, Daniel's hands shook slightly as he reached for hers. His voice, when it emerged, was steady yet filled with the raw intensity of anticipation that had been building for years. "Evelyn, from the moment our paths first crossed, I have known that my life would never be the same. You are my heart, my anchor, my joy. Today, in front of everyone, I promise to walk beside you, to hold you through every storm, to celebrate every sunrise, and to love you with all that I am, for all our days."

Evelyn's eyes glistened, tears threatening to spill, and she clasped his hands tightly, feeling the tremor of suspense that had always existed between them—a tension that now transformed into the certainty of commitment. "Daniel," she whispered, voice thick with emotion, "I have prayed for this. I have hoped for this. I have waited for this. You are my heart, my peace, my joy, and my home. Today, I promise to stand beside you, to walk with you through every challenge, to celebrate every triumph, and to love you with everything I am, for all our days."

The officiant's words echoed gently, drawing the suspense to a peak before releasing it entirely. "By the power vested in me, and by the love that has brought you together, I now pronounce you husband and wife."

A collective breath seemed to release throughout the chapel. Daniel and Evelyn faced each other, tears streaming freely, hands intertwined, hearts pounding, and for a moment, the suspense of all their waiting, all their near-misses, all their prayers and fears and hopes, exploded into the pure, overwhelming joy of fulfillment.

As they shared their first kiss as husband and wife, the world around them seemed to shimmer—the soft lighting of the chapel, the muted strains of music, the gentle rustle of guests' applause—all faded into insignificance. The suspense of years of anticipation, of near-misses and almosts, had transformed into the uncontainable, beautiful certainty of a love that had been tested, nurtured, and finally realized.

The reception that followed was a vibrant tapestry of laughter, tears, and celebration. Friends and family circled them, showering congratulations and admiration, but Daniel and Evelyn moved through the crowd as if suspended in their own world. Every touch, every look, every word spoken to them carried the weight of their journey, the suspense of love finally arriving at its rightful destination.

Later, as they stole a quiet moment away from the crowd, overlooking the city skyline from the terrace, Evelyn leaned her head against Daniel's chest, feeling the rhythm of his heart, the solidity of his presence. "We prayed for this," she whispered. "Every night, every quiet moment, every doubt and fear—we prayed that we would find this, that we would find each other."

Daniel held her tighter, the suspense of their past—the near-misses, the anxious waiting, the cautious hope—melting into the warmth of certainty. "And now we have," he said softly. "We have each other, and nothing else matters. This is the wedding we prayed for, the life we prayed for, and the love that was worth every second of suspense."

As the night deepened and the city lights twinkled like a reflection of their journey, Daniel and Evelyn danced slowly under the stars, each step a testament to patience, faith, and the quiet power of prayers answered. Every glance, every touch, every heartbeat was a reminder of the suspense that had defined their love—moments of almost, moments of waiting, moments of doubt—and how, in the end, it had all led to this breathtaking, irreplaceable certainty: a wedding they had prayed for, and a love that would endure for all their days.

60

FOREVER BEGINS QUIETLY

The night had folded itself gently over the city, draping skyscrapers and streets in a soft, velvety darkness. The last echoes of the wedding—the laughter, the music, the clinking of glasses—had faded into memory, leaving Daniel and Evelyn alone in the quiet of their first night as husband and wife. The room they entered was warm and welcoming, softly lit by a single lamp that cast a golden glow across the walls. The suspense that had defined their journey—the long months of anticipation, the near-misses, the subtle hesitation of timing—had now transformed into a gentle, comforting rhythm, yet it remained, a tender reminder of how far they had traveled to arrive at this precise, fragile, perfect moment.

Evelyn closed the door behind them, and the sudden stillness of the room made her heart flutter. The thrill of the day—the culmination of years of waiting and praying, the suspense of what the future might hold—hung palpably in the air. She looked at Daniel, who stood still for a moment, his eyes sweeping over her as though committing every detail to memory: the curve of her smile, the soft shimmer of her hair, the light of vulnerability and strength intertwined in her gaze.

"Can you believe it?" she whispered, voice trembling. "After all of this... it's just us now."

Daniel stepped closer, the faint rustle of his movements mingling with the quiet heartbeat of the night. "I can't believe it, not fully," he said softly, brushing a stray strand of hair from her face. "It feels like the world has changed, like time has stretched and compressed all at once. We prayed for this, we waited for this, and yet... it's still almost unreal."

Evelyn's fingers reached for his, intertwining with a natural ease that came from years of knowing, of longing, of navigating the spaces between them with care. The suspense that had once felt heavy, a weight pressing on their chests, now felt like a tender hum beneath the surface—a reminder of their resilience, their patience, and the quiet thrill of love finally realized.

They moved together toward the window, standing side by side and looking out at the city below. The streets, now quiet, were reflected in the glass alongside their silhouettes, a visual echo of two lives moving in parallel yet now united. Every light in the distance, every faint sound of life, seemed infused with meaning, a subtle acknowledgment that the universe had conspired to bring them to this exact point.

"I keep thinking about all the times we almost missed each other," Daniel said, voice low and reflective. "The bus that left too early, the messages I didn't send, the hesitations I let linger... Every almost was terrifying, but now I see they were all part of the path that led us here. And now... now we can walk it together."

Evelyn pressed her forehead gently against his chest, feeling the steady rhythm of his heartbeat, a grounding force that carried both reassurance and exhilaration. "Every suspenseful moment, every delay, every fear we felt—it all brought us to this," she murmured. "And even though it was agonizing sometimes, it made this... this certainty feel like a miracle."

Daniel leaned down, capturing her lips in a kiss that was both gentle and electric. It was a kiss that carried the weight of anticipation, the thrill of fulfilled longing, and the quiet intimacy of two hearts that had fought through suspense and doubt to finally rest together. The world outside their room disappeared; only the sound of breath, the rhythm of hearts, and the soft murmur of affection existed in the sacred space they had created.

They pulled back just enough to look at one another, sharing a quiet laugh that was more relief than humor, more wonder than jest. The suspense of the day, the months of longing and uncertainty, had now distilled into this serene, fragile moment of peace. Yet even in tranquility, there was a subtle, thrilling tension—the kind that comes when a life has just shifted, when two paths have converged, and the future stretches ahead like an uncharted map, full of promise and mystery.

Daniel led Evelyn to the bed, the soft fabric of the sheets cool beneath their fingers, the room imbued with the faint scent of flowers and candle wax that lingered from the celebration earlier. Every detail, from the gentle hum of the heater to the soft glow of the lamp, seemed curated to frame this exact night—a night suspended between memory and the first breath of forever.

Sitting side by side, they shared stories and reflections from the wedding day, the conversation flowing effortlessly despite the exhaustion of hours filled with emotion. They laughed at small mishaps, remembered moments of suspense during the ceremony, and marveled at how the smallest gestures—the way they had exchanged glances, the way Daniel had nearly fumbled the ring, Evelyn's first nervous step down the aisle—had all seemed monumental in the moment. Every story they recounted carried the subtle thrill of suspense, the delicious tension of a love story that had been long awaited yet still felt astonishingly new.

Hours passed almost imperceptibly. They talked about the future—the dreams they had nurtured individually, the aspirations they now shared, the places they would see, the home they would create. The suspense of planning, of imagining, of weaving two separate lives into a cohesive whole, was a quiet undercurrent, thrilling in its uncertainty yet comforting in the certainty of commitment. Every decision they discussed, from mundane choices like paint colors to monumental considerations like family planning, carried a weight that was both exciting and humbling, a reminder of how profound the act of union truly was.

Finally, they lay back, limbs entangled, breathing synchronized, the suspense of the day giving way to a deep, contemplative stillness. Evelyn traced the line of Daniel's jaw with her finger, marveling at how familiar yet astonishing it felt to have him so close, so tangible. "Do you realize," she whispered, "that all those moments we almost missed each other... they were preparing us for this? For the quiet, for the forever we're beginning now?"

Daniel nodded, brushing a strand of hair from her face. "Every suspenseful heartbeat, every anxious pause, every almost... It was all part of the story, leading to this perfect, quiet forever. And now that we're here, I know one thing: no suspense, no waiting, no fear, could ever diminish what we have. It's real. It's ours. And it begins now, quietly, gently, but with all the force of everything we've ever hoped for."

The night deepened, the city lights outside flickering faintly as if winking at them, acknowledging their passage into a new chapter. Daniel held Evelyn close, feeling the steady rise and fall of her chest against his, the warmth of her skin, and the quiet, electric hum of contentment that comes when suspense is finally replaced by certainty. They didn't need to speak; the quiet said everything—the prayers answered, the anticipation fulfilled, the long journey rewarded.

In that soft, suspended stillness, they fell asleep wrapped in one another, hearts beating in quiet sync, a subtle thrill of the unknown lingering even in repose. It was the suspense of possibility now transformed into the gentle certainty of presence: forever had begun quietly, beautifully, irrevocably. The near-misses, the waiting, the careful navigation of hearts and timing—all of it had led to this singular, perfect night.

And as dawn approached, painting the sky in hues of pink and gold, Daniel and Evelyn dreamed together, side by side, the promise of shared mornings, quiet laughter, and unending love stretching infinitely before them. Their forever had begun—not with fanfare, not with loud declarations, but with the soft, electric intimacy of two hearts finally, unequivocally, and beautifully united.

www.ingramcontent.com/pod-product-compliance
Lightning Source LLC
Chambersburg PA
CBHW070204120726
47909CB00001B/247

* 9 7 8 0 2 3 4 9 5 4 6 8 3 *